REAL ESTATE

*the text of this book is printed
on 100% recycled paper*

ABOUT THE AUTHOR

I. Edward Weich is Professor of Business Administration and Director of the Real Estate Institute at C. W. Post Center of Long Island University, and previously taught at Hofstra University. Dr. Weich received his B.B.A. at the City College of New York and his L.L.B. and J.S.D. at the Brooklyn Law School of St. Lawrence University, and did post-doctoral work at the University of Miami Law School, Harvard Law School, and Hofstra University. He has been a member of the Bar of the State of New York since 1937 and has been admitted to practice before the United States Court of Military Appeals and the United States Supreme Court. He has also published a text on Property and Casualty Insurance.

REAL ESTATE

I. EDWARD WEICH, J.S.D.

BARNES & NOBLE BOOKS

A DIVISION OF HARPER & ROW, PUBLISHERS

New York, Hagerstown, San Francisco, London

L. C. catalogue card number: 66–23152
ISBN: 0-06-460060-2

80   20 19 18 17 16 15 14 13

Printed in the United States of America

To my wife, Gertrude;
and to our children,
Mervyn D., Stephen Robert, Rosemary, and Jan;
and to our grandchildren,
Douglas Lloyd, Beverly Jean, Deborah Lynn,
Craig Ian, and David Scott

PREFACE

In recent years, there has been a greater awareness of the impact of activity, in the field of real estate, on all levels of society. No longer are the principles and practices in this field the exclusive preserve of the real estate executive, the college business major, the realtor or the business manager; they are also of increasing interest to the small home owner, the small investor, the real estate salesman, the student, and those people entering the industry.

It is the purpose of this book to present a concise, cogent, non-technical, understandable, and authoritative exposition of the principles and practices in real estate. It is written primarily to allow the reader to acquire a background in the fundamentals of this exciting industry.

Many persons have contributed materially to the completion of this text. To try to mention them all would undoubtedly lead to inadvertent omissions. To them all, then, my sincere thanks.

My special thanks to President R. Gordon Hoxie, Dean Eugene Arden, and Professor T. Henry Murphy of C. W. Post College.

Appreciation is acknowledged to the Security Title and Guaranty Company for their permission to use appropriate real estate forms.

The author also wishes to express his thanks to Mrs. Billie Brown, Miss Rosalie Adaschik, Miss Janet Tomaiko, and Mrs. Patricia DiGangi of the secretarial staff at C. W. Post College for their assistance.

I.E.W.

Uniondale, New York

FOREWORD

Good text books on real estate are rare. This is mainly due to the paucity of available authors combining the necessary practical experience with the ability to express themselves clearly. In the following pages Dr. Weich has done an admirable and difficult job of effecting the desired combination.

The subject of real estate currently covers an immense spectrum. The age of specialization in which we are living has not overlooked real estate, and today there are nearly as many specialists in the field of real estate as in the medical profession. Within the main headings of this text are important and complex subdivisions or areas. Actual experience in these areas, rather than a treatise on the subject, will always be preferable, but the author has set forth an able and professional condensation of the many facets and tools of today's varied real estate picture.

In addition to its merits as a textbook, this work will be a valuable reference and comprehensive checklist for the practicing real estate man. The author is to be commended for his contribution to constructive and basic real estate learning.

James D. Landauer
Chairman
James D. Landauer Associates, Inc.

CONTENTS

1   The Real Estate Business and the Market   1

2   Property Rights and Interests   5

3   Agency and Brokerage   19

4   The Real Estate Office and Operations   34

5   Salesmanship and Advertising   41

6   Legal Aspects of Real Estate Transactions   46

7   The Contract of Sale   64

8   Deeds   84

9   Title Search and Insurance, Closings and Recording   92

10   Bonds and Mortgages   100

11   Liens, Easements and Other Encumbrances   112

12   Miscellaneous Real Estate Instruments   120

13   Taxes and Assessments, Valuation and Appraisal   136

14   Property Management   147

15   Leases: Landlord and Tenant   151

16   Subdivisions and Developments   163

17   Current Trends in Real Estate   167

    Appendix Real Estate License Laws (New York State, California, and Florida)   188

    Review Questions and Answers   198

    Bibliography   229

    Index   231

Charts and Real Estate Instruments

Interests in Realty   6

Descent in Distribution of Estate of an Intestate   15

Contract of Sale   66–68

Full Covenant & Warranty Deed   87
Bargain and Sale Deed   87–88
Quitclaim Deed   88
Closing Statement   97
Bond   101
Mortgage   106–108
Affidavit of Title   120–122
Assignment of Mortgage   123
Extension Agreement   127–130
Release of Mortgage   131–132
Subordination Agreement   134–135

REAL ESTATE

1

THE REAL ESTATE BUSINESS AND THE MARKET

The real estate business represents a diversity of enterprise involving real property. Real property may be defined as land, along with its appurtenances and improvements. The land itself is fixed and unique, in that there can be no two parcels alike. *Appurtenances* are those incidental interests which attach to and pass with the land, such as trees, easements, and rights of way. Manmade *improvements* also belong to real property if they are permanently attached to the land; examples are buildings, bridges, swimming pools, and the like.

Legally, land includes not only the soil and everything permanently erected thereon, but everything above and within the earth. The earth's limits, both upwards and downward, are indefinite in extent; therefore, crops are part of real property, as are oil, minerals, and gases in the subsurface. Buildings or improvements may be built in the airspace over the land to the limit allowed by local building codes. These rights to the air space and surface may be used by the landowner or sold or leased by him to another, just as any other portion of his real property.

THE REAL ESTATE BUSINESS

Real estate enterprises may be involved in marketing, brokerage, management, finance, construction, and appraisal. Marketing consists of placing property, or interests in real property, with the consumer. Brokerage is the negotiation of the transfer of title to or an interest in real property and represents that phase of real estate activity engaged in by most people in the real estate business. Property management is closely related to the marketing function. Real estate financing involves negotiations with commercial and savings banks, savings and loan associations, mortgage and insurance companies to provide funds for a particular real estate project. Construction refers to the erection of permanent improvements upon the land, including its sub-

1

divisions and developments. Appraisal concerns itself with estimating the value of real property.

The Real Estate Profession. Most of the people who are in the real estate business consider themselves members of a profession. Standards are dictated not only by statutory requirements but also by the self-imposed regulations of the various trade and professional associations. The National Association of Real Estate Boards and its affiliates is a nationwide organization with branches in every state. Affiliated organizations are the American Institute of Real Estate Appraisers, the Institute of Real Estate Management, the Institute of Farm Brokers, the National Institute of Real Estate Brokers, the American Society of Real Estate Counselors, the Society of Industrial Realtors, and the International Real Estate Federation.

Organizations not affiliated with the Real Estate Boards, but which carry on collateral work of importance to the real estate business are: the National Association of Home Builders, the American Bankers Association, the United States Savings and Loan League, the Society of Residential Appraisers, the Mortgage Bankers Association, and the Life Insurance Association of America. Many of these organizations provide educational programs and maintain standards of practice.

The National Association of Real Estate Boards, in order to guarantee high standards of practice, adopted in 1924 an official code of ethics, which has been revised periodically and kept up to date. Every local organization which becomes affiliated with the Association is required to adopt and enforce the code. Its principal objectives are to regulate relationships between those in the real estate business and the public, such as those between brokers and owners.

THE REAL ESTATE MARKET

The real estate market is created as buyers and sellers find the means to translate their wishes to buy and sell into action. The market is ordinarily classified according to the particular use of the property, such as residential, commercial, industrial, and agricultural. Each of these categories may be concerned with either the purchase and sale of the properties themselves or the rental of property for specific periods of time.

The real estate market may also be classified according to

whether the property involved is income producing or non-income producing. Income producing properties range from modest two-family houses to multi-million dollar developments. Here, the distinguishing factor is that buyers and sellers are primarily interested in an investment opportunity. The important considerations are net return and income potential. Non-income producing properties are obtained primarily for residential occupancy by the owner. Some properties combine income and residential potential—e.g., two-family or small multi-family residences and farms.

The Mortgage Market. The mortgage market is one extremely important factor which influences the real estate market. Since real estate purchases are seldom made with a large percentage of cash, the ability to buy is largely determined by the ability to borrow money. When there is a shortage of mortgage money available and the liquidity of the mortgage money is "tight," buyers need more cash to buy, and this immediately reduces the number of prospective buyers. When mortgage money is "loose," i.e., readily available, buyers need less cash to buy, and this increases the number of prospective purchasers. The action of the Federal Government in securing FHA and VA mortgages has made these mortgages exceedingly attractive and has had the effect of increasing the availability of mortgage money and supporting the real estate market as long as the interest rates on mortgages are such that funds for investment would not do better elsewhere. Conversely, if funds could do better elsewhere, because of higher interest rates, they would leave the mortgage market and cause a tightening of the flow of the financing dollar.

Supply and Demand in Housing. The law of supply and demand as it relates to housing is another principal factor affecting the real estate market. Since housing is one of the more permanent types of property, the size of the total inventory can be controlled by adapting the rate of construction to the need. Booming conditions may develop temporary surpluses, but, by and large, the housing inventory is apt to be adequate. Demand for housing is influenced by the size and income level of the population. A rising level of income, even if there were no increase in population, could support considerable building activity. Also, newly established families, or an increase in population in any particular area would increase the demand for housing, provided that there had been no decline in the level of income.

Real estate activity generally occurs within a loosely defined market framework. The real estate specialist must know his commodity. He must judiciously use his resources, skill, experience, and judgment in bringing together the market participants—i.e., those who buy or sell or otherwise participate in real estate transactions.

2

PROPERTY RIGHTS AND INTERESTS

Real property, strictly interpreted, is that right or interest which an individual has in real estate—here defined as anything that is fixed, permanent, and immovable, such as land and its attachments—to the exclusion of everyone else. *Estates in realty* refer to the rights of ownership, use, and possession of real estate. A right of ownership usually reflects permanency, whereas rights of use and possession refer to estates of a more temporary nature. Rights and interests in real property may consist of estates, easements, and such miscellaneous interests as licenses and franchises. Diagrammatically they would appear as on page 6.

INTERESTS IN REALTY

Interests in real estate may be classified according to: (1) duration of the right, (2) time of becoming effective, (3) number of holders, (4) legal or equitable rights, and (5) property rights.

Duration of the Right. Estates classified according to the duration of the right may be either *freehold* or *less than freehold*.

A *freehold* estate is one that continues forever, or for the life of one individual, or for the lives of more than one individual.

An estate *less than freehold* is one that continues for a period longer or shorter than one person's lifetime. It should be borne in mind that it is possible for an estate less than freehold to run for a longer term than a freehold estate; consequently, a life estate may last only one year (if the life tenant dies at that time), whereas a lease for a number of years may remain in force throughout a longer period.

Freehold Estates. Freehold estates may be: (1) of inheritance, i.e., one which, upon the death of the holder, still continues and descends to the heirs of the holder, or (2) not of inheritance, i.e., one which terminates at the death of the holder and descends as specified when the estate is created.

Fee Simple. The most common freehold estate of inheritance

5

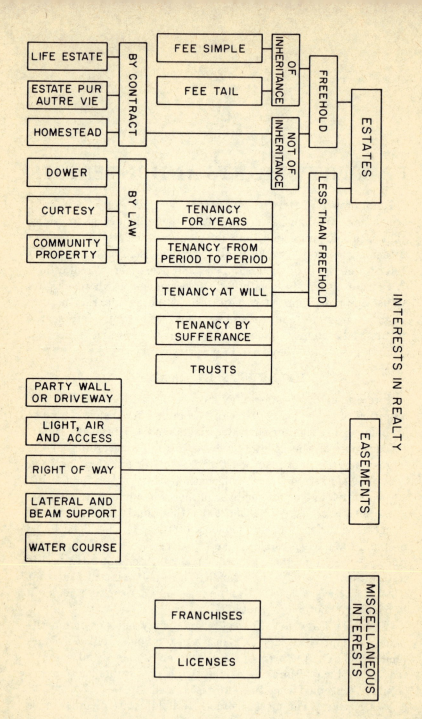

is the *fee simple absolute,* also commonly referred to as a *fee simple* or a *fee.* This is the highest estate in real property. It gives the holder an absolute right in real property subject only to limitations imposed by the state. He can make any use of it he pleases, except that he may not act contrary to state laws. He may transfer it by will, deed, gift, sale, or otherwise. This estate is independent of time limitations, since the owners and heirs may enjoy its use forever. The owner of a fee simple absolute may restrict or even alienate his rights by his own acts or by his failure to act—such as failure to pay consideration, mortgage installments, taxes, or debts—which thus lead to foreclosure and sale.

Fee Tail Estate. This type of estate can be passed down to no one but the heirs of the body, i.e., direct descendants of the original owner. Since this type of estate restricts the alienation of real property, it has been abolished in most of our states and has been replaced by fee simple absolute or life estates with remaindermen, by operation of law.

Life Estate. A life estate gives the tenant full power to use and control the land and buildings as long as he lives, but thereafter his interest is nullified. Since the death of the life tenant terminates the estate, the sale or mortgage of the life tenant's interest gives the grantee or mortgagee doubtful value. The use of life insurance, with the mortgagee or grantee as the beneficiary and the life tenant as the insured, would be a practical method of shifting the risk of loss (due to the termination of the estate) to the insurance company.

A life estate may be predicated on the life of someone other than the tenant, such as the life of the grantor or the tenant's wife. This is known as an *estate pur autre vie.* If the tenant dies while the person by whose life the estate is measured is still alive, the heirs of the tenant inherit the estate until its termination.

Community Property. Community property laws recognize both separate property and community property; the laws prevail primarily in states where Spanish influences were strong. *Separate property* is comprised of the following: all property which the wife or the husband owned before marriage; and any property passing to her or to him afterward, either by inheritance or by gift. Such property is solely under the control of the spouse who is the owner thereof, and there can be no claim or interference therein by the other spouse.

After the marriage, newly acquired property (except gifts and inheritances) is attributed to the combined efforts of both the wife and the husband and constitutes their *community property*. The husband and wife are partners or owners in common of this property. There is no dower or curtesy in community property states. If there is a severance of the marital relationship, by divorce or otherwise, an equal division of the property is required.

Homestead Rights. These rights provide that the homestead shall not be subject to seizure in order to satisfy creditors. Homestead rights have originated recently, that is, during the last one hundred years, and were unknown at common law. Homestead laws prevent the loss of a home, by a forced sale, for the payment of the debts of the owner; they do not apply, however, to the foreclosure and sale of property because of default in the payment of mortgages or taxes. Generally, homestead rights apply only to real property which is used by a family for no other purpose than that of a home. Homestead rights may be alienated by sale, mortgage, or release, except where such alienation is contrary to state law.

Dower and Curtesy. Dower is a life estate, given to a surviving wife, in one-third of the real property owned by the husband during their married life. This right is inchoate, that is, it only attaches upon the death of the husband; however, the property cannot be sold or mortgaged unless the wife joins in the deed or mortgage and gives her consent. The right of dower ceases upon the death of the wife.

Curtesy is similar to dower except that it applies to a surviving husband who is entitled to a life estate in *all* of the property left by his wife, provided however that there is a child, born alive, of the marriage.

Dower and curtesy were abolished in New York State on September 1, 1930, but for marriages contracted prior to that date, the rights still survive. Although several states still retain this survival of common law rights as originally intended, most states have modified them with statutory provisions.

ESTATE LESS THAN FREEHOLD. Estates less than freehold are those that last for a certain or uncertain number of years. They are also called leasehold estates or *chattels real,* that is, personal estates in real property. The owner of the fee is called the *landlord* and the estate holder is called the *tenant.* Estates less than freehold may be classified as follows:

Estate for Years. This estate continues for a fixed period of time or a term—e.g., a commercial lease.

Tenancy at Will. This is an estate which continues at the will of either the landlord or the tenant.

Tenancy from Year to Year, or from Month to Month. The duration of this estate depends on the terms stipulated in the lease.

Tenancy by Sufferance. This estate is created when a tenant who has entered possession rightfully, holds over wrongfully. Both the tenants at will and by sufferance may be removed by the landlord after thirty days' written notice.

Statutory Tenant. This estate, created by the emergency rent laws, which were passed because of the housing shortage and emergency, means that a landlord cannot remove a tenant whose lease has expired, as long as the tenant continues to pay rent; during that period of tenancy the tenant is deemed a statutory tenant.

Time of Becoming Effective. *Estates in expectancy,* as distinguished from estates in possession, represent rights whose benefits can be enjoyed only at a future time. The exact date can be set forth in the instrument which creates the estate; or the date may be indefinite, depending upon a contingency that cannot be anticipated. Estates in expectancy may be classified as *reversions* and *remainders.*

REVERSION. If an owner has passed his ownership rights on to someone else for a number of years, or for life, or until a stated event happens, the return of those rights to the owner constitutes a reversion. Let us assume that Adams has granted Brown a life estate with reversion to Adams, his heirs or his assigns. Upon the death of Brown the ownership of the property will revert to Adams. This is known as a *definite* reversion, as Brown must die at some future date. A definite reversion is devisable and assignable. Reversionary rights may also be *indefinite,* or only a possibility. For instance, if Adams, the owner of a fee, transfers his property to Brown, for a specific purpose, with the stipulation that the property would revert to Adams if the purpose of the transfer were abandoned, or if the grantee were to violate the terms of the transfer, then, upon either the abandonment or violation of the terms of the transfer, the property would revert to Adams. Since this reversion is only a possibility, and thus an indefinite estate, it is not assignable; but the rights in the reverter may pass to the heirs of the owner of the reversion if he dies.

REMAINDERS.   A remainder is a deferred estate going to someone other than the original owner. It may be definite as to amount and time, but it does not become effective until the expiration of a previous estate. The previous estate is a grant of possession of the same property to another person. A remainder differs from a reversion in that a reversion goes back to the original grantor, whereas a remainder goes to a third person. Both usually arise after the expiration of a life estate. When the life tenant dies, the remainderman takes over and may receive either a fee simple, a life estate, or an estate for years. A remainder may be vested or contingent.

Vested Remainder.   This is an estate which is fixed and definite; only the possession is deferred. In the situation where Able grants his property to Baker with Carter as remainderman, there is a vested remainder in Carter, since Baker must die some day. Carter may sell, transfer, or assign his right as remainderman prior to possession.

Contingent Remainder.   In this estate it is necessary for a stipulated contingent event to occur before possession or title can pass to the remainderman. If the contingency does not occur, no rights accrue. Let us assume, for instance, that a widow leaves a life estate to her son with the proviso that the remainder will go to a charity if the son dies without issue. Since the son may die with issue and thereby negate the remainder, this estate is a contingent remainder. Or, in order to regulate the life pattern of his heirs, a father may specify that his daughter shall inherit the remainder, provided that she marries by a certain age, or marries a certain man.

Many states have *mortmain* statutes and rules against perpetuities to prevent the governing of estates by a "dead hand" of a deceased, or to prevent the alienation of real property for an indefinite future period of time.

Number of Holders.   If there is but one individual owner of a parcel of real property, he is known as an *owner in severalty*.

Where there are two or more owners, they may be classified as follows:

TENANTS BY THE ENTIRETY. This tenancy comes into existence when a husband and wife take title to property jointly. Although nothing is stipulated regarding the tenancy, the presumption is, in law, that they are joint tenants enjoying the right of survivorship.

JOINT TENANTS. This tenancy usually occurs where two or more persons are deeded land in such manner that they have one and the same interest, which begins at one and the same time, and the land is held by one and the same undivided possession. In a joint tenancy, there is the right of survivorship, which means that if one of the joint tenants dies the survivor becomes the owner of the entire fee.

TENANTS IN COMMON. In this tenancy both tenants enjoy joint possession of the property but have separate and distinct titles. Each tenant can separately alienate his interest and there is no right of survivorship. It is not necessary for the estates to be created at the same time, nor do the interests of the tenants have to be equal.

TENANCY IN PARTNERSHIP. This tenancy occurs where real property is bought with partnership funds and title thereto is taken in the name of the partnership. The property does not have to be recorded in the name of one or more of the individual partners.

TRUSTS. Trusts are usually described according to the purpose for which they are created.

A *testamentary* trust is one that is created under the terms of a will by the testator, the property owner, who entrusts his property to a trustee for the benefit of the named beneficiaries.

A *living* trust is one in which the property owner transfers the legal ownership and management of land to a trustee. Usually the benefits go to the property owner while he is alive; upon his death the benefits go to his heirs or designated beneficiaries.

A *land* trust is one in which the true owner acquires title to property in the name of a trustee; the true owner's name is usually not disclosed. A trustee-beneficiary agreement is set up in a separate contract which is not recorded; thus, the equitable owner, as beneficiary, may conceal ownership of the property from his wife, relatives, or creditors.

CORPORATE REAL ESTATE. This applies to real property owned by a corporation. A corporation, which is an artificial legal entity, has the implied power to buy or hold real property for the conduct of the corporate business. The corporation may buy, sell, or mortgage real property in accordance with the statutory regulations of the state. Usually the consent of the stockholders is also required.

Legal or Equitable Rights. Estates may also be classified as *legal* or *equitable.* This distinction arises from the methods employed to enforce the rights of the individual. Legal rights are enforced in a court of law and equitable rights in a court of equity. (In New York there are no separate courts of law and equity, but in dealing with a claim the court considers whether the theory of the action is legal or equitable.) Legal decisions require the use of either the statutes or the common law. In decisions based on equity, the paramount question involves fairness rather than the strict and narrow interpretation of the statutory law. Form is not the decisive factor.

For instance, in some states a mortgagee is recognized as the legal owner of real property and the mortgagor as the equitable owner, who is entitled to receive the legal title upon satisfaction of the mortgage according to its terms. We also find examples of legal and equitable ownership in the administration of trust estates. When a trust is created by the settlor, the legal title is conveyed to the trustee and recorded in his name. The equitable title, however, rests with the beneficiaries of the trust.

Property Rights. Estates may also be classified according to the property rights therein. These rights may be either corporeal or incorporeal.

CORPOREAL RIGHTS. These imply full and exclusive possession and use of the land, within the limits of the instrument establishing the right. A freehold estate in land is an example of a corporeal right.

INCORPOREAL RIGHTS. These rights, which include easements, licenses, and franchises, do not imply legal title to real estate; they merely indicate the use one individual may make of property belonging to another person.

Easement. In an *easement* someone who is not the owner is granted the right to use the land for a stated purpose. For example, in a utility easement the owner of land may agree to allow a utility company to erect poles and draw wires over his property for the purpose of supplying electricity to the area to be serviced.

License. A *license* is a right granted by one party to another permitting the use of the former's property by the latter for a specified time and for a specified purpose. A license may be oral, express, or implied. It is usually revocable at will and expires with the sale of the property. It usually does not create an estate in the land; however, if the licensee has gone to considerable expense in the process of using his license, the owner may not readily revoke it without reasonable compensation. A storekeeper who advertises merchandise for sale impliedly gives the public a license to enter his store to consider a purchase.

Franchise. A *franchise* is a privilege, usually granted by the government to specified parties, to use public lands for such purposes as are set forth in the franchise. Franchises are frequently granted to public utilities for the purpose of providing a public service to a community.

VOLUNTARY AND INVOLUNTARY ALIENATION OF REAL PROPERTY

Alienation of real property refers to the transfer of the interest in and/or the title to real property by its owner to another. The transfer of the interest in real property may be by voluntary alienation or by involuntary alienation.

Voluntary Alienation. Voluntary alienation occurs under any one of the following conditions:

SALE. This is the normal commercial real estate transaction.

CONTRACT OF SALE. This is an agreement to be later consummated by the delivery of a deed.

GIFT. The gratuitous delivery of a deed to property from a parent to a child, or from one person to another, is a transfer of interest by gift.

MORTGAGE. This is considered to be a form of voluntary alienation in many states. The legal title to real property is conveyed by trust deed to the mortgagee as security for a loan. This title is subject to divestiture upon the repayment of the loan by the mortgagor.

LEASE. Whether a lease is for life or for a period of years, it is considered to be a form of voluntary alienation of the property for the period of the lease, subject to reacquisition by the lessor at termination.

DEDICATION. A dedication is any transfer of real property to the public. Land may be dedicated by an individual or any property owner. Most commonly, a subdivider or developer may voluntarily deed land and improvements to the municipality, after providing street, curbs, and gutters. Thereupon, the burden of future upkeep would be assumed by the public authorities. There must be an intent by the grantor to give the property to the public and the public must be willing to accept the property.

WILL. Real property may be voluntarily alienated in accordance with the desire of the testator and provide for the disposition of his property to take effect at the time of his death, if the will is executed according to the formalities required by law. Through his will, the owner may pass title to his real estate to the devisees of his choice. Title to real property left in a will is passed by the executor who executes an executor's deed to effectuate the transfer.

DESCENT. This means alienation of property by operation of law. In situations where the owner of real property dies without leaving a will, or leaves an invalid will, or leaves a will that does not provide for the disposition of his real property, the property of the intestate is distributed in accordance with the laws of the state. This distribution is based generally upon the degree of consanguinity. New York, for example, provides for distribution in the event of intestacy in accordance with the chart on page 15.

Involuntary Alienation. The following are the principal ways in which an interest in real property can be transferred by involuntary alienation, i.e., without the owner's volition:

JUDICIAL PROCESS. Transfer or forfeiture through judicial process may entail (1) a *tax sale* to enforce the lien of unpaid taxes, (2) a *public sale* as the result of actions to enforce liens and judgments, unpaid mortgages, foreclosures, or unpaid judgments, and (3) an action under the terms of the *Bankruptcy Act*, whereby the Trustee in Bankruptcy acquires title to the bankrupt's property as of the date of the filing of the petition in bankruptcy. (The Trustee is empowered to give a trustee's deed to the new purchaser.)

ADVERSE POSSESSION. A resident of land may claim title

DESCENT AND DISTRIBUTION OF ESTATE OF AN INTESTATE UNDER §83 OF THE STATE OF NEW YORK DECEDENTS ESTATE LAW AS AMENDED

APPLIES AFTER 3/1/64

HUSBAND OR WIFE	CHILDREN OR DESCENDANTS	FATHER	MOTHER	BROTHERS SISTERS OR DESCENDANTS	SURVIVING GRANDPARENTS	UNCLES OR AUNTS	FIRST COUSINS	FIRST COUSINS ONCE REMOVED	FIRST COUSINS TWICE REMOVED
$2,000 IN MONEY OR INTANGIBLE PERSONAL PROPERTY AND 1/2 OF THE RESIDUE	1/2 RESIDUE (ONE CHILD OR DESCENDANTS OF ONE CHILD)*	S	S	S	S	S	S	S	S
$2,000 IN MONEY OR INTANGIBLE PERSONAL PROPERTY AND 1/3 OF THE RESIDUE	2/3 RESIDUE (TWO OR MORE CHILDREN OR THEIR DESCENDANTS)	S	S	S	S	S	S	S	S
$25,000 AND 1/2 RESIDUE	N OR D	1/4 RESIDUE	1/4 RESIDUE	S	S	S	S	S	S
$25,000 AND 1/2 RESIDUE	N OR D	1/2 RESIDUE	D	S	S	S	S	S	S
$25,000 AND 1/2 RESIDUE	N OR D	D	1/2 RESIDUE	S	S	S	S	S	S
ALL	N OR D	D	D	S	S	S	S	S	S
D	ALL	S	S	S	S	S	S	S	S
N OR D	N OR D	1/2	1/2	S	S	S	S	S	S
N OR D	N OR D	ALL	D	S	S	S	S	S	S
N OR D	N OR D	D	ALL	S	S	S	S	S	S
N OR D	N OR D	D	D	ALL	S	S	S	S	S
N OR D	N OR D	D	D	N OR D	ALL IN EQUAL SHARES	S	S	S	S
N OR D	N OR D	D	D	N OR D	D	ALL IN EQUAL SHARES	S	S	S
N OR D	N OR D	D	D	N OR D	D	N OR D	ALL IN EQUAL SHARES	S	S
N OR D	N OR D	D	D	N OR D	D	N OR D	N OR D	ALL IN EQUAL SHARES	S
N OR D	N OR D	D	D	N OR D	D	N OR D	N OR D	N OR D	ALL IN EQUAL SHARES

*THIS PROVISION AND THE $2,000 IN MONEY OR INTANGIBLE PERSONAL PROPERTY DO NOT APPLY WHERE THE SURVIVING SPOUSE EXERCISES THE RIGHT OF ELECTION PURSUANT TO §18 DECEDENTS ESTATE LAW.

NOTE: DOWER AND CURTESY ARE ABOLISHED. WIDOW MAY TAKE (ELECT) DOWER IN LIEU OF SHARE IN FEE WHERE INCHOATE RIGHT OF DOWER EXISTED PRIOR TO SEPTEMBER 1, 1930.

PERSONS MORE REMOTELY RELATED TO THE DECEDENT THAN THOSE SET FORTH ABOVE DO NOT INHERIT. IN SUCH CASE, REAL PROPERTY PASSES TO THE PEOPLE OF THE STATE OF NEW YORK. PERSONAL PROPERTY IS PAID TO THE COMPTROLLER OF THE STATE OF NEW YORK.

ABBREVIATIONS: S = SURVIVING   N = NONE   D = DECEASED

thereto without any deed or color of title, which may be superior to that of the holder of the recorded title, by acquiring title by adverse possession. Title by adverse possession is acquired if a person holds land and maintains: (1) *actual, hostile,* (2) *open* and *notorious,* (3) *exclusive,* (4) *continuous* and *uninterrupted* possession of the land, (5) *under a claim of right,* (6) for a *statutory period* (varying from seven to thirty years) as provided by the law of the state in which the property is located.

Adverse possession is in essence a statute of limitations that bars the true owner from asserting his claim to the land, where he has remained silent and has done nothing to oust the adverse occupant during the statutory period.

Elements of Adverse Possession. The requirement that the possession of the claimant be open, notorious, and actual means there is no doubt in the mind of the ordinarily prudent person that it is just that. By hostile and adverse possession we mean that the possessor must exercise all acts of dominion over the land, not only against the world but also against the owner, if the opportunity presents itself. The possessor must treat his claim as superior and not subordinate to that of the record owner. This possession must be to the exclusion of the true owner. Continuous and uninterrupted possession means that there has been no abandonment of the property during the statutory period. The right that an adverse possessor has in the property may be handed from one to another without any break during the statutory period. This is known as *tacking,* that is, the continuity of possession is connected by a privity of estate: by grant, devise, descent, or judicial decree.

If the claimant can prove all of the foregoing conditions, he has good title to the property; all the rights of the record owner cease. The title relates then back to the date of the original possession. It may be risky to buy from one who holds title by adverse possession since there is no record of ownership. It may be difficult for the new owner to establish his title, inasmuch as persons who could prove his claim may have died. In order to quiet the title, one may apply to a court of competent jurisdiction for a *declaratory judgment,* whereby the rights of the adverse occupant may be judicially established.

The justification for the doctrine of title by adverse possession lies in the fact that it is undesirable to permit a person whose rights are being invaded to procrastinate in bringing an action to enforce his rights, until facts are forgotten, witnesses are dead, and the invading person has changed his position in the justifiable belief that the one whose rights have been invaded has abandoned his cause of action. If a person wishes to protect his rights, he should act diligently.

Exceptions. The doctrine of adverse possession cannot be asserted against land owned by the United States government, or land owned or used for a public purpose. Nor may it be asserted against a remainderman until the termination of the previous estate. Nor may an owner in common claim adverse title against a co-owner.

SQUATTERS' RIGHTS. People who settle on land without a claim of title or legal right are known as squatters; they cannot acquire title by adverse possession. However, if they are permitted to occupy land for more than the statutory period, they could thereby obtain an *easement by prescription* to use and hold the land until death or removal.

EROSION. Erosion is the wearing away of land through the processes of nature. Natural forces may erode the soil gradually and result in loss of title to the land. Thus a landowner can lose his interest in the land if the sea continues to encroach on it.

ACCRETION. Other natural forces may slowly and imperceptibly cause added increments of soil to be deposited on an owner's land, in which case he acquires title to the additional soil—a frequent occurrence on lands adjacent to large bodies of water.

EMINENT DOMAIN. The state has the power to appropriate real property from private persons for public use upon the payment of a just and reasonable compensation, determined in accordance with the law of the state. Upon payment the title to the land and property is transferred to the state. These proceedings are known as *condemnation proceedings*. The right of the state or federal government to take land in this manner is derived from the Constitution of the United States or of the particular state.

ESCHEAT. It is basic to the law of real property that title or ownership to property must always be vested in someone. Therefore, when an owner dies intestate and leaves no heirs or legal claimants, his property reverts to the state under the doctrine of *escheat*.

CONFISCATION. In times of war, powers are usually granted to the executive department of the government to take over property of enemy aliens, in order to prevent giving aid and comfort to the enemy. This involuntary alienation of real property is called *confiscation.*

3

AGENCY AND BROKERAGE

Basically, every real estate broker is an agent negotiating with some third person on behalf of his principal. Although he may not be expert in the law of agency, he should know the nature of his obligations under the law.

THE LAW OF AGENCY

An agency is a three party relationship, whereby one person, known as an agent, acts for another, known as a principal, in dealing with third persons.

Classification of Agencies. Agencies may be classified as follows: (1) express or implied, depending upon the manner of the appointment; (2) actual or ostensible, depending upon the reality of the appointment; (3) general or special, depending upon the scope of the authority; and (4) by type, depending upon the nature of the employment.

EXPRESS OR IMPLIED. An express agency is one in which the agent's authority is created by a written contract or oral designation; a written Power of Attorney is an example of an express agency. An implied agency is one in which the authority of the agent is inferred from the surrounding circumstances.

ACTUAL OR OSTENSIBLE. If an agency is either express or implied, it is an actual agency. An ostensible agency is one that is implied by operation of law, regardless of the principal's wishes, in order to prevent injustice to innocent third persons. For example, if one person permits another to hold himself out as the former's agent, and an innocent third person, relying thereon and acting on the belief that an agency exists, changes his position to his detriment, the law will not allow a denial of the agency. The effect would be the same as if there had been an actual agency. The first person would be legally estopped (prevented) from denying the agency. (This relationship is also referred to as an agency by estoppel.)

GENERAL OR SPECIAL.   In a general agency, the agent has broad authority to represent his principal, and broader powers to bind his principal. In a special agency, the agent's authority is limited to a specific task or series of tasks, and he has a more limited power to bind his principal.

BY TYPE.   In real estate, the types of agents most frequently encountered, according to the nature of their employment, are the salesman, who is engaged to sell real or personal property for his principal, and the broker, who is a special agent usually engaged to negotiate the sale of real or personal property, but has neither authority to change the principal's terms nor authority to extend credit or make warranties unless he obtains the express consent of the principal.

Other types of agents are delegates, factors or commission merchants, and mercantile agents.

Distinctions between Agents and Others.   Several important distinctions between agents and others must be pointed out.

AGENT AND EMPLOYEE OR SERVANT.   The difference between agent and employee is often difficult to describe. In theory, an agent may bind his principal by contract, whereas a servant or employee may not do so. If the servant or employee is given the authority to bind the master or the employer by contract, however, then the agency relationship also exists.

AGENT AND INDEPENDENT CONTRACTOR.   An agent is subject to supervision and control by his principal, who is liable for the contracts and torts of the agent arising in the course of the employment. An independent contractor is not under supervision or control by the one who employs him, and the latter is not responsible for the contracts or torts of the independent contractor since the latter has complete charge and supervision of the work being done for the employer.

AGENT AND TRUSTEE.   An agent has no title to the property he handles, whereas a trustee has the legal, though not the equitable, title to the property in his custody. An agent acts in the name of the principal, whereas a trustee acts in his own name. The authority of an agent may usually be revoked by the principal at any time, whereas the authority of a trustee is retained until the purpose of the trust is fulfilled; the trustee may be removed, however, for cause.

AGENT AND SUBAGENT.   An agent derives his authority from his principal, whereas a subagent derives his authority from an agent who is, expressly or impliedly, authorized to appoint sub-agents.

AGENT AND AN ESCROW HOLDER. An agent acts for a principal in dealing with third parties. He cannot act for both the principal and the third party if their interests conflict. An escrow holder acts for the two adverse parties in accepting and holding some instrument, money, or thing of value such as a deed, document of title, or securities. An escrow holder's authority cannot be revoked except with the consent of all the parties.

The Principal. Whatever a person may do for himself, he may do through another; therefore, one may appoint an agent to do for him anything that he may legally do for himself.

THE INFANT AS PRINCIPAL. Since an infant can enter into a valid contract, which however may be voidable at his option, he may act as a principal. The agency thus created, like other agreements made by an infant, is voidable.

THE CORPORATION AS PRINCIPAL. Since a corporation is an artificial entity, or a fictitious person, it cannot act except through human agency; the human agent who represents the corporation is, by necessity, competent to act as a principal.

THE INSANE PERSON AS PRINCIPAL. The same rules that apply to the ability of an insane person to contract apply also to his ability to make a contract of agency.

The Agent. Any person, except the completely incapable, may be an agent. The infancy of an agent is no defense to the principal's liability since the agent is merely the conduit of the transaction, and not a party thereto. Only the legal capacity of the principal or the third person is material. The only qualification that an agent need possess is the mental and physical capacity to exercise the authority delegated to him.

CREATION OF AN AGENCY. An agency may be created through appointment or ratification (the acts of the parties), or by estoppel or necessity (the operation of law).

Agency by Appointment. The principal may appoint an agent by either written, oral, or implied contract. The agency contract may be oral or implied except where it is required to be in writing by the Statute of Frauds. The Statute of Frauds requires that an agency contract not to be performed within one year from the date of making, must be in writing. If an agent's duties involve the making of contracts governed by the Statute of Frauds, the state statutes will usually indicate whether his authority must be in writing.

Agency by Ratification. Ratification, in agency, is the approval of an unauthorized act done by an agent. A situation where an agent has acted without authority, or beyond the scope of his authority, may be later approved by the principal either in writing, orally, or by implication. A principal may ratify whatever an agent may *lawfully* do, although that act may be the subject of a civil suit. Thus, in addition to lawful contracts, he may ratify the agent's torts and be held liable therefor. By the same token, the principal cannot ratify the agent's crimes or be liable unless he aided, abetted in, or authorized the illegal act.

Agency by Estoppel. An agency will be implied in law when a person holds himself out to be authorized to act as the agent of another, and the latter, knowing that the agent is in fact not authorized, allows a third person to enter a transaction in reliance thereon, whereby the third person suffers a detriment. The law will estop, or prevent, the denial of the agency.

Agency by Necessity. An agency will be implied in law where a situation exists or an emergency arises which makes it necessary to presume an agency as public policy. For example, the law will imply an agency of a child to pledge his parents' credit for the purchase of necessaries, where the parents fail to supply them.

Relationship between Principal and Agent. The relationship between principal and agent arises generally out of a contract, although an agent may act gratuitously. No formality is required to create the relationship.

DUTIES AND OBLIGATIONS OF PRINCIPAL TO AGENT. If there is an express contract between the principal and the agent, it will set forth the obligations between parties, as well as the scope of the agent's authority to act on the principal's behalf. If there is no express contract, or, if the contract is silent as to some terms, then certain presumptions arise as a matter of law. Among the more important duties of a principal to his agent are: (1) the duty to compensate his agent, (2) the duty to reimburse the agent for expenses, (3) the duty to indemnify the agent against risks, and (4) the duty to pay damages for breach of the agency contract.

Duty to Compensate the Agent. In the absence of a conditional agreement, or in situations where there is a gratuitous agency, the principal is legally obligated to compensate his agent for services rendered. If there is no definite agreement, the agent is entitled to receive the reasonable value of his services, commensurate with his ability. If an agent is hired on the contingency that he is to be paid only if he produces a certain result, the agent is not entitled to payment unless the result is achieved. If an agent is given a drawing account against commissions, and there is no specific agreement that the drawing account is a loan or an advance to be returned in any event, then the drawing account is equivalent to a salary and need not be repaid to the employer if no commissions are earned.

Duty to Reimburse Agent. A principal is obligated to reimburse his agent for all authorized expenses incurred during the existence of the agency.

Duty to Indemnify Agent. If the agent reasonably or necessarily assumes risks during the existence of the agency, the principal is obligated to reimburse him for same.

An agent has a lien for reimbursement and for indemnity on account of advances, expenses, and losses, but not usually for his services rendered unless so provided for in his contract. This lien applies to monies of the principal in the hands of the agent.

Duty to Pay Damages for Breach of the Agency Contract. If the principal breaches his contract of agency, he is obligated to pay the agent all the damages that reasonably flow from the breach. The agent, however, is not entitled to speculative damages, and is obligated to keep the amount of damages to a minimum.

DUTIES AND OBLIGATIONS OF THE AGENT TO THE PRINCIPAL. Among the more important duties of an agent to his principal are: (1) loyalty and good faith; (2) obedience; (3) skill, care, and diligence; and (4) duty to account.

Loyalty and Good Faith. The relationship of an agent to his principal is fiduciary, meaning that he must exercise the highest degree of loyalty and trust. Violation of this relationship may mean loss of compensation, reimbursement, indemnification, or lien. An agent should therefore not serve two principals with conflicting interests, except with the knowledge and consent of both; nor should he have a personal interest adverse to his principal's.

Obedience. If an agent is engaged to perform routine duties, he must obey his principal's instructions to the letter; if he is allowed to use his discretion, he must use his best judgment in following instructions. If a principal suffers damages caused by an agent who exceeds his instructions, the agent may be held liable therefor.

Skill, Care, and Diligence. An agent is required to exercise that degree of skill, care, and diligence commensurate with the nature of the task. An agent who undertakes a particular agency impliedly warrants that he has the necessary skill and will exercise the necessary care and diligence to perform the task properly.

Duty to Account. The agent is obligated, if he collects money for a principal, to render to the principal prompt notice of same, and make remittance either at once or as per custom or agreement. If the agent is permitted to retain the principal's funds for a period of time, as a fiduciary, he must not commingle these funds with his own but must keep them in a separate, special account—unless he has the principal's authority to commingle these funds.

Third Parties. Third parties are persons with whom the agent negotiates on behalf of his principal.

Liability of Principal to Third Parties. A principal is liable to third parties on the contracts made by his agent if one of the following conditions exists: (1) the contract was expressly or impliedly authorized; or (2) the contract, though unauthorized, was ratified; or (3) the contract was such that the third party had a right to assume that the agent was duly authorized.

Liability of Principal on Contracts of General Agents. The principal is liable on contracts made by his general agent, though unauthorized, if the agent had apparent authorization and the third person is unaware that the agent is exceeding his authority.

The authority to conduct a transaction usually includes authority to do those acts which are incidental to it, or accompany it, or are reasonably necessary to it. For example, an agent who has possession and authority to sell personal property has the implied authority to fix the price, terms, and warranties, and to deliver possession and accept payment. But he does not have the implied authority to mortgage the property or sell it on credit.

The authority merely to sell or solicit sales, however, does not carry with it the authority to make collections, unless the agent possesses the goods and has proof of that authority. Likewise, an agent who has the authority to pay bills for a principal does not have the implied authority to borrow money, even though the money may be needed to pay the principal's bills.

An agent who is authorized to collect is not authorized to collect anything but money; if he is permitted to take checks, he has no authority to cash them.

Whether or not a principal becomes liable to subagents or employees hired by a general agent depends upon the actual or apparent scope of the general agent's delegated authority.

Liability of Principal on Special Agent's Contracts. A principal is liable to third parties on a contract negotiated on his behalf by a special agent only if the agent has been expressly authorized to execute the contract.

LIABILITY OF AN AGENT TO THIRD PARTIES. An agent is personally liable to third parties for:

1. Breaching a duty common to all persons.
2. Acting for an incompetent or non-existent principal.
3. Acting for an undisclosed principal.
4. Misrepresenting the extent of his authority.
5. Receiving money wrongfully, through fraud, mistake, misrepresentation, and the like.
6. Assuming personal obligations.
7. Committing a tort.

LIABILITY OF THIRD PARTY TO PRINCIPAL AND AGENT. A third party is bound to a principal by the contracts of the agent, regardless of whether the principal is disclosed or undisclosed, except in those cases wherein there is a representation that there is no agency.

Since the contract made by an agent is on behalf of his principal, the third party is liable thereon only to the principal and not to the agent.

The Undisclosed Principal. An undisclosed principal is one whose identity is not disclosed to the third party at the time the contract was made, even though the third party knows that the agent is acting for a principal. Where an undisclosed principal is not known at the time of the contract, but is later discovered by the third party, the latter has the option of holding either the agent or the undisclosed principal liable on the agency contract; he cannot hold both liable.

The undisclosed principal is not liable for the acts of his agent if the contract has been fully executed by the agent and if the agent has exceeded or acted outside of the scope of his authority, or if the agent has signed a negotiable instrument (since no person can be a party to a negotiable instrument unless his name appears on it).

Termination of the Agency. An agency may be terminated under the following conditions: (1) in accordance with the terms of the contract of agency; (2) by the acts of the parties, that is, by mutual agreement or revocation by the principal (unless the agency is coupled with an interest), or by renunciation by the agent; and (3) by operation of law, that is, when there is illegality of the subject matter, destruction of the subject matter of agency, termination of the purpose of agency, death or incapacity of one or both of the parties, dissolution of the business, and bankruptcy or insolvency of the principal.

Termination of an agency will not bind third persons who have transacted business through the agent, unless due notice of the termination is received.

REAL ESTATE BROKERAGE

The Real Estate Broker. A real estate broker is a professional agent who is engaged in the business of procuring the purchase or sale of land, who acts as an intermediary between seller and purchaser, or who negotiates loans on real estate.

The real estate broker's relationship to the public requires a high degree of competency and trustworthiness; therefore, most states require that he establish his ability and integrity and be licensed before he is permitted to engage in the business.

The real estate broker, although an agent for many different principals in negotiating the sale of their properties, is nevertheless an independent businessman with reference to the operation of his office. Generally, the broker's duty is to find a buyer who is ready, willing, and able to purchase the property, either according to the terms of the listing contract, or on other terms acceptable to the principal. Although the broker does not have the authority to bind his principal to a contract of sale or to make a conveyance of real property, such authority may be delegated to him.

The Real Estate Salesman. The real estate salesman works out of the office of a real estate broker. The salesman is usually the one who makes the sales talks and representations which induce the prospect to contract to purchase a property. It should be pointed out that the relation between the broker and salesman, as well as that between the owner of property listed for sale and the broker listing the property, is that of principal and agent. In the absence of a statute requiring that such contracts be in writing, an oral contract creating such a relation is enforceable.

Listing Contracts. The employment of a broker as an agent authorized to find a buyer for real property is known as a listing. In a majority of states (New York included), the listing contract need not be in writing, unless, by its terms, it is not to be performed within a year. However, many risks and misunderstandings may be avoided by the use of a carefully drafted and well-rounded listing contract. Specimen forms are usually available through local real estate boards; a contract may also be drafted by a competent attorney.

KINDS OF LISTING CONTRACTS. There are five commonly used types of listing contracts: (1) open listing, (2) multiple listing, (3) net listing, (4) exclusive agency listing, and (5) exclusive right to sell listing.

Open Listing. An open listing is one which is given to any number of brokers, without liability to compensate any except the one who first secures a purchaser ready, willing, and able to meet the terms of the listing or who first secures the acceptance by the seller of a satisfactory offer made by the buyer. The sale of the property automatically terminates this listing.

Multiple Listing. A multiple listing is one whereby a real estate broker who is a board of exchange member brings his listing(s) to the attention of the other members; if a sale results, the commission is divided among the broker bringing the listing, the broker making the sale, and the listing bureau.

Net Listing. A net listing is one in which the owner specifies the price below which he will not sell the property, and the price at which a broker will not receive a commission; the broker receives the excess over and above the net listing as his commission. Most states frown upon the practice of net listings. In New

York, for example, §175.19 of the regulations of the Department of State provides that "No real estate broker shall make or enter into a 'net listing' contract for the sale of real property or an interest therein."

Exclusive Agency Listing. An exclusive agency listing is an agreement of employment between the owner of property and a broker, to the exclusion of all other brokers. If a sale is made by another broker during the term of the listing, the broker holding the exclusive agency is entitled to a commission, despite the fact that a commission may be payable to the broker who effected the transaction. However, the owner retains his right to sell the property himself without paying a commission.

Exclusive Right to Sell Listing. An exclusive right to sell listing is an agreement between an owner and a broker under which the exclusive right to sell the property for a specified period is granted to the broker. If a sale is made during the term of this agreement, whether by the owner himself or any other broker, the listing broker is nevertheless entitled to a commission.

The Broker's Employment by the Seller. The broker is usually the agent of the seller and must look to him for the payment of his commission.

DURATION OF EMPLOYMENT. The employment of a real estate broker may or may not be for a definite time, depending upon the terms of the employment contract or listing. If the time is fixed, the owner may not without risk cancel the broker's authority prior to the expiration date. Where no time is fixed for the duration of the broker's agency, either party acting in good faith may terminate the broker's employment at will. To avoid risk, the owner should notify the broker that his employment is terminated. This notice may be oral, written, or implied.

Whether the broker's authority is for a fixed or unspecified time, it is in any case terminable if one or more of the following conditions exists:

1. The purpose of the employment not accomplished within the *specified* time.
2. Where time is not specified, the purpose of the employment not accomplished within a *reasonable* time.
3. The death or insanity of principal or broker.
4. The bankruptcy of the principal or broker.

5. The destruction of the subject matter.
6. Sale by another broker.
7. Broker's fraudulent conduct for his own benefit.

DUAL EMPLOYMENT. Ordinarily a broker may represent only one principal. But a broker may be employed by both the buyer and the seller of real estate (neither of whom can avoid paying a commission) if they know that the broker is acting for both parties and give their consent.

COMMISSIONS. In order that a broker be entitled to a commission for a sale or lease, his services must be shown to be the procuring cause for the transaction. A broker is not entitled to his commission until there has been a meeting of the minds of the buyer and the seller on all of the material terms of the contract, such as price, amount of cash as down payment, amount and number of mortgages and their duration, the rate of interest to be paid on the mortgage, and the rate of amortization of the mortgage.

The mere fact that a broker introduces a buyer to a seller does not entitle the broker to a commission if he does not consummate an agreement and the transaction is subsequently negotiated by another broker.

If an owner has given the broker, in his listing, the full and complete terms upon which he is willing to sell his property, and not merely the asking price, the broker's duty is fulfilled, and his commission is earned when he produces a customer who is "ready, willing, and able" to comply with the terms fixed by the owner. (The words "ready" and "willing" mean that the buyer is prepared to enter into a contract in accordance with the terms set by the seller. The word "able" means that the buyer has the financial ability or the wherewithal to consummate the deal.) If the owner has listed the property for sale and has not fixed the price, or has not set the terms, leaving them to be determined thereafter, the broker's commission is not earned until the customer produced by him reaches an agreement with the owner upon the price and the terms upon which the sale can be made. It is therefore not necessary that a contract in writing be actually signed by all the parties, but rather that their minds have met upon all the essential terms of the agreement to purchase. In a controversy regarding commissions earned, the execution of a writing simplifies the proof of claim. Therefore, a well-drafted and executed binder would be as valuable as a contract of sale for such a purpose.

It is also a customary practice among brokers to agree that they are not entitled to commissions until title has actually been conveyed or the deal fully consummated, provided that the failure thereof is not due to any arbitrary or capricious act of the owner.

Rate of Commission.   The commission to be received by a real estate broker is not regulated by statute, nor legally fixed by the local real estate board. The commission, which in most areas is usually 5 or 6 per cent of the sales price, is generally mutually agreed upon by the owner and the broker. In the absence of such agreement, the broker is entitled to commissions at the rate customarily paid for similar services in the community where the services are rendered. Commission rates adopted by a real estate board merely govern the members of the board in their charge for their services; the community may follow or disregard the board's regulations. It is customary, however, for the public to accept the schedule of commissions promulgated by the real estate board, thereby creating prevailing or customary rates of commission, which will be recognized by the courts.

Conflicting Claims for Commission.   Where an owner employs a number of independent brokers to negotiate a transaction, only the broker who was the procuring cause of the sale or lease (i.e., first induced the customer to agree to the owner's terms) is entitled to a commission, regardless of whether a commission had already been erroneously paid to another broker. In an exclusive agency or exclusive right to sell listing, the listing broker is entitled to his commission, at least by way of damages, on a sale or lease by another broker during the existence of the listing.

Disclosure of Customer.   Where the seller does not require the broker to disclose the identity of the buyer, the broker is not bound to do so. However, if a broker does not identify the buyer and, after negotiations have failed, the seller negotiates the deal with that buyer independently of the broker, the broker is not entitled to a commission.

When Commission Is Earned.   Unless the contract provides otherwise, the broker earns his commission when he produces a buyer who is ready, willing, and able to buy on the seller's terms, even if these terms differ from those in the original listing contract.

Deferment of Commissions. The parties may agree that although the broker has been the procuring cause of the sale and has found a buyer who is ready, willing, and able to buy on the seller's terms, the commissions are not payable in the event that the sale is not consummated by a transfer of title. This waiver must be in writing, but does not require a valuable consideration. However, this waiver of commission is not enforceable if the seller does not consummate the transaction, unless the parties provide to the contrary.

Default by Owner or Seller. The broker's client cannot, in bad faith, terminate the broker's employment so as to consummate the transaction himself. The broker cannot thus be deprived of his commission. The broker is also entitled to his commission if the owner refuses to sign the contract of sale on the terms he had proposed; or if the title is unmarketable, because of some defect; or if the owner has misrepresented or mistakenly stated the size of the property; or if the owner is guilty of a misstatement of the amount of the rentals.

If the agreement provides that the buyer is to pay the commission, and the broker finds a buyer who is ready, willing, and able to perform on the owner's terms, but the owner refuses to perform, then the broker is entitled to the payment of the commission by the owner.

If the buyer refuses to take title because of ordinary street encroachments, the broker is not entitled to his commission, but if the sale is prevented by encroachments upon abutting owners he is entitled to compensation for his services.

Default by the Customer. Unless the customer is ready, willing, and able to comply with the terms of the agreement to buy or lease, the broker is not entitled to his commission. If a contract is consummated between the buyer and the seller, the broker's right to a commission is not affected by the customer's refusal, failure, or inability to perform. But the seller may justifiably refuse to enter into a contract or pay the broker where the buyer is an irresponsible dummy (a dummy being a person apparently acting for himself while, in reality, he is acting on behalf of another).

If the agreement provides for the commission to be paid by the buyer, then the latter is liable to the broker for the commission if he fails or refuses to complete the transaction; he continues to remain liable even when the transaction is not closed because there is a defect in the seller's title.

Broker's Duties. The broker has distinct obligations to both the client (principal) and the third person (customer), as follows:

To THE CLIENT. The relationship between broker and client is governed by the law of principal and agent; generally, the broker has the following responsibilities:

1. To exercise good faith and reasonable diligence and such skill as is generally possessed by persons of ordinary capacity engaged in the same business.
2. To make no secret profits by deceiving his employer.
3. To be loyal to his employer and account fully for transactions wherein the latter was defrauded.
4. To reveal all offers of purchase received.
5. To disclose the name of the purchaser, if the owner requests it, or lose his commission.
6. To take no incompatible position with his employer, i.e., buying the property for himself or any partnership or corporation in which he is interested without complete disclosure.

To THE CUSTOMER. The broker should guard against inaccuracies in representations to customers, such as a misstatement of a material fact made with intent to mislead the customer. This would constitute fraud and would justify the refusal of the buyer to take title and would afford the owner a good defense to the broker's claim for a commission.

DEPOSIT MONIES. Deposit monies coming into the hands of brokers and belonging to others are trust or fiduciary funds. This money belongs to the owner and must not be commingled by the broker among his own funds. It must be kept in a separate account and duly accounted for to the owner, unless there is an agreement to the contrary.

The broker is usually an agent of limited authority and must act in accordance with his authority. By taking a listing, a broker has the authority to find a purchaser and be a negotiator or intermediary. However, in such an instance, the broker does not have the authority to accept a deposit on behalf of the seller, unless he is specifically granted such authority. If he accepts such a deposit, he does so on behalf of the buyer, and the said deposit remains the property of the buyer until the offer is accepted. Upon acceptance of the offer, the deposit becomes the property of the seller, and the broker is no longer responsible to the buyer for returning it.

If the broker accepts a deposit from a buyer, with the condition that he secure suitable mortgage financing in order to complete the purchase, and there is further provided an escape clause in the contract whereby the deposit is refundable in the event that the mortgage loan is not obtained, then the deposit money is the property of the buyer until the financing is obtained.

Where the purchase of one property is conditioned upon the sale by the purchaser of property he already owns, a deposit paid on account of that contract remains the property of the buyer until the condition is performed.

Retention of the deposit by the broker in either of these instances, wherein the conditions have not been met and refund demanded, would be an unethical act and a demonstration of improper conduct on the part of the broker sufficient to warrant disciplinary action under the License Law. If the buyer arbitrarily causes the failure of the condition or the contingency, then the broker is not obligated to return the deposit.

If the condition or contingency is frustrated by the act of the seller, the broker will be entitled to his commission and he may retain the deposit; the buyer then will have a right of action against the seller for the return of the amount of the deposit, unless the broker agrees to return the deposit to the buyer in the event that the transaction is not completed.

The real estate broker must at all times consider the interest of those he represents as paramount to his own interests.

4

THE REAL ESTATE OFFICE
AND OPERATIONS

The operation of a real estate office involves many diverse activities. In this chapter we shall consider the principal participants, i.e., the broker and salesman, the organization of a real estate business, the scope of operations to be engaged in, and, briefly, real estate license law.

BROKER AND SALESMAN

The real estate broker and salesman play an important role in the community; they are usually the center of real estate activity and are charged with a strong public obligation. The real estate broker, usually assisted by several real estate salesmen, engages in a diversified variety of services relating to one or more types of real estate activity.

Broker, Realtor, and Salesman. As defined in real estate license law, the *broker* is a person, firm, or corporation licensed by the state to act, for a fee or other valuable consideration, as an intermediary to bring parties together and assist them in negotiating a contract relating to real estate. He endeavors to arrange for a "meeting of the minds" between buyer and seller. In addition he is also cognizant of land values, construction, and financing. He must be trustworthy, competent, and aware of his responsibility to the community. *Realtor* is a coined word which may be used only by an active member of a local real estate board which is affiliated with the National Association of Real Estate Boards.

In real estate license law the *salesman* is a person licensed by the state to be employed by a real estate broker on a salary and/or commission basis for the purpose of conducting real estate negotiations under the broker's supervision.

TYPES OF REAL ESTATE BUSINESS

After a salesman has passed the broker's examination, he may decide to open a real estate office. His first question then may be, as it often is in business: How shall the real estate office, as a business, be organized? Although the question cannot be categorically answered, there are many considerations. One of the most important is the impact of taxes. Also important are such matters as efficiency and flexibility of operation, license and license fee requirements, personal liability, continuity of the life of the business, amount of capital investment, and government control.

A business may take one of several forms: an *individual proprietorship* is the easiest to organize; the *partnership* form permits the pooling of capital, talent, skill, experience, and contacts of the co-owners; and the *corporation* attracts larger capital investments. A broker must evaluate the extent of his needs and the area of his operations and then select the type of organization which best suits his particular venture.

Individual Proprietorship.   By far the great majority of businesses are sole or individual proprietorships, which have the obvious advantages that the business is easiest to organize, the control is absolute, and there is a flexibility of operation. This type is a one-man organization. The broker receives all the profits and has the satisfaction of independence, a form of "psychic income." An individual proprietor may use either his own or a trade name; if the latter is used, the assumed name must be registered with the clerk of the county and the real estate license will be issued in that name. A disadvantage of individual proprietorship is that the business operations are necessarily limited by the amount of capital investment and the extent of the proprietor's experience. Its success depends heavily upon the owner's continuous personal attention to the business.

Partnerships.   The *partnership* form is usually desirable when two or more licensed brokers, whose qualities are complementary, decide to pool their resources and talents, experience, and business contacts. As in the case of the individual proprietor, there is no federal income tax on the organization per se, although each of the partners as an individual entrepreneur is taxed on his share of the income. There is, however, complete personal liability of each for all the debts of the business, and the acts of one partner acting *within the scope of his authority* in the business legally bind all other partners. The death of one partner dissolves the partnership. All partners must be licensed real estate brokers.

Corporation. The advantage of the *corporation* is that it limits personal liability, particularly in instances where the business entails financially risky activities beyond the field of brokerage as such. If the firm engages extensively in building and construction or subdividing and developing real property or real estate, there may be substantial advantages in the corporate form: stockholders have limited liability; capitalization is relatively easy; and the organization may have a perpetual life. On the other hand, this form of organization entails the costs of legal and statutory fees for incorporation; taxes are also an expense factor since a stock transfer tax must be paid. In addition taxes are paid on income, both by the corporation on its profits and by the stockholder on his dividends. Further, because of the limited liability features, credit is sometimes difficult to obtain.

SCOPE OF OPERATIONS

Real estate offices may conduct a general real estate business or they may specialize in a particular field.

Important Activities. In many large offices the scope of real estate activity may be wide and various and cover the following important services:

1. Sales. Negotiating sales of real property, usually on behalf of the owner for a commission or fee, or finding for a buyer a specific piece of real property. This activity is the most common type of service rendered.

2. Exchange. Negotiating the trade of two or more parcels of real property.

3. Financing. Assisting in the procurement of funds from lenders to expedite the purchase or sale of real property.

4. Management. Assuming responsibility for the custody, care, control, and preservation of the real property and insuring the maximum continuous net return from the real property, for the owner, during its economic life.

5. Leases. Securing rental property for tenants or finding tenants for property owners who wish to rent.

6. Appraising. Estimating the fair and reasonable value of real property.

7. Subdivisions and Development. Planning and constructing residential, multi-family, business, and industrial properties.

The larger offices may also have the following departments, each with its own supervisory personnel: (1) selling, exchanging, and obtaining listings for sales; (2) renting and leasing; (3) mortgage financing; (4) management; (5) appraisal and valuation; (6) farm and agricultural land; and (7) industrial and commercial properties.

Real estate offices must of course provide for the routines of internal operations: stenographic and clerical work; accounting and auditing; office management; and maintenance of office plant (library, maps, publications). The office personnel will include at least one licensed real estate broker and usually one or more licensed salesmen, as well as clerical and administrative personnel as needed.

Areas of Activity.   Most real estate brokers confine their area of activity to the neighborhood, town, or city in which their office is located. This concentration of activity gives the broker the time and opportunity to become expert in local conditions and situations. Although there are some brokers who operate on a state or nationwide basis, this type of activity is limited to a group that has created an organization which is usually beyond the resources or means of the average broker. The more extended the area of operations, the greater the need for more knowledge and larger staffs; the operating costs are also higher.

Location and Operation.   The most common location for a real estate office is the street level in a primarily transient area. Location plays an important role in attracting passers-by.

It is self-evident that a real estate office should be presentable, well-furnished, and should exhibit a general appearance of efficient operation. Files and records should be accurately kept, up-to-date, and readily available. The personnel of the office should be readily available to the clientele, and areas of privacy should be set aside for occasions when privacy is required. Coordination of office activities with few waste motions will make for smooth operations.

Practical Aspects.   Certain practical aspects of the real estate business may seem obvious, yet are often overlooked or underestimated. Without any consideration of these points, however, a new office may have difficulty getting off the ground, and may not long continue to function.

Capital Requirements.   Enough capital should be available for purchase of furniture and fixtures and for operating and living expenses during a period of six months. It is most desirable to go into business debt free or with a minimum of borrowing.

Operating Expenses. The usual operating expenses include rent, advertising, telephone and utilities, salaries, supplies, entertainment, and taxes (including license fees, social security, unemployment and income taxes).

Listings. The life blood of a real estate office primarily engaged in sales and resales is the securing of listings. The most common methods of obtaining listings are as follows: (1) personal contact, including telephone calls; (2) newspaper advertisements; (3) contact with financial institutions; (4) "For Sale" signs or advertised sales in the community; (5) news items of persons moving from the community; (6) obituary columns and reports; (7) other brokers and/or multiple listing bureaus. It should be noted that although advertising may not be one of the most effective methods of obtaining listings, nevertheless it is extremely useful in establishing the firm name and good will, and holds an important place in the operations of the business.

Real Estate as a Profession. The real estate profession is particularly well-suited to individuals who do not shrink from hard work and long hours, or a good deal of bell-ringing. There is a place in this field for one who is eager to study and learn. It is not a so-called desk job involving a nine to five routine with regular lunch periods and coffee breaks.

The rewards, both tangible and intangible, are limitless. There is no ceiling on what a qualified and capable real estate man can earn in dollars and cents. The intangible rewards derive from professional competence, personal satisfaction from a job well done, and respect earned from clients and colleagues.

REAL ESTATE LICENSE LAW

Each state has enacted its own laws for the licensing of real estate brokers and salesmen. The purpose of licensing statutes is to protect the public from dishonest practices, from unscrupulous persons, and from costly blundering by incompetent real estate agents. It also minimizes fraud and fraudulent practices in real estate transactions and promotes higher standards of efficiency and trustworthiness in the real estate brokerage business. (Detailed information with regard to the Real Estate License Law, as it applies particularly to the State of New York, is given in Appendix I.)

Constitutionality. Since real estate license laws generally operate to prevent individuals from pursuing a vocation and restrict the right to engage in the real estate business, many attacks on their constitutionality have been made over the years. Nevertheless, the broad basic concepts of these laws have been established almost universally as valid and constitutional.

Regulating Bodies. Each state supervises the licensing of real estate brokers through a regulating body. This body may be a real estate commission or a broker's board, or a separate department, or some other department given such responsibility as a part of its regular functions. In New York State, for example, licensing is regulated by the office of the Secretary of State.

Qualifications for License. The regulating body in each state determines the qualifications for licensing. Prime consideration is given to age, citizenship, residency, competency, and good reputation and character. Experience, preparation, education, and other background factors are important requisites.

Examinations. Practically all states require that an applicant for a broker's license take and pass a written examination to become qualified for licensing. Delaware requires merely the successful passing of an accredited course in real estate. New Hampshire is the only state that does not require a written examination.

Bond and Surety. The states are about evenly divided as to the policy of requiring the posting of a bond or surety by a broker. The amount of the bond required ranges from $1,000 to $5,000, with most such states requiring $1,000 from salesmen and $2,500 from brokers.

Fees. About half the states require an examination fee, ranging from $3 to $25. All states, however, impose a license fee on an annual or biennial basis, ranging from a low of $5 in some states to a high of $50 in others, with an average fee of $20 to $25. Renewal fees are usually the same as the licensing fees.

Expiration Dates. Nearly every state provides that all licenses expire on the same specified date. In some states licenses expire one year from the date of issue, and in Massachusetts licenses expire on the birthday of the licensee.

Suspension or Revocation of Licenses. Since the right to issue a license carries with it a reciprocal right to suspend or revoke it, all states have specific regulations providing penalties for certain violations, such as fraud, incompetence, untrustworthiness, and failure to obey the law.

Non-residents. Most states make provision for the licensing of non-resident brokers. Some have reciprocal arrangements with other states that offer their brokers licensing privileges. Many will license non-residents if they comply with the statutes of their own states.

5

SALESMANSHIP AND ADVERTISING

Although salesmanship in real estate may be regulated by legal formalities, the principles involved are little different from those concerning the sale of other articles of value (except that the money involved in real estate transactions is usually greater). Many books have been written in the fields of salesmanship and advertising generally. In this chapter we shall endeavor to present those phases of salesmanship that are particularly relevant to real estate transactions.

SALESMANSHIP

A large part of a real estate broker's activity is centered around negotiating the sale (or exchange) of real property for his principal. The art of selling is, therefore, at the core of the business operation. Selling involves perspicacity, aggressiveness, and hard work. Real estate selling is highly competitive. The competition stems not only from brokers or salesmen of other firms, but from the brokers and salesmen within the firm as well. There is always the record of one's own past performance. In the real estate field, the selling function runs the gamut from prospecting for properties and buyers to negotiating between buyer and seller, and to the final closing of the transaction.

Personal Qualities. The broker or salesman should bring personal qualities of tact, diplomacy, and good judgment to each business transaction, and he should be able to direct and manage himself as well as be directed and managed. Since the costs of maintaining a salesman are substantial, selection of a qualified person is a matter of vital concern to the broker. Even though most salesmen are paid on a commission basis, a lack of qualifications may result in financial loss to the firm. Some of the sought-after qualities of a salesman are: suitability to the business, ability to direct and manage business activities, personality, sales ability, intelligence, imagination, and persistence.

Some offices are large enough to require the services of a sales manager, who is able to assist in selecting salesmen and to train them to continue to grow on the job. The manager should have the confidence of his staff, be able to anticipate and solve problems, hold staff meetings, cooperate in securing prospects, and assist in negotiations and closings. He should possess a warm personality and an interest in people, and he should have a good working knowledge of real property and brokerage rules. Imagination and persistence are attributes that cannot be overlooked. Most importantly, he must have the ability to sell. He must be able to sell not only his product but his prospect as well.

A successful broker or salesman must be prepared to sell. Education, experience, and ability are vital factors. Other factors that contribute to successful selling are a knowledge of the buyers in the area, a knowledge of the general real estate market and business conditions, and an understanding of motives that influence buying. Some of the dominant motives for buying a residential home are the desire for economy and comfort, the love of children, and pride of possession. Inducements for the purchase of commercial property include the expectation of profit and the presence of guarantees of a continuous satisfactory return on the capital investment.

Knowledge of the Product. A factor in selling anything is a sound knowledge of the product. This is no less true in the real estate business. The broker or salesman should always inspect and investigate what is offered and analyze all the factors that could affect any anticipated transaction. The listing of a property should be complete and accurate. It has been said that "a house well listed is a house half sold." When he is listing a house, the broker should inspect the property thoroughly and make sure that the house is salable at the proposed terms. "A picture," said Confucius, "is worth 10,000 words!" In the absence of a camera a precise mental picture may be a reasonable substitute.

Prospects. Since one cannot sell unless he has a prospective customer, prospecting is a very important phase of the selling process. The sources of prospects are limitless. Some of the more commonly used methods of obtaining prospects depend upon advertising, personal contacts, previous inquiries, speculators and real estate operators, tenants in apartment houses managed by the broker or cooperative brokers, inquiries among neighbors, and publicity and public relations.

After securing a prospect, the salesman or broker should qualify him. First he should determine his needs and make an effort to correlate them to the available listings. The art of qualification demands discernment, diplomacy, and tact. The "window shoppers" and the curious must be separated from the buyers. Discussions with the prospect should elicit essential information, and yet not be offensive. A prospect may resent one's prying into his personal affairs; yet, besides checking his name and address, one must ascertain his business affiliation, average income, marital status, family make-up, location preferences, likes and dislikes, and religious and education affiliations.

After he has qualified the prospect, the broker is in a better position to show available properties. He knows the range of price the prospect can afford, the type of house, the number of rooms, the location, the services required, and the community facilities needed. Thus, much time and wasted effort can be avoided. If the prospect is a married couple, care must be taken to show the property to both parties together. The prospect should always see the physical property. Rarely will one spouse feel free to make a decision without the advice and consent of the other. Showing the property to both avoids delay and procrastination and increases the chances of immediate action.

Showing the Property.   Properties should be shown in their most favorable light. Appearances play an important role in this phase of the selling project. In the spring or summer, greater emphasis must be placed on the landscaped portions of the property. If the property is occupied, the neatness and cleanliness of the interior should be made a matter of concern. Also, an occupied house makes a better impression on a prospective purchaser than a vacant one. If the premises are in need of repairs or repainting, the broker should remind the seller that the cost of repairs usually is recovered in the purchase price.

The salesman should not show too many homes at one time since that only confuses the prospective purchaser; on the other hand, showing too few properties may unduly hamper the opportunity for comparison. It is necessary to take into consideration at all times the prospect's likes and dislikes, and to concentrate on showing properties best suited to his needs and desires.

In showing the property, the salesman will allow the prospect to convince himself that the property meets his needs and requirements. The salesman must think and act in terms of the prospect's problems; in other words, it is simpler to have the prospect sell himself than try to sell to him. Less time should be spent in talking about the property and more time given to answering the client's questions. Although sales talk is a necessary ingredient of the relationship, one should know when to stop talking. Overselling is risky and often disastrous.

The salesman should have the ability to convince the prospect of the benefits and the advantages of the product. Not only is truthfulness in describing and evaluating the product morally essential, but misstatements by the salesman can often be injurious. All questions should be thoroughly and honestly answered, all objections rationally explored, and an atmosphere of relaxed negotiation maintained—all this being accomplished while discussion emphasizes the factors of need, desire, interest, anticipation, and, finally, positive action. It is unwise to engage in technical discussions or to "talk over the prospect's head." Many a broker-client relationship has started off wrong because the broker, either by accident or design, talked down to the listener. Furthermore, it is poor judgment to argue with a prospect; one may win the argument but lose the deal.

The salesman should always try to obtain some offer from the prospect. If an offer is to be rejected, the broker should never do it; he should wait for the principal, the owner of the property, to make the decision.

After all preliminaries have been concluded, the test of a real salesman is found in his ability to close the deal. When is the most favorable psychological moment to ask the prospect, "When would you care to take possession?" Experience and, perhaps, intuition will assist the broker or salesman to pose this question at the most auspicious time and to receive an affirmative response.

One last point: An alert broker is always on the lookout for business. He should be active in community organizations, especially the chamber of commerce, and in religious and educational programs.

ADVERTISING

The purpose of advertising is to mold the customer's thinking along the lines preferred by the advertiser and thus to elicit a favorable decision. It is used basically for bringing realty to the attention of the prospective buying public, for paving the way to a possible sale, and for creating and maintaining good will.

Advertising is a presentation in a newspaper or a magazine or by television, radio, billboard, or direct mail; it is the consummation of conscious effort on behalf of the advertiser to create sufficient interest in the buyer's mind for the product. In this context it includes, besides the conscious use of the spoken and printed word, such factors as word of mouth, good will, and good public relations.

Types of Advertising. Real estate advertising may be classified as *specific,* meaning that it relates to the sale of a definite parcel of real estate. In addition, much real estate advertising is *institutional,* stressing the overall advantages of owning real estate property. Many brokers concentrate on *name* advertising, that is, on keeping the name of the broker in the public eye. Brokers use advertising therefore in many different ways to emphasize the advantages of the services he can render.

Some brokers, unfortunately, engage in unethical advertising, that is, advertising properties for which they have no listings or some which are not available or do not even exist. This practice, used basically to build up prospect lists, is considered unprofessional and misleading by reliable brokers.

Advertising Policy. A real estate firm's advertising policy must consider the following: what shall be emphasized, what media shall be used, what appeals shall be made, and how much shall be spent. A good program is determined in advance, yet is flexible enough to allow for a change in mid-stream. In an advertising budget, the expenditures are usually projected on a probable future volume of activity. Naturally, expenditures will be adjusted in the light of business fluctuations.

A formula has been devised to express the epitome of good advertising. A successful advertisement must attract *A*ttention, arouse *I*nterest, create a *D*esire, and inspire *A*ction. The first letters of Attention, Interest, Desire, and Action create the acronym Aida, generally referred to as the AIDA formula in advertising.

Specifically, real estate advertising should appeal to pride of ownership and status in the community, and to a sense of thrift, security, and comfort resulting from home ownership.

6

LEGAL ASPECTS OF
REAL ESTATE TRANSACTIONS

In this chapter we shall discuss some of the principles of the law of contracts and of crimes and torts with which one engaged in the real estate business should be acquainted. It is not intended, however, that this information should supersede in any way competent legal advice from an attorney, when needed.

CONTRACTS

Almost all transactions involving the sale, purchase, exchange, lease, or mortgage of real estate require a written contract. Examples of contracts include purchase and sale contracts, listing contracts, land contracts, deeds, mortgages, and leases.

The contract is the basic legal instrument in all real estate transactions. A knowledge of the law of contracts, as well as a knowledge of the manner in which the contract is used, is essential if owners, sellers, purchasers, brokers, and salesmen are to protect their own interests and to be aware of the effects of the contract on their rights and obligations.

Definition of a Contract.   A *contract* is an agreement whereby one party acquires a legal right to an act or a forbearance on the part of another. Unless there is a promise to do something or refrain from doing something which gives to the promisee a right in the future conduct of the promisor, there can be no contract.

For example, a written instrument acknowledging the receipt of a sum of money in payment for certain services has been held to be a receipt and not a contract, on the ground that it is a mere admission of a past transaction, containing no promise to do anything or to refrain from doing anything.

For a valid contract to exist, there must be both an *agreement* and a resulting legal *obligation*. An agreement is the expression of an intention by two or more persons to change the legal relationship between them. If, in the expression of the intention, a legal obligation is not imposed, there is only an agreement. If a legal obligation is imposed, the agreement becomes a contract.

Elements of a Contract. In order to have a contract, the parties thereto must include certain elements. Lacking any of these, there is no contract. These requisites are: mutuality of assent, legal capacity of the parties to contract, consideration, and legality of subject matter. To these elements is sometimes added: contracts to be in writing (a most important provision in real estate contracts since the Statute of Frauds and state real property laws are involved).

MUTUALITY OF ASSENT. Mutuality of assent means that an offer by one party must be accepted by the other, or by a meeting of the minds of the parties; otherwise no contract will result. After an offer has been made it may be revoked, rejected, or accepted. Situations also exist wherein the parties have apparently entered into a contractual agreement, but in reality have not done so.

The Offer. An offer may be oral or written and must fulfill certain requirements. If it is to serve as the basis for a contract, it must be seriously intended as such, communicated to the offeree, and definite and certain.

Since offers must be seriously intended as such, a mere expression of an intention or willingness to do some act in the future is not an offer. An offer differs from an intention in that it expresses or imports a willingness on the part of the offerer to incur a legal obligation to the one to whom it is made.

Offers involving social functions—e.g., to a tea or a dance, or to a baseball game—are not valid offers. Similarly, "invitations to trade"—e.g., advertisements, price lists, circular letters, and advertisements for bids on building projects—are not valid offers.

The offer must be communicated to the offeree, since he cannot accept an offer of which he has no knowledge. If an offer is made to someone, it can be accepted only by him and not by anyone else. For example, if Able offers to sell his house to Baker for $10,000, and Carter accepts Able's offer, Carter's acceptance would not constitute a contract.

If an offer is made to the public, e.g., in a real estate bulletin or newsletter, anyone who gains knowledge of the offer and accepts the terms outlined may consummate a valid contract. But suppose Able offers a group of lots for $500 to a select group on a mailing list, and Carter, without knowledge of the offering, seeks to purchase a lot at that price. Later, upon learning of the offering, Carter sues in specific performance. He cannot win the suit, since he was not aware of the offer, and his intention to buy the lot did not place any obligation upon Able to sell it to him.

The offer must be definite and certain. If an indefinite or uncertain offer is accepted, it cannot be said that the minds of the parties have fully met on all terms of the contract. A contract which leaves such matters as price and the contract period to be settled by future agreement is unenforceable because of its indefiniteness. An agreement to reach an agreement is no agreement at all.

If a vague offer is accepted, it cannot furnish the basis for a contract because such an offer in a contract would make it difficult to determine whether or not a breach had been committed.

Revocation of an Offer. An offer may be revoked (withdrawn) before it is accepted, with the following exceptions:

1. An option (e.g., a promise to hold an offer open) is binding if there is consideration.
2. In some states (e.g., New York) a written option is binding without consideration.
3. In some states (where seals are recognized) an option under seal is binding, as the seal imports consideration.

An offer may be revoked under the following circumstances:

1. Expressly, either orally or in writing.
2. By the lapse of a specified time, which is stipulated in the offer.
3. By the lapse of a reasonable time, if no time for acceptance is stipulated in the offer.
4. By the death or insanity of the offerer.
5. By the destruction of the subject matter of the offer.
6. By a legal prohibition following the offer.

Rejection of an Offer. An offer is extinguished by rejection, and cannot thereafter be accepted unless it is renewed. The rejection may be:

1. Flat or categorical, e.g., by affirmative action or statement by the offeree.

2. By a counter-offer. The new offer extinguishes the first offer; if the new offer is not accepted, the counter-offerer cannot then reinstate the first offer by subsequent acceptance.

Acceptance of an Offer.   In order to create a binding contract there must be an unambiguous acceptance, showing a clear intention to accept the offer in every particular, precisely as made. An intended acceptance which changes the place, time, or terms of payment, or the time and place of delivery, is inoperative as an acceptance of the offer.

If one accepts a written offer, by signing a document for instance which he later claims he had had no fair opportunity to read, he is bound by his acceptance and cannot hide behind the defense of ignorance. Inability to read what one signs, because of defective eyesight, is no defense. If, however, a signature to a contract has been procured by fraud or trickery, the contract is unenforceable.

An offerer cannot compel an offeree to speak or act by threatening to construe silence as an acceptance. In some instances, however, silence accompanied by other circumstances may be considered an acceptance where the offeree in some manner takes advantage of the offer by exercising rights of ownership or control of the subject matter of the offer, where the offeree intends to accept, or where a course of conduct has been established so as to spell out an acceptance.

Reality of Consent.   There are situations in which there exist an offer and an acceptance and the parties to an agreement have apparently consented to the same thing, whereas in reality they have not done so. The apparent consent of one or both parties to the agreement may have been given under such circumstances as to make it no true expression of their will.

The cases in which lack of real consent may arise are those in which there is mistake, misrepresentation, fraud, duress, or undue influence.

Mistake.   Mistake arises where the parties do not mean the same thing, or where, though meaning the same thing, they have formed erroneous conclusions as to the subject matter (in some important particular) which involves the very essence of the agreement. In such cases there is no true meeting of the minds because the apparent agreement is based upon the assumption of the existence of some fact which, in reality, does not exist. The effect of mistake is to render the contract void, and if the contract is executed, in whole or part, an action may be maintained to recover what has been paid.

Misrepresentation.   A misrepresentation is a statement of fact, not actually true, but believed to be true by the party making it. Also, in the absence of proof of fraud, a misrepresentation may include an intentional false statement as well as an innocent misstatement of fact. A misrepresentation of a material fact renders a contract voidable at the option of the party to whom the misrepresentation was made.

Fraud.   Fraud is a false representation of a material fact made with the knowledge of its falsity or with reckless disregard of the truth, or made with the intention that it be acted upon, relied upon by another, and acted upon by him to his injury or damage. Fraud renders a contract voidable at the option of the injured party. (A notable exception to this rule is the two-year incontestability clauses in life insurance policies. In a life insurance contract, the insurance company waives its right to void a policy for fraud discovered more than two years after the policy's inception date.) An injured party may also affirm the contract and sue for damages, or he may rescind the contract and demand the return of what he has put in and himself return that which he has received.

Duress.   To constitute duress there must be some actual or threatened exercise of power which is possessed, or believed to be possessed, by the party exacting or receiving the consent from another, the danger being one from which the latter can obtain immediate relief only by making the contract. A contract which has been entered into under duress is voidable at the option of the victim.

Undue Influence.   Undue influence is a term used to refer to the power which one party wrongfully exercises over another in attempting to control the judgment and to influence the action of such other person in order to benefit himself. The only effect of undue influence is to render the contract voidable at the option of the oppressed party.

LEGAL CAPACITY OF THE PARTIES TO CONTRACT.   Legal capacity on the part of both parties to a contract is essential in order to make it enforceable. The question of legal capacity may arise in any of the following cases:

Federal and State Governments. The capacity of the federal and state governments to contract is co-extensive with the duties and powers of those governments. Only for purposes of government do they have full contractual capacity.

Foreign states and sovereigns. Foreign states and sovereigns may make contracts and sue thereon, but they can only be sued when they voluntarily submit to the jurisdiction of the court.

Corporations. A corporation has contractual capacity only within the powers granted to it by its charter. Contracts not within the corporation's chartered powers are said to be *ultra vires,* i.e., beyond the power of the corporation to act.

Infants. The term *infants,* as it is used in law, refers to all persons under twenty-one years of age. As a rule, the contracts of infants are voidable; that is to say, they may be disaffirmed or ratified at the option of the infant. An infant may hold an adult to a contract, but an adult cannot bind an infant to an agreement. The defense of infancy exists only for the protection of the infant and cannot be put forth in behalf of adult claimants. It should be noted that a contract to convey real estate executed by an infant can be disaffirmed only after the infant attains his majority. Nevertheless, an infant can at his own option disaffirm all other contracts either at any time during his minority or within a reasonable time after he attains his majority.

Infants are liable for necessaries, but only to the extent of their reasonable value. Necessaries include food, clothing, shelter, medical attendance, ordinary education, and similar essentials. (Excessive or duplicate quantities are excluded from liability.) What constitutes a necessary depends upon the infant's station in life.

Insane Persons. The legal test of insanity as a factor affecting the validity of a contract is the ability of the person whose sanity is in question to understand the nature and the effect of a particular transaction. Contracts made by a person after he has been adjudged insane are *void.* Before such adjudication, they are *voidable.*

The liability of an insane person for necessaries is the same as that of an infant.

Drunken Persons. A contract made by a person who, at the

time, was in such a state of intoxication as not to know what he was doing or what would be the consequences of his act is *voidable*. Slight intoxication does not affect the validity of a contract; it must be sufficient to destroy an understanding of the terms of the contract.

If a person is adjudged a habitual drunkard, and the court appoints a committee to act for such a person, contracts entered into by the adjudged incompetent during the existence of the commission are *void*.

Spendthrifts. Generally speaking there is no restraint on the power of a spendthrift to contract. In several states, however, such persons may be placed under guardianship, in which event they no longer have a right to make contracts on their own behalf.

Married Women. At common law a married woman formerly had no power to contract in her own name, since her property and rights went to the husband upon marriage. Today most of the common law disabilities of married women in the United States have been removed.

Aliens. As a rule, aliens have the same rights and powers to contract as citizens. Since commercial intercourse between subjects of belligerent countries is impractical in wartime, contracts with enemy aliens which had been made before the outbreak of war are usually suspended until after hostilities, while such contracts made during a state of war are void.

Convicts. A contract made by a convict undergoing a sentence of imprisonment, even if the sentence imposed is a life term or the death penalty, is valid. (In New York State, a person sentenced to life imprisonment is deemed civilly dead; he cannot enforce a contract but he remains liable for its obligations and creditors could proceed against his estate.)

CONSIDERATION. Anything of value given in return for a promise may constitute consideration. Value may take the form of a benefit to the promisor or a detriment to the promisee. Without consideration a promise is a *nudum pactum* (a naked pact, a bare agreement) without force in law.

Good consideration will support an executed contract whereas only *valuable* consideration will support an executory contract. The courts do not concern themselves with the adequacy of consideration. Executed or *past* consideration will not support a promise.

Good consideration, which may be defined as one founded on natural love and affection between near relatives, is prevalent in conveyancing a deed of real property from a father to a son. *Valuable* consideration is indicative of a *quid pro quo*, something for something. It does not need to be money or property value that one gets from the contract, although these are usually the subject of consideration. Doing something that one has a right to do, or refraining from doing what one has a right to do, has been held to be valuable consideration. As to *adequacy* of consideration, the courts do not look upon consideration as an exchange of values. The courts do not renegotiate contracts but only interpret them. If a man is a good bargainer and made himself a profitable deal, he is entitled to his bargain. *Past* consideration arises where a person has already been benefited and at the time he received such benefit he was under no legal obligation to pay for it. If he subsequently promises to pay for the favor, he gains nothing by making the promise, nor does the promisee do anything to support the promise; therefore, there is no consideration to support the promise.

LEGALITY OF SUBJECT MATTER. The law will not enforce an agreement to do what the law says must not be done; therefore, a contract to perform any act prohibited by law would be void. Thus, gambling contracts are void. Contracts, including negotiable instruments, made on Sundays or holidays (but not consummated or calling for performance on such days) are valid unless specifically prohibited by a state statute. Contracts made on any day calling for performance on Sunday or legal holidays are usually unenforceable unless the work is required for public convenience and necessity.

CONTRACTS REQUIRED TO BE IN WRITING. At common law no contract was required to be reduced to writing. The common law recognized only two classes of contracts: those under seal and those not under seal. (The former were considered more dignified than the latter.) In order to be enforceable under the Statute of Frauds, a contract for the sale of land or for transfer of an interest in land must be in writing and signed by the party to be charged, i.e., the party to be held on the contract.

Classification of Contracts. Contracts may be classified in the following categories:

EXPRESS AND IMPLIED. An *express* contract is one expressed

in words, spoken or written. An oral contract is expressed in spoken words, whereas a written contract is expressed in writing.

An *implied* contract is one that is inferred from the conduct of the parties. Here the agreement is arrived at by an interpretation of the acts and conduct of the parties. Implied contracts must be distinguished from those obligations created by law, which do not require the assent of the party upon whom the obligations are imposed. The latter obligations, founded upon a legal fiction and not true contracts, are referred to as contracts *implied in law*. Implied contracts are contracts *implied in fact*.

The quasi-contract is an example of a contract implied in law and evolves from the theory that, if a person is in possession of money or its equivalent, belonging to another, the law will create a fictitious contract to restore the same to its rightful owner, although no such contract was in fact made or intended by the parties concerned. The basis for a recovery in an action of quasi-contract is the unjust enrichment of one party at the expense of another. The remedy, generally, is a money judgment for the amount of the unjust enrichment.

EXECUTORY AND EXECUTED. An *executory* contract is one in which the conditions have not been fully performed, i.e., something remains to be done in the future by one or both of the parties to the contract.

An *executed* contract is one in which the conditions have been fully performed, i.e., nothing remains to be done by either party.

UNILATERAL AND BILATERAL. A *unilateral* contract is one with an offer which promises payment in return for an act. The performance of the act denotes acceptance of the offer, consummating the obligations under the contract. For example, if owner Able says to broker Baker, "I will pay you a six per cent commission if you will sell my house," this is a unilateral contract. The obligation to pay a commission will become binding if the broker sells the house.

A *bilateral* contract is one in which a promise is given in exchange for another. An offer that calls for a reciprocal promise can be accepted only by a promise of the offeree.

JOINT, SEVERAL, AND JOINT AND SEVERAL. A *joint* contract is one made by two or more promisors acting as one to fulfill an obligation, or made by two or more promisees acting as one to require performance. A *several* contract is one which applies individually to any one of a number of promisors or promisees. Each promisor or promisee has a separate right or duty of compliance with respect to the same obligations. A *joint* and *several* contract is one in which two or more persons bind themselves as one party and also separately, as individuals. For example, if five persons sign a contract reading, "We hereby agree . . . ," such an obligation is joint and all must be sued together or none at all. If they had signed, "We and each of us agree . . ." or "I hereby agree . . .," that contract would be joint and several; all, or any one, could be sued in case of controversy.

VALID, VOID, AND VOIDABLE.   A *valid* contract is one satisfying all legal requisites for a contract. All the parties are bound and the court will lend its aid to the enforcement of the contract. A *void* contract is one which can have no legal effect. The parties thereto are in the same position as they would have been if no agreement had been made. This term is self-contradictory, since an agreement which produces no legal obligation cannot properly be called a contract. A void contract is a nullity and can be neither ratified nor enforced. A *voidable* contract is one that may be disaffirmed at the option of one of the parties. A good illustration arises in the contract between an infant and an adult, other than for necessaries. Although the infant may treat the contract as a valid one, and if desired may hold the adult to his promise, the adult cannot, if the infant so decides, hold the infant to his promise, since the latter has the right to disavow his obligation under the contract on the ground of his infancy.

UNENFORCEABLE OR ENFORCEABLE.   An *unenforceable* contract is one which, although valid, is incapable of such proof as is required by law. In this class are found oral contracts which are required by the Statute of Frauds to be evidenced by a writing. Such contracts, though incapable of enforcement, are regarded as valid for many purposes and may become enforceable at some future time if the requirements of proof are met. For instance, an oral contract within the Statute of Frauds (p. 56) may become *enforceable* at a later date by reason of a written acknowledgment of its terms signed by the party against whom the obligation is sought to be enforced.

CONTRACTS OF RECORD AND UNDER SEAL (SPECIALTIES).   A contract of record is one entered into before some court "of record." Two leading examples are *judgments* and *recognizances*. A judgment is an official determination by a court justice, and is enforceable by execution only in the state where rendered. For the purpose of enforcing a judgment in another jurisdiction, it is treated as a contract. A bail bond is an example of a recognizance.

A contract under *seal*, also called a *specialty* or *covenant*, is a contract solemnized by adding a seal to one's signature. The seal may be a wax impression, the word "seal" or initials L. S., a scroll, a disc, or other symbol. Under the common law, such contracts possessed greater force than ordinary contracts, and this is still true today in several states, particularly with regard to the question of consideration and the Statute of Limitations. The force and effect of a seal is rapidly becoming obsolete. In real estate practice, the two most common forms of contracts under specialties are *deeds* and *bonds*.

Statute of Frauds. In 1677 a statute was enacted in England entitled "An act for the prevention of frauds and perjuries" (29 Car. 11 c. 3). This act has been more generally referred to as the Statute of Frauds. Its object was to prevent certain fraudulent practices which were commonly endeavored to be upheld by perjury. Specifically, it required contracts for the sale of an interest in land to be evidenced by a writing; otherwise, they were unenforceable.

The fourth and seventeenth sections of the statute have been enacted by most of the states, although with slight deviations. Hence, in all states of the union, contracts for the sale of real property are required to be in writing, but this is not true with respect to contracts for the sale of goods. The Statute of Frauds is in force in this country only in those states whose legislatures have adopted it and only to the extent covered by the legislation. It is not a part of our heritage of common law which governs many of our legal relationships, irrespective of legislation. In the state of Maryland, however, by virtue of Article V of its Declaration of Rights (which declares in force in Maryland all English statutes enacted prior to July 4, 1776, and applicable to local circumstances), the Statute of Frauds became a part of the law.

Parol Evidence Rule. This rule means that once parties have reduced an agreement to writing, they are bound by the writing and are not allowed to offer any proof of an oral agreement contradicting the terms of the writing.

EXCEPTIONS TO THE PAROL EVIDENCE RULE. Four exceptions

to the Parol Evidence Rule occur where proof is offered for the purpose of:

1. Showing a non-contractual relationship or going to the very existence of a written contract and destroying it.
2. Showing that the enforcement of the contract was dependent upon a condition precedent, which condition has not been fulfilled.
3. Clearing up ambiguities, omissions, and obscure matters.
4. Showing that the written contract had subsequently been modified for a consideration.

Assignment of Contracts. Generally, all contracts, except those which stipulate to the contrary or those which create a personal relationship, are assignable. An assignment need not be in any special form and, like a gift, requires no consideration.

RIGHTS OF ASSIGNEE. An assignee acquires only such rights as the assignor has, and is subject to any defenses which the other party to the contract may have had against the assignor.

Discharge of Contracts. The term *discharge of contract* relates to the methods by which the contractual tie may be loosened and the parties wholly freed from their obligations. Contracts may be discharged by operation of law, agreement, performance, and breach.

OPERATION OF LAW. Contracts discharged by operation of law generally relate to those which are discharged in the following ways:

Impossibility of Performance. When performance is impossible, a contract is void—for example, an agreement for the sale of a house which subsequently is destroyed by fire.

Merger. Merger refers to the absorption of a thing of lesser importance by a greater, whereby the lesser ceases to exist, but the greater is not increased. For example, a simple contract for the sale of real property is merged in a subsequently executed deed delivered in full performance of the contract. Such a deed supersedes the contract.

Alteration of the Instrument. A material alteration destroys the instrument and, if fraudulently made, there can be no recovery on the original obligation by the wrongdoer. For instance, if a deed is materially altered by addition or erasure, it is discharged —i.e., set aside—provided that the alteration is made by a party to the contract, or his agent, intentionally and without the consent of the other party.

Bankruptcy. By virtue of the National Bankruptcy Act, a discharge in bankruptcy releases the bankrupt from all his contractual obligations.

AGREEMENT. An agreement may be discharged by recission, a substituted contract, or a provision in the contract.

Recission. An executory bilateral contract may be rescinded before breach by mutual consent of the parties. If the contract is fully executed by one party, the other cannot be released from his obligation without giving some consideration to the one who performed.

Substituted Contract or Novation. The parties to a contract may abandon it by mutual agreement and substitute in its place a new and different contract. However, the new agreement altering, canceling, supplementing, or supplanting the former contract requires a new consideration to support it.

Provision for Discharge Contained in a Contract. A contract may contain stipulations providing for its discharge upon the occurrence of certain events or at the option of one of its parties. These provisions are, in their very nature, conditions subsequent. They may be made operative by the non-fulfillment of some term of the contract, the occurrence of a particular event, or the exercise by one of the parties of an option to terminate the contract.

PERFORMANCE. The most usual method of discharging a contract is by performance. Questions most frequently arising in connection with the performance of contracts are: time of performance, time of the essence, satisfactory performance, substantial performance, performance by payment, and tender of performance.

Time of Performance. If a contract specifies no time for performance, it must be performed within a reasonable time. What constitutes a reasonable time depends on the circumstances of each individual case. Where the contract specifies a time for performance, the question whether or not non-performance within the time limit prescribed by the contract discharges the contract would depend upon whether time was "of the essence," i.e., made a material term or condition thereof.

Time of the Essence. Where the parties have expressly stipulated that time is to be regarded as the essence of the contract, the failure of one party to perform within the prescribed time discharges the contractual obligation of the other. But where time is neither expressly, nor by implication, of the essence of the contract, the failure or inability of one party to perform within the time designated does not give the other party any right to rescind or abandon the contract, but only the right to recover damages in consequence of the breach.

Satisfactory Performance.   In the absence of specific provisions to the contrary, performance is deemed satisfactory if it would satisfy the ordinary, reasonable person under the circumstances.

Substantial Performance.   If a bona fide effort is made to comply fully with the terms of a contract, and there has been no willful or intentional departure from such terms, and the deviations, defects, or omissions are only minor, then recovery will be allowed based upon substantial performance; however, offsetting damages because of such deviations, defects, or omissions may be sustained.

Performance by Payment.   Under the terms of a contract, performance by payment is subject to the following provisions:

Place.   In the absence of an agreed place of payment, it is the duty of the debtor to seek out his creditor in order to make payment.

Money.   If the contract requires the payment of money, such payment extinguishes the debt and discharges the contract. A payment in counterfeit money does not discharge the debt. If the debtor mails his payment to the creditor, he does so at his own risk. If, however, the debtor sends the money as directed by the creditor, it is at the creditor's risk and the debt is discharged, even though the remittance is lost.

Check or Note of Debtor.   It is a question of intention whether or not the payment of a debt by a check or note of the debtor acts as a discharge of the debt. If the note is accepted expressly as absolute payment, it will discharge the debt. In the absence of such agreement, the check or note is only a conditional payment and not an absolute one.

Application of Payments.   Where a person owes several debts or items to another, he has a right to direct to which item any payment which he may make shall apply. If the debtor does not make his wishes explicit, then the creditor may apply the payment to whatever debt he pleases. Where neither the creditor nor the debtor applies the payment to any particular debt or item, the law will make the application. There is a judicial conflict in interpreting whether the application should be for the benefit of the debtor or the creditor. The common law favors the creditor, the civil law the debtor. In New York State, the courts have shown a preference for the civil law rule, and they apply the payment in a way which would be most beneficial to the debtor.

Tender of Performance. A tender is an offer to do what a party has promised to do but is prevented from doing by acts of the other party. A tender is sufficient if it unconditionally meets the requirements of a contract. If it deviates in any particular from the contract, it is not sufficient. A sufficient tender would have the effect of stopping interest and shifting the cost of the suit to the other party.

The debtor may offer his creditor any of the following monies, in any amount for the payment of private debts: silver dollars, fractional coins (half dollars, quarters, dimes), minor coins (nickels, pennies), and treasury notes.

BREACH OF CONTRACT. A breach of contract arises upon the refusal of a party to recognize the existence of a contract or upon his commission of an act inconsistent with its terms. The effect of a breach of contract is to give rise to a new obligation, namely, to compensate the injured party and frequently to relieve the latter from his obligations under the contract. It does not have this effect where the breach relates only to a subsidiary part of the contract.

Rights of Party Discharged. Where a party to a contract is discharged by a breach committed by the other party, he may:

1. Consider himself exonerated and resist an action brought against him for non-performance on his part.
2. Sue at once for such damages as he has sustained, without showing performance on his part.
3. Sue on *quantum meruit* and thereby recover the reasonable value of the part of the contract that he has performed.
4. Sue in specific performance.
5. Request arbitration.

Damages. Damages is recompense for a wrong. In a breach of contract it represents the loss directly and naturally resulting from the breach. It excludes, therefore, speculative, remote, or possible losses which cannot be shown to have resulted directly from the breach.

Damages are of the following types:

1. *General* damages, such as might accrue to any person similarly injured.
2. *Special* damages, such as did in fact accrue to the particular individual by reason of the particular circumstances of the case.
3. *Liquidated* damages, which constitute the compensation which the parties have agreed must be paid in satisfaction of the loss or injury which will follow from a breach of contract. (They must bear a reasonable proportion to the loss; otherwise, they would be construed to be a penalty and thus unenforceable.)
4. *Nominal* damages, which arise when a wrong is established but no real damage is proved. (A judge or jury may award nominal damages, sometimes fixed at six cents).

The measure of damages for the breach of contract is the loss which the injured party can prove he sustained as a result of the breach. In a contract for the sale of goods the measure of damages is usually the difference between the contract price and the market price of the goods at the time and place of the breach.

Binders.   In general real estate practice, the question often arises whether a binder, or binder agrement, is a contract enforceable against the parties thereto, which complies with the Statute of Frauds.

Binders are instruments which are usually executed by a purchaser and seller of real property prior to the execution of a more formal contract for the sale of real property. If the binder contains all of the material terms of the agreement, is properly signed, and imposes legal obligations on the parties, it is despite its simplicity a valid contract for the sale of real property, provided that there is nothing further for the parties to do but enter into the more formal contract called for by the binder agreement. Lacking the essential elements, the binder would simply represent a receipt of a sum of money in contemplation of the execution of a valid contract for the sale of real property.

CRIMES AND TORTS

Definition of a Crime. A crime is an act or omission forbidden by law and punishable upon conviction by death, imprisonment, fine, or other penalty.

CRIMES RELATING TO REAL ESTATE. The following discussion of crimes pertains to the real estate business and should be known to people in the field.

Fraudulent practices. Many crimes against business involve fraudulent practices, such as obtaining property by fraudulent pretenses (trick or devices), passing bad checks, issuing false credit statements, making false claims in advertising, and making transfers of property to defraud creditors.

Forgery. Forgery is another type of prevalent crime against business. It includes such acts as signing another person's name to a negotiable instrument, counterfeiting stocks, bonds, or warehouse receipts, and the like. Changing of trade marks, falsification of public records, and alteration of deeds, leases, mortgages, wills, or any other document of legal import constitute forgery.

Definition of a Tort. There is a close relationship between torts and crimes. A tort is a wrongful act which is injurious to a fellow member of society. The same act may be both a tort and a crime. For instance, an assault upon an individual may be prosecuted both civilly and criminally.

TORTS RELATING TO PROPERTY. Property and property rights are of such importance to society that they are protected against unwarranted interference by others. Some examples of torts against property are trespass to real property, trespass to personal property, conversion, and deceit.

Trespass to Real Property. Any entry by a person, or anything done that causes entering or the act of remaining or permitting anything to remain on the land of another, is a trespass—unless permission is granted or the entry is privileged. Actual pecuniary harm is not an essential element of this tort; however, if no harm is done, only nominal damages can be recovered. At common law it was held that the right to land extended from the center of the earth to the heavens. This rule has been modified since the advent of aircraft. The temporary invasion of the air space over one's land is privileged if it is done in a reasonable manner and within the requirements of the state statutes; however, if anything is dropped from an aircraft, or there is a forced landing, then there is liability for the actual damages which result.

Trespass to Personal Property. Any intentional and harmful meddling with personal property, or deprivation of the use thereof for an appreciable length of time, is a trespass, unless it is privileged or done with the consent of the injured party.

Conversion. Conversion is the unlawful dominion over, or the unlawful appropriation of, the personal property of another. The nature of this tort is the wrongful deprivation of a person's right to the possession of his personal property.

Deceit (fraud). The tort of deceit (fraud) is based upon injury resulting from a misrepresentation of a material fact (knowingly made with intent to deceive) which is relied upon to the injury of the defrauded party.

7

THE CONTRACT OF SALE

The primary function of the contract of sale is to reduce the preliminary parol understandings of the parties to writing, and to comply with the Statute of Frauds and the statutes of most states which require, as in New York, that "the sale of real property, or an interest therein, is void unless the contract, or some note or memorandum thereof, expressing the consideration, is in writing, subscribed by the party to be charged, or by his lawful agent, thereunto authorized in writing."

A sale of real property may be consummated by the delivery and acceptance of a deed even though the parties have not entered into a prior contract. However, this procedure is fraught with hazard, since any questions regarding the negotiations prior to the sale are left to the memories of witnesses, and conditions to take effect subsequent to the sale are left to the honor of the parties. The absence of a contract is very unsatisfactory in case of controversy.

A contract of sale of real property *must* contain, at the least, the following elements: mutuality of consent, i.e., an offer and an acceptance by parties with the capacity to contract; consideration, i.e., a *quid pro quo;* a legal subject matter; and a form in accordance with statutory law. These are the minimal features that are absolutely necessary to the consummation of a valid contract.

The validity of a contract is to be judged by the law of the state where executed, and a contract which is effective in a state where made is effective in every state, provided it is not contrary to the public policy of the state. In addition, contracts of sale executed on Sundays are valid.

ANALYSIS OF THE CONTRACT OF SALE

Contracts of sale may take many forms. The elements here presented are those of a rather complete contract (see p. 66), and make the contract more safe and certain. Printed forms are most helpful because they attempt to describe fully the obligations and terms in a complete and accurate statement, so that transfer of title in real estate may be effected smoothly.

Date. The contract begins by setting forth the date of its execution. Although the date is not absolutely essential to the validity of the contract, it has importance where time limits exist for compliance with certain provisions of the contract.

Parties. The parties to a contract are generally referred to as the seller and the purchaser, both of whom must be legally competent to contract.

The Seller. In many states, if the seller is a married man and acquired title * to property prior to or during marriage, his wife's name should appear also, as both must execute the instrument; otherwise, the purchaser cannot enforce performance of the contract should the wife subsequently refuse to sign. The wife's signature is necessary in order to release her dower rights. It is also necessary to have the wife join in the contract with the husband in all states having community property laws or homestead rights. Where the property is owned by husband and wife in a tenancy by the entirety, or otherwise, the wife must join on the contract as one of the sellers. If the seller, or sellers, dies before the closing of the title, the heirs or executors may properly execute and deliver the deed.

The Purchaser. The name and address of the purchaser should be set forth in full. When the contract has been executed and delivered, the purchaser becomes the equitable owner of the property. In the event of the death of the purchaser before closing, the heirs succeed to his interests and the deed must be prepared and delivered accordingly.

A statement should be inserted representing that the seller owns the property. If the seller merely holds a contract of sale from the record owner, this should be stated, with a warranty that good title can be delivered. Thereafter, mutuality of agreement is expressed by a statement to the effect that the seller agrees to sell and the buyer agrees to purchase the property.

Description. The correct description should be set forth in

---

* In New York State, dower rights may attach if property was acquired prior to September 1, 1930.

THIS AGREEMENT, made the   day of   , nineteen hundred and
BETWEEN

hereinafter described as the seller, and

hereinafter described as the purchaser,

WITNESSETH, that the seller agrees to sell and convey, and the purchaser agrees to purchase, all that certain plot, piece or parcel of land, with the buildings and improvements thereon erected, situate, lying and being in the

This sale includes all right, title and interest, if any, of the seller in and to any land lying in the bed of any street, road or avenue opened or proposed, in front of or adjoining said premises, to the center line thereof, and all right, title and interest of the seller in and to any award made or to be made in lieu thereof and in and to any unpaid award for damage to said premises by reason of change of grade of any street; and the seller will execute and deliver to the purchaser, on closing of title, or thereafter, on demand, all proper instruments for the conveyance of such title and the assignment and collection of any such award.

The price is

      Dollars, payable as follows:

      Dollars,

on the signing of this contract, by check subject to collection, the receipt of which is hereby acknowledged;

      Dollars,

in cash or good certified check on the delivery of the deed as hereinafter provided;

      Dollars,

by taking title subject to a   mortgage now a lien on said premises in that amount, bearing interest at the rate of   per cent per annum, the principal being due and payable

      Dollars,

by the purchaser or assigns executing, acknowledging and delivering to the seller a bond or, at the option of the seller, a note secured by a purchase money   mortgage on the above premises, in that amount, payable

together with interest at the rate of   per cent

per annum payable

Any bond or note and mortgage to be given hereunder shall be drawn on the standard forms of New York Board of Title Underwriters for mortgages of like lien; and shall be drawn by the attorney for the seller at the expense of the purchaser, who shall also pay the mortgage recording tax and recording fees and pay for and affix to such instruments any and all revenue stamps that may be necessary.

If such purchase money mortgage is to be a subordinate mortgage on the premises it shall provide that it shall be subject and subordinate to the lien   of the existing   mortgage   of $, any extensions thereof and to any mortgage   or consolidated mortgage   which may be placed on the premises in lieu thereof, and to any extensions thereof provided (a) that the interest rate thereof shall not be greater than   per cent per annum and (b) that, if the principal amount thereof shall exceed the amount of principal owing and unpaid on said existing mortgage   at the time of placing such new mortgage or consolidated mortgage, the excess be paid to the holder of such purchase money mortgage in reduction of the principal thereof. Such purchase money mortgage shall also provide that such payment to the holder thereof shall not alter or affect the regular installments, if any, of principal payable thereunder and shall further provide that the holder thereof will, on demand and without charge therefor, execute, acknowledge and deliver any agreement or agreements further to effectuate such subordination.

If there be a mortgage on the premises the seller agrees to deliver to the purchaser at the time of delivery of the deed a proper certificate executed and acknowledged by the holder of such mortgage and in form for recording, certifying as to the amount of the unpaid principal and interest thereon, date of maturity thereof and rate of interest thereon, and the seller shall pay the fees for recording such certificate.

Said premises are sold and are to be conveyed subject to:

    1. Zoning regulations and ordinances of the city, town or village in which the premises lie which are not violated by existing structures.

    2. Consents by the seller or any former owner of premises for the erection of any structure or structures on, under or above any street or streets on which said premises may abut.

    3. Encroachments of stoops, areas, cellar steps, trim and cornices, if any, upon any street or highway.

All notes or notices of violations of law or municipal ordinances, orders or requirements noted in or issued by the Departments of Housing and Buildings, Fire, Labor, Health, or other State or Municipal Department having jurisdiction, against or affecting the premises at the date hereof, shall be complied with by the seller and the premises shall be conveyed free of the same, and this provision of this contract shall survive delivery of the deed hereunder. The seller shall furnish the purchaser with an authorization to make the necessary searches therefor.

The following are to be apportioned:
(1) Rents as and when collected. (2) Interest on mortgages. (3) Premiums on existing transferable insurance policies or renewals of those expiring prior to the closing. (4) Taxes and sewer rents, if any, on the basis of the fiscal year for which assessed. (5) Water charges on the basis of the calendar year. (6) Fuel, if any.

If the closing of the title shall occur before the tax rate is fixed, the apportionment of taxes shall be upon the basis of the tax rate for the next preceding year applied to the latest assessed valuation.

If there be a water meter on the premises, the seller shall furnish a reading to a date not more than thirty days prior to the time herein set for closing title, and the unfixed meter charge and the unfixed sewer rent, if any, based thereon for the intervening time shall be apportioned on the basis of such last reading.

The deed shall be the usual
deed in proper statutory short form for record and shall be duly executed, acknowledged, and have revenue stamps in the proper amount affixed thereto by the seller, at the seller's expense, so as to convey to the purchaser the fee simple of the said premises, free of all encumbrances, except as herein stated, and shall also contain the covenant required by subdivision 5 of Section 13 of the Lien Law.

All sums paid on account of this contract, and the reasonable expenses of the examination of the title to said premises and of the survey, if any, made in connection therewith are hereby made liens thereon, but such liens shall not continue after default by the purchaser under this contract.

All fixtures and articles of personal property attached or appurtenant to or used in connection with said premises are represented to be owned by the seller, free from all liens and encumbrances except as herein stated, and are included in this sale; without limiting the generality of the foregoing, such fixtures and articles of personal property include plumbing, heating, lighting and cooking fixtures, air conditioning fixtures and units, ranges, refrigerators, radio and television aerials, bathroom and kitchen cabinets, mantels, door mirrors, venetian blinds, shades, screens, awnings, storm windows, window boxes, storm doors, mail boxes, weather vanes, flagpoles, pumps, shrubbery and outdoor statuary.

The amount of any unpaid taxes, assessments, water charges and sewer rents which the seller is obligated to pay and discharge, with the interest and penalties thereon to a date not less than two business days after the date of closing title, may at the option of the seller be allowed to the purchaser out of the balance of the purchase price, provided official bills therefor with interest and penalties thereon figured to said date are furnished by the seller at the closing. If at the date of closing title there may be any other liens or encumbrances which the seller is obligated to pay and discharge, the seller may use any portion of the balance of the purchase price to satisfy the same, provided the seller shall have delivered to the purchaser at the closing of title instruments in recordable form and sufficient to satisfy such liens and encumbrances of record, together with the cost of recording or filing said instruments. The purchaser, if request is made within a reasonable time prior to the date of closing of title, agrees to provide at the closing separate certified checks as requested, aggregating the amount of the balance of the purchase price, to facilitate the satisfaction of any such liens or encumbrances. The existence of any such taxes or other liens and encumbrances shall not be deemed objections to title if the seller shall comply with the foregoing requirements.

If a search of the title discloses judgments, bankruptcies or other returns against other persons having names the same as or similar to that of the seller, the seller will on request deliver to the purchaser an affidavit showing that such judgments, bankruptcies or other returns are not against the seller.

In the event that the seller is unable to convey title in accordance with the terms of this contract, the sole liability of the seller will be to refund to the purchaser the amount paid on account of the purchase price and to pay the net cost of examining the title, which cost is not to exceed the charges fixed by the New York Board of Title Underwriters, and the net cost of any survey made in connection therewith incurred by the purchaser, and upon such refund and payment being made this contract shall be considered canceled.

The deed shall be delivered upon the receipt of said payments at the office of

at   o'clock on   19

The parties agree that
brought about this sale and the seller agrees to pay the commission at the rates established or adopted by the Board of Real Estate Brokers in the locality where the property is situated.

It is understood and agreed that all understandings and agreements heretofore had between the parties hereto are merged in this contract, which alone fully and completely expresses their agreement, and that the same is entered into after full investigation, neither party relying upon any statement or representation, not embodied in this contract, made by the other. The purchaser has inspected the buildings standing on said premises and is thoroughly acquainted with their condition.

This agreement may not be changed or terminated orally. The stipulations aforesaid are to apply to and bind the heirs, executors, administrators, successors and assigns of the respective parties.

If two or more persons constitute either the seller or the purchaser, the word "seller" or the word "purchaser" shall be construed as if it read "sellers" or "purchasers" whenever the sense of this agreement so requires.

IN WITNESS WHEREOF, this agreement has been duly executed by the parties hereto.

In presence of:

NOTE: FIRE LOSSES. This form of contract contains no express provision as to risk of loss by fire or other casualty before delivery of the deed. Unless express provision is made, the provisions of Section 5-1311 of the General Obligations Law will apply. This section also places risk of loss upon purchaser if title or possession is transferred prior to closing.

full and in detail. The true political or territorial locality must be included. The description should be a formal, legal one. Generally, property is described in any one of the following four methods: lot and block number, metes and bounds, government survey, and monuments.

LOT AND BLOCK NUMBER. Every map, or plat, filed by a subdivider or developer with the clerk of the county in which the property is located, usually contains lot and block numbers. Sometimes only lot numbers are required. After the acceptance of the plat by the proper authorities, the owner of the subdivision may from that time forth describe the property by lot and block number when conveyed. For example, if a map is filed under the title "Map of Kensington Gardens, Village of Hempstead, Nassau County, New York" the description may read: "Lot #417, Block 23 of the Map of Kensington Gardens, Village of Hempstead, Nassau County, New York, surveyed by John Teas, L. S. and C. E., Hempstead, N. Y., July 2, 1962 and filed in the office of the Clerk of the County of Nassau, July 6, 1962 on page 806, Liber 4143."

Anyone desiring to know the exact size of the lot can get the information in the county clerk's office where the plat is filed.

METES AND BOUNDS. The description by metes (measures) and bounds (directions) is a method of defining boundaries, often used in conjunction with, and in addition to, description by lot and block. The property is described by beginning at a certain point and measuring and indicating the length of the boundaries of the property until the point of beginning is again reached. For example, a metes and bounds description of the property located in Hempstead, New York, and mapped below would be:

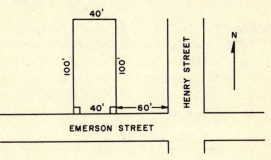

All that lot or parcel of land with the buildings and improvements thereon in the Village of Hempstead, County of Nassau, State of New York, bounded and described as follows:

Beginning at a point on the northerly side of Emerson Street distant 60 feet westerly from the corner formed by the intersection of the northerly side of Emerson Street with the westerly side of Henry Street, running thence northerly and parallel with Henry Street 100 feet; running thence westerly and parallel with Emerson Street 40 feet; running thence southerly and again parallel with Henry Street 100 feet to the northerly side of Emerson Street; running thence easterly along the northerly side of Emerson Street 40 feet, to the point or place of beginning.

GOVERNMENT SURVEY. The government survey, which is also referred to as the geodetic or rectangular survey, was adopted by Congress after the Revolutionary War. It is used primarily in the states that came into the union after the original thirteen colonies. This system is based upon a grid of north, south, east, and west

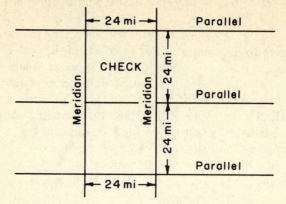

lines established by the Bureau of Land Management in Washington, D. C. The north and south lines are called meridians; the east and west, parallels. The distance between parallels and meridians is twenty-four miles in each direction, and each twenty-four square mile unit is called a *check*. Above is an illustration of a check in relation to parallels and meridians.

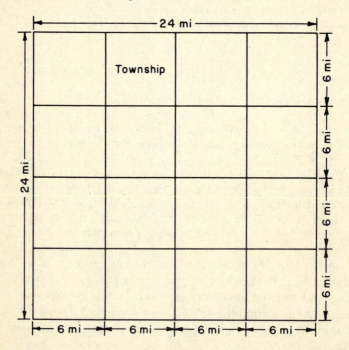

The Check. Every check is divided into sixteen townships of six miles square, as in the illustration at the bottom of page 70.

Base Line. Certain parallels, in accordance with the designation made by the state, are indicated as base lines. The townships, or tiers as they are sometimes referred to, are numbered and designated as being either north or south of the base line. In the illustration below, the townships designated T. 1 S. refer to the first row of townships (hence, tiers) south of the base line. T. 2 S. refers to the second tier, and so on. All the townships in the same tier north or south of the baseline have the same numerical designation.

TOWNSHIPS NORTH OF BASE LINE					PARALLEL
				T. 4 N.	N
			T. 3 N.		
		T. 2 N.			
	T. 1 N.				
BASE LINE					BASE LINE
	T. 1 S.	T. 1 S.	T. 1 S.	T. 1 S.	
TOWNSHIPS SOUTH OF BASE LINE	T. 2 S.	T. 2 S.	T. 2 S.	T. 2 S.	
	T. 3 S.	T. 3 S.	T. 3 S.	T. 3 S.	
	T. 4 S.	T. 4 S.	T. 4 S.	T. 4 S.	PARALLEL

Since the designation T. 1 S. refers to all of the townships located in the first tier south of the base line, the location of a particular township in that tier is pinpointed by its location in the range, east or west of a principal meridian.

Principal Meridians, Ranges. In addition to designating certain parallels as base lines, the state also designates certain meridians as *principal meridians.* Just as townships are numbered as being north or south of the base line, they are also numbered as being east or west of the principal meridian. The rows of townships east or west of a principal meridian are called *ranges,* and each range is identified with a number, as illustrated below:

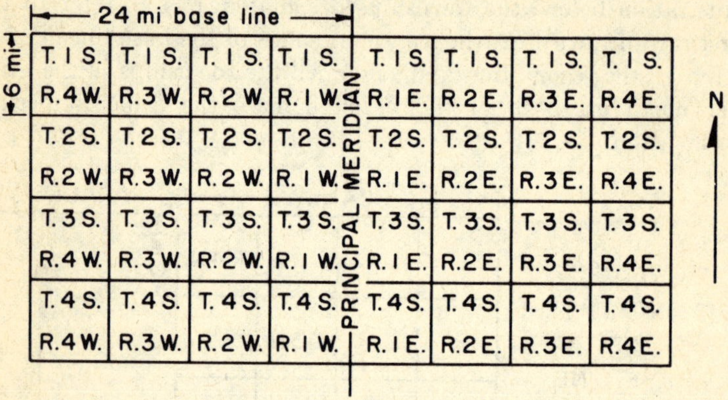
24 mi base line
6 mi
T. 1 S. R.4 W.
T. 1 S. R.3 W.
T. 1 S. R.2 W.
T. 1 S. R. 1 W.
T. 1 S. R. 1 E.
T. 1 S. R.2 E.
T. 1 S. R.3 E.
T. 1 S. R.4 E.
T. 2 S. R.2 W.
T. 2 S. R.3 W.
T. 2 S. R.2 W.
T. 2 S. R. 1 W.
T. 2 S. R. 1 E.
T. 2 S. R.2 E.
T. 2 S. R.3 E.
T. 2 S. R.4 E.
T. 3 S. R.4 W.
T. 3 S. R.3 W.
T. 3 S. R.2 W.
T. 3 S. R. 1 W.
T. 3 S. R. 1 E.
T. 3 S. R.2 E.
T. 3 S. R.3 E.
T. 3 S. R.4 E.
T. 4 S. R.4 W.
T. 4 S. R.3 W.
T. 4 S. R.2 W.
T. 4 S. R. 1 W.
T. 4 S. R. 1 E.
T. 4 S. R.2 E.
T. 4 S. R.3 E.
T. 4 S. R.4 E.
PRINCIPAL MERIDIAN
N

A township bearing the designation T. 2 S., R. 3 W., would be that township in the second tier south of the base line, and in the third range west of the principal meridian.

Townships, Sections A township consists of an area of thirty-six square miles which is further divided into thirty-six square mile tracts which are designated as *sections* and numbered as in the illustration below:

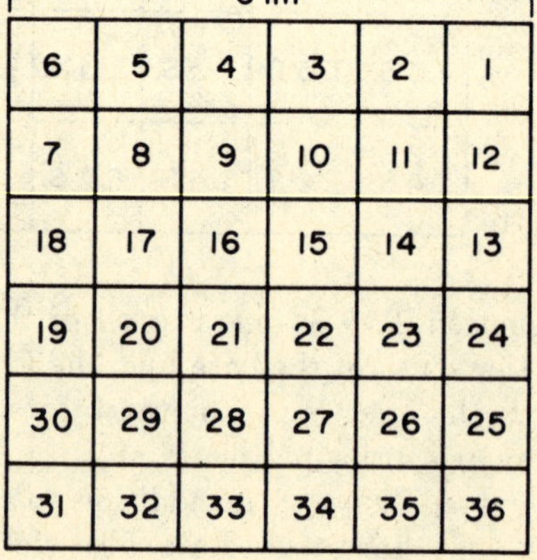
6 mi
6 5 4 3 2 1
7 8 9 10 11 12
18 17 16 15 14 13
19 20 21 22 23 24
30 29 28 27 26 25
31 32 33 34 35 36

All sections of townships are numbered in the same manner. A section, one mile square, contains 640 acres. When a parcel of land less than a section is to be described, the section is then quartered as illustrated below:

|← 1 mile →|

NW $\frac{1}{4}$ 160 acres	NE $\frac{1}{4}$ 160 acres
SW $\frac{1}{4}$ 160 acres	SE $\frac{1}{4}$ 160 acres

N ↑

A section of 640 acres may be further subdivided as follows:

W $\frac{1}{2}$ N $\frac{1}{2}$ NW $\frac{1}{4}$ 40 acres	E $\frac{1}{2}$ N $\frac{1}{2}$ NW $\frac{1}{4}$ 40 acres	NW $\frac{1}{4}$ NE $\frac{1}{4}$ 40 acres	W $\frac{1}{2}$ NE $\frac{1}{4}$ NE $\frac{1}{4}$ 20 acres	E $\frac{1}{2}$ NE $\frac{1}{4}$ NE $\frac{1}{4}$ 20 acres

S $\frac{1}{2}$ NW $\frac{1}{4}$ 80 acres	N $\frac{1}{2}$ S $\frac{1}{2}$ NE $\frac{1}{4}$ 40 acres

	W $\frac{1}{2}$ S $\frac{1}{2}$ S $\frac{1}{2}$ NE $\frac{1}{4}$ 20 acres	E $\frac{1}{2}$ S $\frac{1}{2}$ S $\frac{1}{2}$ NE $\frac{1}{4}$ 20 acres

SW $\frac{1}{4}$ 160 acres	SE $\frac{1}{4}$ 160 acres

N ↑

Table of Land Measures

Linear:	1 link	= 7.92 inches
	1 rod	= 25 links, 16½ feet, 5½ yards
	1 chain	= 100 links, 66 feet, 4 rods
	1 mile	= 5,280 feet, 320 rods, 80 chains
Square:	1 acre	= 160 square rods, 10 square chains, 4,840 square yards, 43,560 square feet
	1 section	= 640 acres, 1 square mile
	1 square mile	= 640 acres
	1 township	= 36 square miles

MONUMENTS. Real property may be described by marking and designating the corners of landed property with visible natural monuments, such as stones or trees. Generally, however, corner monuments may be established by a surveyor using an iron pipe, filled with concrete and set in the ground, and then using reasonably permanent characteristics of the property. The land illustrated in the diagram below would be described as follows:

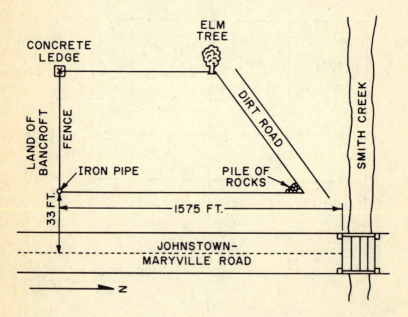

Beginning at an iron pipe sunk in the ground, 33 feet west of the center line of a highway running from Johnstown to Maryville

and distant 1,575 feet south of the north face of the south abut-
ment of the bridge over Smith Creek; running thence west along a
fence and by the land of one Bancroft to the cross cut in the
center of a concrete ledge; running thence north and at right
angles to the fence to an elm tree; running thence northeast along
a dirt road to a pile of rocks; thence south and back to the iron
pipe, the point or place of beginning.

Street Rights. If the property fronts on, or adjoins, a
street and if the title of the owner extends to any portion of the
highway, the following clause is usually included:

This sale includes all right, title and interest of the seller of, in
and to any land lying in the bed of any street, road or avenue
opened or proposed, in front of or adjoining said premises, to the
center line thereof, and all right title and interest of the seller in
and to any award made or to be made in lieu thereof and in and
to any unpaid award for damages to said premises by reason of
any change of grade of any street; and the seller will execute and
deliver to the purchaser, on closing of title, or thereafter, on demand, all proper instruments for the conveyance of such title and
the assignment and collection of any such award.

Financial Arrangements. Since the real property laws of all
states provide that a contract for the sale of real property is void
unless a consideration is expressed therein, the terms of payment
should be clear, unambiguous, and stated in full detail. The required clause should contain a statement of the total purchase
price and how it is payable. Upon the signing of the contract, it
is customary for the purchaser to give the seller at least 10 per
cent of the purchase price as a down payment. The balance is due
on the closing date. If the balance is to be paid in full upon closing, the seller will provide that the purchaser bring it in the form
of cash or a certified check. If part of the balance is to be paid by
cash or certified check and the remainder by the seller's taking
title subject to an existing mortgage or mortgages, or subject to
and assuming same, this will be stated and the liens identified. If
the seller agrees to lend the purchaser a portion of the balance of
the purchase price, then a purchase money mortgage will be used
and the terms and conditions will here be delineated.

When the purchaser takes a deed "subject to" a mortgage, he
cannot be held personally liable on the bond for a deficiency

judgment, in the event of a subsequent foreclosure of the mortgage, unless he later executes an extension agreement. If the purchaser takes "subject to" a mortgage and expressly "assumes" and agrees to pay it, then he becomes personally liable on the bond, at the option of the mortgagee; he will also be liable for any deficiency judgment. This assumption clause will read as follows: $[amount of balance of- assumed mortgage] . . . by the purchaser taking title subject to an existing mortgage which the purchaser assumes and expressly agrees to pay."

The question of taking title "subject to" a mortgage or "subject to and assuming" a mortgage is entirely a matter of agreement at the time the contract is signed. The insistence upon the signing of an assumption agreement will depend upon the value or projected value of the property in relation to the mortgage. If the value of the property is adequately in excess of the existing mortgage, and there is little possibility that there will be any excessive depreciation during the term of the mortgage, this matter is purely academic.

If the purchase money mortgage clause is inserted, the seller may refuse to deliver title in the event the contract is assigned or sold, or he may insist that the purchaser under the contract execute the bond if this is done. If the contract were silent on the subject of whether the purchaser is to pay all mortgage charges, it might be assumed that the seller intended to pay them; however, it is customary for the purchaser to pay all these charges because the seller will accept a mortgage in lieu of cash, for the convenience of the purchaser. These costs, therefore, should justifiably be borne by the purchaser. It is good practice, however, to dispel any misunderstanding by making these terms unequivocal.

"Subject to" Clauses. A "subject to" clause is one which, by agreement, will in some form or manner limit or restrict the conveyance of the fee simple absolute to the grantee. These clauses should be accurately expressed. A few examples of "subject to" clauses follow.

MORTGAGES. If the purchaser agrees to accept a title which gives him less than absolute ownership of the property, as in the situation wherein the premises were sold subject to an existing mortgage and/or a purchase money mortgage, the complete right, title, and interest of the grantee in the property is subordinate to the rights of the mortgagee. If there is no complete compliance with the terms of the mortgage, the mortgagee may cause the property to be sold, after proper judicial action, for the purposes of satisfying the mortgage obligation.

COVENANTS OR RESTRICTIONS. If any covenants or restrictions exist against the property, the appropriate clause might be as follows: "subject to covenants and restrictions, if any, of record affecting said premises, not violated by the existing building or buildings thereon, or by the manner of occupancy thereof, and not rendering the title unmarketable."

TENANTS AND LEASES. If tenants are on the property, their exact status should be set forth as follows: "subject to monthly tenancies" or "subject to a lease made to . . . dated . . . expiring . . . with or without option to renew upon the following terms . . ." as the case may be.

Each lease should be initialed in the deed for identification, and an adjustment made if there is a security deposit under any lease. (Any concessions under leases should also be incorporated in the contract, and a list of tenancies set forth in full with representations as to rentals paid and the day of the month when payable. Any arrears in rent should also be shown.)

IMPLIED WARRANTY. On the theory of implied warranty, to protect the seller, some contracts are made with the following "subject to" clause: "It is understood and agreed that there is no representation, either express or implied, made by the seller as to the condition of the property or to what uses it may be applied, and that the purchaser has inspected the premises and knows the condition thereof and agrees to purchase it, 'as is.'"

Another "subject to" clause of value to a seller who is an executor, administrator, trustee or other person or corporation acting in a fiduciary capacity is as follows: "The seller represents that in executing this contract it is acting in its capacity as a . . . (state fiduciary capacity) and is unwilling to be bound in any other capacity."

UNOPENED STREET. It has been held that the failure to mention an unopened street is good cause for rejection of title; thus, in such a situation the following clause should be inserted: "subject to the proposed opening or widening of any street or avenue abutting, adjoining or crossing the property described herein."

TITLE. It is customary for the parties to agree that the buyer will accept title subject to a reputable title insurance company approving and insuring a title offered by the seller.

Personal Property Clause. One of the prime purposes of the contract of sale is to detail the conveyance of real property and all of the fixtures and articles of personal property attached to, appurtenant to, or used in connection with, the property. Usually, there is confusion or misunderstanding regarding the nature and extent of the personal property included in the sale, unless specifically stated in the contract. It is good practice, therefore, to set forth an itemized list of all such personalty, together with a representation by the seller that, except as stated, the said personal property is owned by the seller, free of all liens and encumbrances.

The usual articles of personalty that may be the subject of the sale are outlined in the standard form. Deletions and additions will be made in accordance with the agreement of the parties.

Reduction Certificate. If there is a mortgage on the premises, the purchaser is entitled to receive proof of the exact status of that lien on the day he takes title to the premises. The seller usually, therefore, agrees to deliver to the purchaser a certificate, commonly referred to as a "reduction certificate," executed and acknowledged by the mortgagee, so that it can be recorded; this instrument certifies the unpaid balance of principal and interest, the date of maturity, and the rate of interest. The seller usually pays the fee for its recording. This instrument protects the buyer against any adverse claims later asserted by the mortgagee, his heirs, or assigns.

Assessment Clause. The contract of sale should provide for the payment of assessments which are unpaid at the time of closing. In most states there is an established custom regarding the payment of assessments which will apply if no such provision is included in the contract. However, misunderstanding can be avoided by including a specific agreement regarding the payment of assessments. A clause commonly used in most standard forms is as follows:

> If at the time of the delivery of the deed, the premises or any part thereof shall be or shall have been affected by an assessment or assessments which are or may become payable in annual installments, of which the first installment is then a charge or a lien, or

> has been paid, then, for purposes of this contract all the unpaid
> installments of any such assessment, including those which shall
> become due and payable after the delivery of the deed, shall be
> deemed to be due and payable and to be liens upon the premises
> affected thereby, and shall be paid and discharged by the seller,
> upon the delivery of the deed.

The above clause completely protects the purchaser and places
the onus upon the seller to convey the premises free and clear of
the entire assessment burdening the property at the time of the
delivery of the deed. Any agreement between the purchaser and
the seller for the apportionment of assessments should be clearly
stated to delineate the intention of the parties.

Apportionment Clause. At the time of the execution of the
contract, the parties should be aware of certain items of expense
or income that, upon the closing of the contract, will either be
prepaid or unpaid, or earned or unearned. The contract should
therefore provide for an adjustment or apportionment of these
items, so that the seller will be reimbursed for those items that he
has prepaid, and will credit the purchaser for those which should
have been paid by them at, or prior to, the closing.

The following items are usually apportioned to the day of
taking title: rents as and when collected; interest on mortgages;
premiums on existing transferable insurance policies; taxes and
sewer rents; water charges; fuel, if any; escrow payment, if any.

Violations of Law or Municipal Ordinances. The following
is the clause customarily inserted in the contract of sale regarding
existing violations:

> All notes or notices of violations of law or municipal ordinances,
> order or requirements noted in or issued by the department of
> housing and buildings, fire, health, labor, or other state or munic-
> pal department having jurisdiction, against or affecting the prem-
> ises at the date hereof, shall be complied with by the seller and the
> premises shall be conveyed free of the same, and this provision of
> this contract shall survive delivery of the deed hereunder. The
> seller shall furnish the purchaser with an authorization to make
> the necessary searches thereof.

Thus, the seller has the obligation to clear up all existing violations, either at the time of the delivery of the deed or subsequently.

Delivery and Kind of Deed.   The usual contract of sale will make provision for the type of deed * which the seller will deliver and which the buyer will accept. The most commonly used deeds are: full covenant and warranty, bargain and sale, bargain and sale with covenants against grantor's acts, and quit claim. A detailed examination of these deeds is made in Chapter 8.

Vendee's Lien.   All sums paid by the buyer (vendee) on account of the contract of sale and the reasonable expenses of the examination of title are liens on the property. These liens, however, do not continue after there is a default on the part of the buyer.

Closing.   The contract of sale will stipulate the time and place of closing the title. It is customary to close at the office of the attorney for the seller, or at the lending institution if refinancing will take place at the closing.

Time will not be considered "of the essence" of a contract unless it is expressly stated therein. Closing dates may, therefore, as a matter of courtesy, be adjourned from time to time, if time is not made of the essence. But the parties or their attorneys should enter into written stipulations setting forth the reasons and designating the party who requested the adjournment. A purchaser may request a reasonable number of adjournments, provided the circumstances are justifiable. The same is true of the seller, but he may not unreasonably withhold the delivery of the deed.

Clauses to Facilitate the Closing.   Frequently, it is the intention of the seller to apply a portion of the balance of the purchase price that he will receive at the closing for the purpose of paying off certain liens and charges which are part of his

---

* But the contract may be silent as to the type of deed to be offered, in which case it is customary, as in New York State, to accept a short form bargain and sale deed with covenants against grantor's acts; in other states this practice will vary in accordance with local custom and usage. The short form, however, minimizes the purchaser's recording costs.

Note also that in New York State the deed must contain the covenant requiring that the seller shall become a trustee for the benefit of any mechanics, workmen, or materialmen who may have performed services or furnished materials, and that he agrees to hold the consideration of the conveyance for their benefit. Most other states have similar protective provisions. By the insertion of this clause, the buyer may safely pay the consideration and is protected against any creditors of the seller.

obligation. The following is a clause customarily used for that purpose:

The amount of any unpaid taxes, assessments, water charges and sewer rents which the seller is obligated to pay and discharge, with the interest and penalties thereon to a date not less than two business days after the closing of title, may at the option of the seller be allowed to the purchaser out of the balance of the purchase price, provided official bills therefor with interest and penalties thereon computed to said date are furnished by the seller at closing. If, at the date of closing title, there are any other liens or encumbrances which the seller is obligated to pay and discharge, the seller may use any portion of the balance of the purchase price to satisfy same, provided the seller shall have delivered to the purchaser at the closing of title instruments in recordable form and sufficient to satisfy such liens and encumbrances of record, together with the cost of recording or filing said instruments. The purchaser, if request is made within a reasonable time prior to the date of closing title, agrees to provide at the closing separate checks as requested, aggregating the amount of the balance of the purchase price, to facilitate the satisfaction of any such taxes, or other liens and encumbrances. The existence of any such taxes or other liens and encumbrances shall not be deemed objections to title if the seller shall comply with the foregoing requirements.

To facilitate further the closing of title, the following clause is used to identify the seller in the event there is a confusion of names:

If a search of the title discloses judgments, bankruptcies or other returns against other persons having names the same as or similar to that of the seller, the seller will, on request, deliver to the purchaser an affidavit showing that the judgments, bankruptcies or other returns are not against the seller.

Broker's Clause. If the sale was brought about by a real estate broker, the contract should identify him and express the obligation of the seller to pay him a commission. In the absence of an express contract between the broker and the seller, the broker will be entitled to the prevailing rate of commission in the community. The usual brokerage contract is for a 6 per cent commission payable if, as, and when title actually passes, provided the seller does not arbitrarily refuse to go through with the sale.

Seller's Liability for Non-conveyance.   The following clause in the contract will limit the seller's liability for being unable to convey title as agreed:

> In the event that the seller is unable to convey title in accordance with the terms of this contract, the sole liability of the seller will be to refund to the purchaser the amount paid on account of the purchase price and to pay the net cost of examining the title, and upon such refund and payment being made this contract is considered cancelled.

Merger.   To avoid any misunderstanding that the executed contract represents the entire agreement between the parties, the following clause is usually inserted:

> It is understood and agreed that all understandings and agreements heretofore had between the parties hereto are merged in this contract, and that the same is entered into after full investigation, neither party relying upon any statement or representation, not embodied in this contract, made by the other. The purchaser has inspected the buildings standing on said premises and is thoroughly acquainted with their condition.

Execution.   All parties to a contract must execute it by signing, because a necessary person who does not sign the contract cannot be compelled to execute a deed. This is particularly important where there are numerous owners. It is not necessary to have the contract acknowledged before a notary public, unless it is to be recorded. However, the signatures are always witnessed.

Miscellaneous Provisions.   The following matters are occasionally encountered and should be included where applicable.

ASSIGNMENT.   Assignments of contract of sale should include all the right, title, and interest of the grantor; they should recite a consideration, and be dated and signed by the assignor and assignee. If the contract is recorded, the assignment must be recorded.

SURVIVAL CLAUSES.   The contract merges in the deed on the delivery thereof; thus, if it is desirable to continue the seller's liability under any representation in the contract, the following sentence can be appropriately inserted after the representation:

"This provision of the contract shall survive the delivery of the deed hereunder."

POSSESSION.   If the seller or one holding under him is to be in possession of all or part of the premises at the time of closing of title, it is good practice to include a representation that the premises will be delivered vacant at the closing of the title; otherwise, there should be a clause to survive the delivery of the deed that the seller will vacate the premises at a specified time and that he will deliver a lease at the closing.

It is not good practice to permit the purchaser to take possession prior to the actual delivery of the deed, since a person who occupies the premises under a contract of sale is not a tenant but a vendee. The relationship betwen vendor and vendee has different legal implications from that of landlord and tenant; for instance, if there were a default on the part of the purchaser, the seller could remove him only by means of an involved action in ejectment, rather than the comparatively simple eviction proceedings. If the purchaser must have possession, the better practice is to have him execute a lease with an option to purchase.

8

DEEDS

The transfer of title to real property is implemented by the execution and delivery of a deed. This is an extremely important real estate instrument in that it represents the indicia of ownership of real property. The deed may be defined, simply, as an instrument in writing, carefully drawn and executed, whereby one party, known as the grantor, conveys real property or an interest therein to another party, known as the grantee, by delivery of the deed to him.

HISTORY OF DEEDS

The deed was developed from the common law of England. Real property at that time was conveyed by "livery of seizin." ("Livery" is synonymous with "delivery": it is the act of delivering legal possession of property.) Thus, if a person wished to convey his possession and ownership of real property to another, he would deliver to the latter, on the land, "in the name of seizin of the land," a handful of earth or a branch or twig of a tree, and at the same time verbally express his intention of making the conveyance. Later, when the Statute of Frauds became part of the law, a writing was required of the transaction and the oral statements were reduced to written instruments. The delivery of the written instrument replaced the symbolic delivery of the handful of earth or the branch of a tree. This writing developed into our present-day deed, which, practically uniformly in all our states, must be executed and delivered to be effective.

ANALYSIS OF THE DEED

Every deed starts with the words "This indenture . . ." Historically, when two parties were concluding a sale of real property, two copies of a deed signed by both the grantor and the grantee would be written on one sheet of paper (usually parchment) side by side. The instrument was then torn in half by a wavy tear, or cut, and each party would receive a part of it. The genuineness of the two parts could be tested by placing them together and examining the indented edges to ascertain if they matched. This method of identification has long since outlived its usefulness; nevertheless, deeds are still referred to as "indentures" regardless of the manner of their execution.

Basic Requirements. Since the deed is another type of contract, it must satisfy certain essential requirements in order to be valid. The formal requirements for a valid deed are not uniform throughout the fifty states in the United States; however, there is a thread of uniformity, in that all deeds must contain the following elements:

PARTIES. The grantor and grantee must have the capacity to contract and should be identified. Some states require the complete addresses of the parties, and it is good practice to include them where possible.

CONSIDERATION. In a deed, consideration is usually stated nominally, such as "for the sum of $10 and other good and valuable consideration." The Code of Ethics of the National Association of Real Estate Boards, however, encourages the naming of the actual consideration. (Nebraska requires the actual consideration to be stated in the deed.)

WORDS OF CONVEYANCE. A granting clause or operative words of conveyance must be included. Words such as "grant and release," "grant and convey," or "grant, bargain, and sell" indicate the intent to convey—e.g., "grant and release unto the party of the second part, his heirs and assigns forever" (or if a corporation, its successors and assigns forever). The word "forever" indicates the conveyance of the fee simple.

DESCRIPTION OF PROPERTY. The four methods most commonly used to describe the premises are: metes and bounds; lot and block number; government survey; and monuments. (These have been described in Chapter 7.)

In addition to the physical description of the property, the deed will include mention of any appurtenances—e.g., right of way, easements, or water rights.

HABENDUM CLAUSE. By this clause, the estate to be taken by the grantee may be limited, that is, any reservations or restrictions will be indicated here. Such reservations and restrictions would include liens and/or exceptions to which the title was subject. The habendum clause states: "TO HAVE AND TO HOLD the premises herein granted unto the party of the second part the heirs or successors and assigns of the party of the second part forever."

There should be concurrency in the estate as expressed in the habendum clause and as expressed by the operative words of conveyance in the granting clause. If there is a conflict between the two clauses, then the latter prevails.

EXECUTION AND ACKNOWLEDGMENT. The deed must be signed by the grantor. If the grantee is to assume the mortgage, he will usually sign, too. If the grantor is a corporation, the signing will be done by one of the officers who is authorized to sign, and he will place the corporate seal on the deed. For individual grantors the addition of a seal is a mere formality. Acknowledgment is the attesting of the signing and signature by a third person, usually a notary public, to prevent the forgery of recorded documents, and is necessary before a deed can be recorded.

Although a deed is drafted and executed and is complete in every detail in accordance with the aforementioned requirements, it will not become legally operative (i.e., title is not conveyed) unless and until it is delivered by the grantor and accepted by the grantee. There must be an intent on the part of both parties to effectuate the conveyance. After delivery and acceptance the grantee will record the deed in the county where the real property is situated.

KINDS OF DEEDS AND CONVEYANCES

Although there are various kinds of deeds, some are more common than others.

Common Types of Deeds. There are many types of deeds used in connection with the conveyance of real property. The most widely used are: full covenant and warranty, bargain and sale, bargain and sale with covenants against grantor's acts, and quit-claim deeds.

FULL COVENANT AND WARRANTY. In this deed, the grantor covenants that: (1) he owns the property (seizin) and has the right to convey it; 2) the purchaser's title will be protected against attack; (3) the premises are free from encumbrances; (4) the grantor will execute and procure any further documents or assurances necessary to perfect title; and (5) the grantor will

THIS INDENTURE, made the   day of   , nineteen hundred and

BETWEEN

party of the first part, and

party of the second **part,**

WITNESSETH, that the party of the first part, in consideration of One Dollar and other valuable consideration paid by the party of the second part, does hereby grant and release unto the party of the second part, the distributees or successors and assigns of the party of the second part forever,

ALL that certain plot, piece or parcel of land, with the buildings and improvements thereon erected, situate, lying and being in the

TOGETHER with all right, title and interest, if any, of the party of the first part of, in and to any streets and roads abutting the above-described premises to the center lines thereof ; TOGETHER with the appurtenances and all the estate and rights of the party of the first part in and to said premises ; TO HAVE AND TO HOLD the premises herein granted unto the party of the second part, the distributees or successors and assigns of the party of the second part forever.

AND the party of the first part, in compliance with Section 13 of the Lien Law, covenants that the party of the first part will receive the consideration for this conveyance and will hold the right to receive such consideration as a trust fund to be applied first for the purpose of paying the costs of the improvement and will apply the same first to the payment of the cost of the improvement before using any part of the total of the same for any other purpose.

AND the party of the first part covenants as follows : that said party of the first part is seized of the said premises in fee simple, and has good right to convey the same ; that the party of the second part shall quietly enjoy the said premises ; that the said premises are free from incumbrances, except as aforesaid ; that the party of the first part will execute or procure any further necessary assurance of the title to said premises ; and that said party of the first part will forever warrant the title to said premises.

IN WITNESS WHEREOF, the party of the first part has duly executed this deed the day and year first above written.

IN PRESENCE OF :

Bargain and Sale Deed

THIS INDENTURE, made the   day of   , nineteen hundred and

BETWEEN

party of the first part, and

party of the second **part,**

WITNESSETH, that the party of the first part, in consideration of One Dollar and other valuable consideration paid by the party of the second part, does hereby grant and release unto the party of the second part, the distributees or successors and assigns of the party of the second part forever,

ALL that certain plot, piece or parcel of land, with the buildings and improvements thereon erected, situate, lying and being in the

TOGETHER with all right, title and interest, if any, of the party of the first part of, in and to any streets and roads abutting the above-described premises to the center lines thereof; TOGETHER with the appurtenances and all the estate and rights of the party of the first part in and to said premises; TO HAVE AND TO HOLD the premises herein granted unto the party of the second part, the distributees or successors and assigns of the party of the second part forever.

AND the party of the first part, in compliance with Section 13 of the Lien Law, covenants that the party of the first part will receive the consideration for this conveyance and will hold the right to receive such consideration as a trust fund to be applied first for the purpose of paying the costs of the improvement and will apply the same first to the payment of the cost of the improvement before using any part of the total of the same for any other purpose.

IN WITNESS WHEREOF, the party of the first part has duly executed this deed the day and year first above written.

IN PRESENCE OF:

Quitclaim Deed

THIS INDENTURE, made the   day of   19

BETWEEN

party of the first part, and

party of the second part,

WITNESSETH, that the party of the first part, in consideration of

One ($1.00) Dollar   , lawful money of the United States, and other good and valuable consideration paid by the party of the second part, does hereby remise, release and quitclaim unto the party of the second part,   and assigns forever,
ALL that certain plot, piece or parcel of land, with the buildings and improvements thereon erected, situate, lying and being in the

---

TOGETHER with all right, title and interest, if any, of the party of the first part of, in and to any streets, avenues and roads abutting the above-described premises to the center lines thereof.
TOGETHER with the appurtenances and all the estate and rights of the party of the first part in and to said premises,
TO HAVE AND TO HOLD the premises herein granted unto the party of the second part,
                              and assigns forever,
AND the party of the first part, in compliance with Section 13 of the Lien Law, covenants that the party of the first part will receive the consideration for this conveyance and will hold the right to receive such consideration as a trust fund to be applied first for the purpose of paying the cost of the improvement and that the party of the first part will apply the same first to the payment of the cost of the improvement before using any part of the total of the same for any other purpose.
IN WITNESS WHEREOF, the party of the first part has   executed this deed the day and year first above written.

IN PRESENCE OF:

forever continue to warrant title. The full covenant and warranty deed is the best type of deed that a purchaser can receive.

BARGAIN AND SALE. In this deed no representation or guarantee of good title is made, but the grantor's title is conveyed absolutely.

BARGAIN AND SALE WITH COVENANTS AGAINST GRANTOR'S ACTS. This deed is the same as the preceding one except that it adds a representation that the title is good and that the grantor has done nothing to encumber it.

QUITCLAIM. This deed is merely a release of any interest a grantor may have in the title. The deed contains no warranties or covenants and is generally used to correct a record to or to convey an interest inadvertently overlooked.

Other Types of Deeds. In addition to the foregoing the following represent various types of deeds that are used in special situations wherein real property is conveyed.

DEED OF GIFT (in some states). This is a conveyance of real property which the grantor makes "for and in consideration of the love and affection" which he bears unto the grantee.

REFEREE'S DEED IN FORECLOSURE. The referee is a court-appointed official whose duty it is to sell the property by virtue of an order of the court, and he is authorized to give a deed to the purchaser.

REFEREE'S DEED IN PARTITION. An action in partition is usually one brought by a joint owner of a parcel of real property to dissolve the concurrent ownership. For example, Able and Baker own real property as joint tenants and Baker brings an action for its partition. At the conclusion of the action the property may be sold by the referee, if so ordered, at public auction and the funds divided according to the respective rights of Able and Baker. The purchaser will be given a referee's deed in partition by the referee.

GUARDIAN'S DEED. A guardian is an official, usually appointed by the court, to convey the interest of an infant in real property. The deed recites the court order appointing the guardian, the application of the guardian to the court for permission to convey the property, and the court order authorizing him to do so.

COMMITTEE'S DEED. This is similar to the guardian's deed, except that it is used with respect to incapacitated persons, other than infants. A committee is usually appointed by the court to administer the affairs of an incompetent person. The committee recites the court order of appointment, the application for permission to sell, and the court order authorizing the sale.

DEED BY ASSIGNEE FOR BENEFIT OF CREDITORS. In the trust agreement between the insolvent debtor and his creditors, an assignee or trustee is appointed for the benefit of creditors; he then marshals the debtor's assets for distribution. The debtor conveys his title to real property to the assignee by deed of assignment; title to the real property can then be conveyed by deed by the assignee for the benefit of·creditors.

DEED OF SURRENDER. This type of deed is used to merge an estate for life or years with either a reversion or a remainder. This can also be done by a quit-claim deed from the life tenant to the remainderman.

CORRECTION DEED (OR DEED OF CONFIRMATION). This deed is used to correct an error in a prior deed. For example, Able conveys to Baker, but there is an error in the description. Upon request, Able will correct the error. This may also be done by a quit-claim deed, explaining the purpose of the instrument. But note that if the seller refuses to correct a description in a deed, a court order may be obtained correcting the error, after an action for the reformation of the instrument.

DEED OF RELEASE. This is a form of quit-claim deed used to convey the street rights of an abutting owner to a municipality. The purpose of the conveyance, recited in the instrument, is to release certain described premises from a dower interest, a reverter for breach of condition subsequent, or a remainder interest.

Covenants. A covenant in a deed is an affirmation or agreement solemnly made by the grantor attesting that certain conditions either exist or do not exist, or that the grantor will perform certain acts to protect the grantee's title, if necessary.

COVENANTS RUNNING WITH THE LAND. These are agreements which pass certain rights and duties to subsequent grantees whenever the real property is conveyed.

Covenant of Quiet Enjoyment. This covenant is construed to mean that the grantee may at all times after conveyance peaceably and quietly have and hold his property without any suit, trouble, molestation, eviction, or disturbance by the grantor or any person claiming under or through him.

Restrictive Covenant. Restrictive covenants are valid except when they are against public policy, or have outlived their usefulness. They are enforceable by injunction. Note that a covenant in a deed restricting further conveyance of the real property to persons of the Caucasian race cannot be enforced by the courts (as set forth in recent decisions of the United States Supreme Court) since it is repugnant to public policy.

Conveyances by Will or Intestacy. If one dies and leaves a will, he will usually have named an executor to carry out his wishes. If one dies without leaving a will, the court will appoint an administrator to distribute the decedent's estate. Both the executor and the administrator are authorized to dispose of the decedent's real property by deed.

Executor's Deeds. Where the owner of real property has died testate, title to his real property may be conveyed by his executor, in accordance with the terms of the will.

Administrator's Deed. In the event of intestacy the distribution of the estate is made by the administrator's deed, executed by the administrator under the supervision of the court.

Transfer of Title by Adverse Possession. An interest in real property may be acquired by occupying land in such a way and for such a period of time that the real owner is barred from recovering title or possession. If a person occupies the land of another for a prescribed time period (in some states the term is twenty years, in New York fifteen years, and in other states even a shorter period of time) and if his possession fulfills specified requirements—claim of title or color of title, hostile to the owner, actual, open, visible and notorious, continuous and exclusive—then at the end of the prescribed period, determined by the Statute of Limitations of the state concerned, the adverse user may convey good title to another.

Stamps on Deed. Federal internal revenue tax stamps on deeds were eliminated on January 1, 1968. The tax had been 55¢ per $500 of equity with a minimum of $1.10. Most states thereupon immediately required state revenue tax stamps on deeds in the same amount. Generally, unless the contract provides otherwise, the tax stamps must be affixed by the seller since this is a tax upon the amount of equity he receives for the conveyance. Although no government agency inspects the deed when conveyed to ascertain whether the proper tax stamps have been placed thereon, it would be foolhardy to neglect to do so as no county clerk would accept for recording, nor would any court enforce a deed that had not been properly endorsed.

9

TITLE SEARCH AND INSURANCE, CLOSINGS AND RECORDING

After the purchaser has signed a contract for the sale of real property, he should obtain the best examination of the title available. No deed or mortgage should be accepted unless the title to the property has been properly searched. Thereafter, the closing may properly take place; after the acceptance and delivery of the deed the grantee will record it so that it becomes effective against the world.

TITLE SEARCH

The title search yields a complete report referred to as an "abstract of title"—a condensed history of the ownership of the land and improvements. It is a summary of the operative parts of all instruments of conveyance affecting the land, title, or interest therein and includes a statement of all liens, charges, and encumbrances or liabilities to which the land is subject.

Purpose of the Title Search. The purpose of having the title searched, and an abstract of title made, is to ascertain whether there are any flaws in the grantor's title or to disclose possible clouds on title, that is, any impairment of the owner's title. The buyer may order the title search at his own expense and for his protection.

If a mortgage is to be placed on the property, the search will be ordered by the mortgagee, at the expense of the mortgagor, because the mortgagee must be assured that the borrower has title to the property. If the lending institution (mortgagee) is a bank, it must ascertain that there are no superior liens on the property. By law, a bank may not lend money on second mortgages. The title search will assure them that their loan is in compliance with the law.

A title search is usually made by a mortgagee or lienor prior to the foreclosure of a mortgage or lien. All parties who have an interest in the subject matter of the foreclosure, because their liens are inferior to that of the forecloser, must be made parties to the action; otherwise, the mortgagee's action against the mortgagor will be defective. The title search will, therefore, reveal the identity of all persons and parties required to receive the service of process in the foreclosure proceedings, and the nature and extent of their interest.

A guaranteed search is preferable, especially in large cities, although inexpensive abstracts of title covering short periods are used under certain conditions. A good title examination, however, cannot be made cheaply or quickly.

Subjects of a Title Search. The title searcher will make an exhaustive investigation and report on the following:

CHAIN OF TITLE. This would be checked through the grantor-grantee index of the property in the proper book (liber) on conveyances as far back as is required. Each deed should be verified for the description of the property, internal revenue tax stamps, the acknowledgment, the date of recording, easements, restrictions, or unusual features.

MORTGAGE INDEX. This file should be checked to ascertain whether a prior grantor had mortgaged the property and, if so, whether the mortgages are still in effect or have been satisfied.

LIS PENDENS. A *lis pendens* is notice of the pendency of a legal action concerning the property; if any are found, the legal action must be discontinued or settled, and the docket marked "cancelled," before title can be passed.

JUDGMENTS. An entered judgment is a lien against the real property of the judgment debtor. The length of time that this lien is valid as a charge against the property depends upon the law of the particular state. The judgments against all grantors who are judgment debtors are reported. The title report will give the names of the judgment debtor and creditor, the attorney for the judgment creditor, the amount of the judgment, and the time and date of entry of the judgment. If a judgment is found against a grantor that is still a charge against the property, it must be satisfactorily disposed of before good title can be passed.

LAND TAXES, WATER CHARGES, AND ASSESSMENTS. These are paramount liens on real estate and are generally paid at, or prior to, closing. The search should reveal the date of the last payment and delinquencies, if any, so that they may be disposed of.

MINOR LIENS. Mechanic's liens, conditional bills of sale, tax liens, and building and loan agreements, must be disposed of if they are a burden on the property.

PETITIONS IN BANKRUPTCY AND CREDITOR ASSIGNMENTS. Bankruptcy petition and assignments are handled in the same manner as judgments and must be satisfactorily disposed of.

SURROGATES COURT SEARCH. If there is an executor or an administrator in the chain of title, the proceedings in Surrogates Court will have to be examined in order to ascertain whether the property was deeded to the right person. Also, it should be ascertained whether all applicable taxes were duly paid.

POSSIBLE DOWER RIGHTS. If a married person owned the property, it will be necessary to ascertain whether dower rights were then still applicable and affected the title. For example, in New York State, dower rights were abolished on September 1, 1930. Many other states have followed New York in abolishing dower; nevertheless, some states still retain this right.

RECORDED LEASE AND TENANCIES. Leases and tenancies will be reported for purposes of determining their effect on the passing of title.

TITLE INSURANCE

In addition to providing the service of searching the title, the title company will, for a premium, guarantee that the title to the property is clear, except for the defects noted in an exception sheet which is prepared as a part of its title report. These defects are not covered by the title insurance policy unless they are specifically omitted from the exception sheet and included in the coverage. Since title insurance companies usually can act with greater speed in searching titles than individuals, lawyers, or abstractors, the title company is a valuable adjunct in expediting real estate transactions. These companies employ highly skilled and competent employees. The premium for title insurance is paid only once, at the inception of the coverage, and the policy holder is protected from losses due to defective title and all legal expenses incurred as long as he, or his heirs or estate, retains an interest in the property.

CLOSINGS

If the contract of sale has been properly drawn and all pertinent matters disposed of, the closing of the title is ordinarily a simple procedure. At the closing the following steps are usually accomplished.

Identity of Parties. The first step is the identification of all persons present. The title report will indicate all parties who are necessary for the signing of the closing instruments. In a simple closing of an unencumbered one-family house being purchased for all cash, the necessary parties will usually include the buyer and his attorney, the seller and his attorney, and the title company representative. If a real estate broker negotiated the sale, he or his agent will usually be present, not as a necessary party to the closing, but to be paid his brokerage commission by the seller. If the property is to be mortgaged, as part of the financing, then the mortgagee and/or his attorney will be present for the purpose of exchanging money loaned to the buyer for duly executed bond and mortgage instruments.

Closing Objections. The title company report will reveal any objections to the seller's title. The seller is obligated to dispose of these satisfactorily in order to convey good and marketable title. Some of the usual objections are: unpaid corporate franchise taxes, unsatisfied judgments against the seller or prior owners in the chain of title, unpaid mortgages, and unpaid taxes. When the buyer is satisfied that all the objections have been disposed of, the parties will then proceed to compute the financial adjustments.

Financial Adjustments. The standard contract of sale provides for the apportionment of certain items as of the date that the title is conveyed. These usually include:

1. Rents as and when collected.
2. Interest on mortgages.
3. Premiums on existing transferable policies of insurance or renewal of those expiring prior to the delivery of the deed.
4. Taxes and sewer rents on the basis of the calendar year for which assessed. (In counties where taxes and sewer rents are assessed on the basis of the fiscal year, the apportionment must be made on that basis.)
5. Water rates on the basis of the calendar year.
6. Fuel.
7. Escrow account, if any, where the title is taken subject to an amortized mortgage.

Except by agreement otherwise, these items are adjusted as of the date of closing. The seller will be entitled to a credit for all charges that he has prepaid; the buyer will be entitled to receive a credit for all sums and charges the seller was obligated to assume and pay to the date of closing, but has not paid. It is customary to assume a thirty-day month in calculating adjustments of interest, taxes, and water charges; rent is usually adjusted on the basis of the actual number of days in the month.

Further, the seller will be entitled to the purchase price, less the amount of cash he has received from the buyer on the signing of the contract, less any outstanding mortgages which are assumed by the buyer. On page 97 is a form of closing statement usually followed by real estate attorneys.

Execution of Closing Instruments. The buyer is entitled to receive a duly executed deed upon the payment in full, by cash or certified check, of the balance due to the seller. The deed is prepared by the seller or his attorney and is examined and approved by the buyer or his attorney and the title company representative. If the buyer must borrow money from a mortgagee to use as part or all of his payment, the attorney for the mortgagee will prepare the bond and mortgage to be signed by the buyer.

Fees at Closing. The fees at closing are required to be paid as follows:

The Seller:
1. State revenue stamps on the deed if required. The fee is usually 55¢ per $500 of equity that the seller is to receive, or fraction thereof. The minimum fee is $1.10, except where no consideration is received; thus, where the deed is granted as a gift or a bequest, there is no fee.
2. Real estate broker's fee, if any.
3. Attorney's legal fee, if any.

The Buyer:
1. Fee for recording the deed.
2. Mortgage tax, if any.
3. Fee for recording mortgage, if any.
4. Legal fee for drawing up bond and mortgage, if any.
5. Title company bill.
6. Survey expense, if any.
7. Attorney's fee, if any.

Seller _____   Seller's attorney _____

Purchaser _____   Buyer's attorney _____

Date of Closing _____   Adjustments as of _____

Closing statement of Premises _____

Credit

Paid on contract	$
First mortgage	$
Interest from _____	
to _____ at %	$
Second mortgage	$
Interest from _____	
to _____ at %	$
Purchase money mortgages	$
Taxes	$
Water rates	$
Rents	$

Total credits $

Debit

Purchase Price	$
Water	$
Taxes	$
Rents	$
Fuel	$
Insurance apportioned	$

Total debits
Less: Total credits

Balance paid to seller $

Paid by seller

Recording expenses	$
Revenue stamps	$

Held in escrow by:

$ as follows:

Paid by Purchaser

Mortgage tax	$
Revenue stamps	$
Record mortgage	$
Record deed	$
Drawing bond & mortgage	$
Title company bill	$
Closing title	$
Other recordings	$
Survey expense	$

Insurance Memorandum

Number Company Amount Premium Expiration Apportionment Remarks

Mortgage Memorandum

First mortgage: Amount $ Held by:
                   Address: Interest rate   %
                   Interest days: Mortgage due:

Second mortgage: Amount $ Held by:
                   Address: Interest rate   %
                   Interest days: Mortgage due:

Taxes payable _____   Water payable _____

Delivery, Acceptance, Recording. After the payment of the closing fees and the balance of the purchase price, the closing instruments are delivered by the seller to the buyer. The buyer may then record the deed, as outlined in the subsequent section.

RECORDING

All states make statutory provision for recording instruments affecting an interest in real property, and there is a good deal of similarity in the recording laws of most of the states. The recording acts are statutes of recordation or registration and provide for the recording of every instrument or writing by which an interest or estate in land is created, transferred, mortgaged, assigned, or satisfied, or by which the title to real property may be affected either in law or in equity.

Purpose of Recording. The purpose of the recording acts is to give actual or constructive notice to the world of the status of the title, as long as there is compliance with the statute. However, the recording acts do not protect purchasers against theft, forged deeds or instruments in the chain of title, fraud, or duress.

The instruments are recorded by either photostating or reproducing the original, and then filing or indexing it in the liber in the office of the register or clerk of the county in which the property is located. If the instrument to be recorded is a deed or a mortgage, it will usually be indexed both as to grantor and grantee, or mortgagor and mortgagee. These indexes will generally be kept both in alphabetical and in chronological order. When the instrument is presented and delivered to the City Register or county clerk for recording, a statutory recording fee is charged, depending on the number of pages in the document. The date and time of day, in hours and minutes, are then stamped on the instrument.

In most states an unrecorded conveyance is void as against a subsequent bona fide purchaser, in good faith and for value, and without notice of the conveyance.

The Torrens System of Recording Title. The Torrens System, where it has been adopted, seeks to provide that a landowner who has been issued a Torrens certificate of title shall, in law, be conclusively presumed to be the owner of the land described in the certificate. Under the Torrens System the law reaches out to the title itself to set it at rest against the rest of the world. The difference between the recording system and the Torrens System is this: under the recording system the deed is registered and is always open to controversy, whereas under the Torrens System the title itself is registered.

10

BONDS AND MORTGAGES

In our present economy, we rarely purchase real property outright, that is, paying all cash. The difference between the purchase price and the amount of money that the buyer pays the seller to convey title to him is usually financed by a lender. As security for the repayment of this loan, the borrower pledges the real property by executing a mortgage, and also pledges his own personal liability by executing a bond.

The bond and mortgage, therefore, are the legal instruments establishing the liability of the borrower to the lender, *in personam* (personally) and *in rem* (property), for the repayment of the obligation. These two instruments are executed, usually simultaneously, upon the granting of the loan upon the property.

BONDS

A bond is the legal instrument executed by the borrower (obligor) acknowledging that he is justly indebted to the lender (obligee) for the amount of money loaned to him by the obligee. Further, the obligor covenants to repay this debt in accordance with the terms established by the agreement of the parties, usually in stated installments of principal, together with interest at an established rate, on the unpaid balance.

In the standard form of bond generally used, the obligor additionally agrees that the whole of the principal sum becomes due, at the option of the obligee, in case of default in the payment of any installment of principal, interest, tax, assessment, or water rate; or upon actual or threatened alteration, demolition, or removal of any building standing on the mortgaged premises; or in case of failure to assign and deliver fire insurance policies after demand in case of fire; or upon failure to reimburse the mortgagee for premiums paid on fire insurance; or upon failure to execute an estoppel certificate upon request.

KNOW ALL MEN BY THESE PRESENTS,

That

hereinafter designated as the obligor, does hereby acknowledge the obligor to be justly indebted **to**

hereinafter designated as the obligee, in the sum of

dollars,

lawful money of the United States, which sum said obligor does hereby
covenant to pay the said obligee, and the executors, administrators, successors or assigns of the obligee,

with interest thereon to be computed from the date hereof at the rate of   per centum
per annum and to be paid on the   day of   19   , next ensuing and
thereafter

IT IS HEREBY EXPRESSLY AGREED, that the said principal sum shall at the option of the obligee become
due on the happening of any default or event by which, under the terms of the mortgage securing this bond,
said principal sum may or shall become due and payable; also, that all of the covenants, conditions and agreements contained in said mortgage are hereby made part of this instrument.

This bond may not be changed or terminated orally. The word "obligor" or "obligee" shall be construed as
if it read "obligors" or "obligees" whenever the sense of this instrument so requires.

DATED the   day of   19   .

IN PRESENCE OF:

The bond refers to the mortgage and its covenants, which are
incorporated into it, by reference; it is not usually recorded.

MORTGAGES

Each state has its own mortgage laws, but all are based on the
common law and follow a basic pattern. The purpose of the mortgage is to create a lien upon the real property that can be properly
recorded so that in the event that there is a default in the repayment of the obligation the property may be sold and the proceeds
used to reimburse the mortgagee.

History. The mortgage of the common law goes back to early
Saxon law; however, the classical common-law mortgage, which

is the forerunner of the present-day mortgage, was not in common use in England until 1400.

The earliest mortgage was a deed which contained a defeasance clause. If the mortgagor defaulted, the mortgagee, who held the deed, was entitled to take possession of the land and would then become the absolute owner. The mortgage instrument was strictly construed, and there could be no appeal to reason or justice, as these pleas were considered immaterial except in cases of extreme hardship. Thus, if a mortgagor who was robbed while en route to pay the mortgagee then entered a plea to the king and tendered payment of the amount due, the mortgagee could be ordered to accept the payment and return the land. The king's prerogative, however, was rarely exercised.

Sometime prior to 1450 these hearings on petitions to redeem mortgaged property after default were delegated to the chancellor, a high church official who was well versed in Roman and Canon law. The chancellor was the "Keeper of the King's conscience," and this idea gradually developed into a separate court called "Chancery Court," which later became known as the Court of Equity.

The attitude that early remedies were available only in instances of extreme hardship, where the default lay beyond the control of the mortgagor, eased with time and an increasingly liberal trend set in so that eventually the courts granted relief in all cases except *laches* (undue procrastination). However, a mortgagor in default, as a prerequisite to seeking relief, was required to pay the court principal, interest, and costs.

This liberal trend placed the mortgagee at a distinct disadvantage, since he could not foretell what the court would consider as laches. To foreclose a mortgagor's right to redeem the property, the mortgagee therefore would institute an action in strict foreclosure, and the court would set a specific time, usually two to six months, within which the mortgagor could redeem his property from foreclosure. If he did not do so, his right to redeem the property was permanently cut off.

The courts increasingly recognized the mortgage as a security device and the mortgagor as the true owner in equity of the property, whereas in law the mortgagee held the title.

Two early developments contributed to mortgage law as we know it today. First, in early English law, Englishmen could not charge interest on money loaned, although foreign money lenders could do so. And second, a conveyance of real property was not valid unless the grantee took possession. When real property was mortgaged, therefore, the mortgagee took possession and, since he could not collect interest, he kept the rents and profits. At a later date, the Chancery Court made the mortgagee account for the rents and profits and apply them to mortgage debt. Thus, a mortgage began to be recognized as valid without possession. The mortgagor was allowed to retain possession, but the mortgagee, who was the title owner, was entitled to possession upon demand.

After the Revolution, the States adopted the laws of England in so far as they were in accord with the social and economic concepts in the States.

Concepts of a Mortgage. There are basically two concepts of mortgages: common law and equity.

COMMON LAW. Under common law the mortgage is considered a conveyance of real property to be defeated by the happening of an event, such as payment. If there is a default, the conveyance becomes absolute.

EQUITY. In equity a mortgage is considered to be the security for the payment of a debt. The mortgagee is the title owner; the mortgagor is the equitable owner who is entitled to the possession and rent and profits of the land. The mortgagor has the right to pay off the debt and redeem the mortgaged land. This right is not cut off until the mortgage has been foreclosed and a decree of foreclosure entered by the court. The early action of foreclosure is in the nature of cutting off the equitable owner's (mortgagor's) equity of redemption and thereby vesting the title absolutely in the mortgagee. These concepts are embodied in the two prevalent theories regarding mortgage extant in the United States today.

Theories of Mortgages in the United States. There are two mortgage theories prevailing in the United States: title and lien.

TITLE THEORY. On executing a mortgage, the mortgagor passes title to the property to the mortgagee, subject to a condition subsequent (e.g., payment of the debt). Upon fulfillment of the condition subsequent, the title to the property reverts to the mortgagor and the mortgage becomes void. The mortgage contains a provision stating that the mortgagor is entitled to retain possession.

LIEN THEORY. Under the lien theory (used in a majority of states), the title remains with the mortgagor. The mortgage that is placed on the property is a lien, or a charge on the title, providing for a sale of the mortgaged premises to satisfy the lien in case of default. The order of priority of mortgages, whether in title or in lien, is similar to that found in deeds, with priority depending upon the order of the recording of the mortgage (assuming there has been no fraudulent recording by the mortgagee). The first lien recorded is the first mortgage. There may also be second and third liens and mortgages, depending upon the order of priority of recording. Second and third mortgages usually are more expensive to acquire than first mortgages, since they are riskier investments; however, they serve an important function where the purchaser does not have enough available cash to consummate the transaction.

Requirements of a Mortgage. The following list summarizes usual mortgage requirements.

1. The date.
2. The names of parties, including addresses.
3. The amount of the debt and a statement regarding how it is to be paid off.
4. A statement that "mortgagor mortgages to mortgagee" the property in question as security for the repayment of the debt.
5. A complete description of the property.
6. A covenant to pay the indebtedness.
7. A covenant to keep the premises insured.
8. A covenant that none of the property will be removed.
9. A covenant to pay taxes as they fall due.
10. An acceleration clause, i.e., a stipulation that if the covenants are not kept or if title is not valid, all installments of the loan will become due immediately and, if they are not paid, foreclosure will ensue.
11. A warranty of title.
12. A covenant by the mortgagor to pay the attorney's fee in case of foreclosure.
13. A stipulation that personal property later acquired will be included in the mortgage.
14. Appointment of receiver clause. (This protects the mort-

gagee during the interval between the commencement of actions and the final order of a court.)

15. Estoppel certificate clause. (This certificate, which must be produced by the mortgagor upon request, verifies the unpaid mortgage balance.)

16. Good repair clause. (If the mortgagor fails to keep the premises in reasonably good repair, or fails to comply with requirements of a governmental department—within a stated period, such as three months—the mortgagee has the option to foreclose.)

17. Sale in one parcel clause. (If the mortgaged property consists of more than one lot, the mortgagee may sell the premises, or such portions as may be affected by the mortgage, in one parcel.)

18. Trust clause. If the mortgagor borrows mortgage money to improve the property, he holds the funds in trust to pay for the improvement, and thus is prevented from not paying for the improvement.

19. Prepayment clause. (Usually inserted at the request of the mortgagor, this clause relates the terms of prepaid interest or stated amounts of mortgage at any time prior to the due date. Many lenders require a payment of a penalty in case of prepayment, and there is customarily a period of notice. The penalty is usually measured by a number of months of interest.)

Since a mortgage is a contract, it must contain the essential elements—i.e., mutuality of agreement, parties with capacity to contract, consideration, a legal subject matter, and a form in accordance with law.

Types of Mortgages. Mortgages may be classified according to the nature of the guaranty, the purpose they serve, the function they perform, or the nature of the mortgage.

FHA. A Federal Housing Administration (FHA) insured loan is one which is insured by the Federal Housing Administration according to the National Housing Act of 1934. Thus, a lending institution can lend a greater percentage of appraised value than in situations where the loan is not thus guaranteed.

V. A. GUARANTEED MORTGAGE. Under the terms of the so-called G. I. mortgage, dating from the Serviceman's Readjust-

This Mortgage, made the   day of

one thousand nine hundred and

BETWEEN

, the mortgagor

and

, the mortgagee

    WITNESSETH, that to secure the payment of an indebtedness in the sum of

dollars,

lawful money of the United States, to be paid

with interest thereon to be computed from the   day of   , 19   , at

the rate of   per centum per annum, and to be paid

according to a certain bond
note

or obligation bearing even date herewith, the mortgagor hereby mortgages to the mortgagee
    ALL

TOGETHER with all fixtures and articles of personal property now or hereafter attached or appurtenant to or used in the operation of said premises, including (but not limited to) plumbing, heating, lighting and cooking fixtures, air-conditioning fixtures and units, ranges, refrigerators, radio aerials, bathroom and kitchen cabinets, mantels, door mirrors, venetian blinds, shades, window screens, awnings, storm windows, window boxes, storm doors, screen doors, mail boxes, weather vanes, flag poles, pumps, shrubbery and outdoor statuary, all of which shall be deemed to be and remain a part of the realty and are covered by the lien of this mortgage. If the lien of this mortgage be subject to a conditional bill of sale or chattel mortgage covering any such property, then in the event of any default in this mortgage all the right, title and interest of the mortgagor, in and to any and all such property is hereby assigned to the mortgagee, together with benefits of any deposits or payments now or hereafter made thereon by the mortgagor or the predecessors or successors in title to the mortgagor in the mortgaged premises.

TOGETHER also with any and all award and awards heretofore made and hereafter to be made by the City of New York or any Municipal or State authorities to the present and all subsequent owners of the premises herein described including any award or awards for any change or changes of grade of streets affecting said premises, which said award and awards are hereby assigned to the said mortgagee, and the legal representatives, successors and assigns of the mortgagee; and the said mortgagee, for the said mortgagee, and the legal representatives, successors and assigns of the ,mortgagee (at its or their option) are hereby authorized, directed and empowered to collect and receive the proceeds of any such award and awards from the authorities making the same and to give proper receipts and acquittances therefor, and to apply the same toward the payment of the amount owing on account of this mortgage and its accompanying bond, notwithstanding the fact that the amount owing on account of this mortgage and said bond may not be then due and payable; and the said mortgagor for the said mortgagor, and the legal representatives, successors and assigns of the mortgagor, hereby covenants and agrees to and with the said mortgagee, and the legal representatives, successors and assigns of the mortgagee upon request by the holder of this mortgage to make, execute and deliver any and all assignments and other instruments sufficient for the purpose of assigning the aforesaid award and awards to the holder of this mortgage, free, clear and discharged of any and all encumbrances of any kind or nature whatsoever.

AND the mortgagor covenants with the mortgagee as follows:

1. That the mortgagor will pay the indebtedness as hereinbefore provided.

2. That the mortgagor will keep the buildings on the premises insured against loss by fire, for the benefit of the mortgagee; that he will assign and deliver the policies to the mortgagee; and that he will reimburse the mortgagee for any premiums paid for insurance made by the mortgagee on the mortgagor's default in so insuring the buildings or in so assigning and delivering the policies.

3. That no building on the premises shall be altered, removed or demolished without the consent of the mortgagee.

4. That the whole of said principal sum and interest shall become due at the option of the mortgagee: after default in the payment of any installment of principal for fifteen days, or after default in the payment of interest for fifteen days; or after default in the payment of any tax, water rate, sewer rent or assessment for thirty days after notice and demand; or after default after notice and demand either in assigning and delivering the policies insuring the buildings against loss by fire or in reimbursing the mortgagee for the premiums paid on such insurance, as hereinbefore provided; or after default upon request in furnishing a statement of the amount due on the mortgage and whether any offsets or defenses exist against the mortgage debt, as hereinafter provided.

5 That the holder of this mortgage, in any action to foreclose it shall be entitled to the appointment of a receiver.

6. That the mortgagor will pay all taxes, assessments, sewer rents, or water rates, and in default thereof, the mortgagee may pay the same.

7. That the mortgagor within five days upon request in person or within ten days upon request by mail will furnish a written statement duly acknowledged of the amount due on this mortgage and whether any offsets or defenses exist against the mortgage debt.

8. That notice and demand or request may be in writing and may be served in person or by mail.

9. That the mortgagor warrants the title to the premises.

10. That the fire insurance policies required by paragraph No. 2 above shall contain the usual extended coverage endorsement; that in addition thereto the mortgagor, within thirty days after notice and demand, will keep the premises insured against war risk and any other hazard that may reasonably be required by the mortgagee. All of the provisions of paragraphs No. 2 and No. 4 above relating to fire insurance and the provisions of Section 254 of the Real Property Law construing the same shall apply to the additional insurance required by this paragraph.

11. That in case of a foreclosure sale, said premises, or so much thereof as may be affected by this mortgage, may be sold in one parcel.

12. If any action or proceeding be commenced (except an action to foreclose this mortgage or to collect the debt secured thereby), to which action or proceeding the holder of this mortgage is made a party, or in which it becomes necessary to defend or uphold the lien of this mortgage, all sums paid by the holder of this mortgage for the expense of any litigation to prosecute or defend the rights and lien created by this mortgage (including reasonable counsel fees), shall be paid by the mortgagor, together with interest thereon at the rate of six per centum per annum, and any such sum and the interest thereon shall be a lien on said premises, prior to any right, or title to, interest in or claim upon said premises attaching or accruing subsequent to the lien of this mortgage, and shall be deemed to be secured by this mortgage and by the bond which it secures. In any action or proceeding to foreclose this mortgage, or to recover or collect the debt secured thereby, the provisions of law respecting the recovery of costs, disbursements and allowances shall prevail unaffected by this covenant.

13. That the mortgagor hereby assigns to the mortgagee the rents, issues and profits of the premises as further security for the payment of said indebtedness, and the mortgagor grants to the mortgagee the right to enter upon the premises for the purpose of collecting the same and to let the premises or any part thereof, and to apply the rents, issues and profits, after payment of all necessary charges and expenses, on account of said indebtedness. This assignment and grant shall continue in effect until this mortgage is paid. The mortgagee hereby waives the right to enter upon said premises for the purpose of collecting said rents, issues and profits, and the mortgagor shall be entitled to collect and receive said rents, issues and profits until default under any of the covenants, conditions or agreements contained in this mortgage, and agrees to use such rents, issues and profits in payment of principal and interest becoming due on this mortgage and in payment of taxes, assessments, sewer rents, water rates and carrying charges becoming due against said premises, but such right of the mortgagor may be revoked by the mortgagee upon any default, on five days' written notice. The mortgagor will not, without the written consent of the mortgagee, receive or collect rent from any tenant of said premises or any part thereof for a period of more than one month in advance, and in the event of any default under this mortgage will pay monthly in advance to the mortgagee, or to any receiver appointed to collect said rents, issues and profits, the fair and reasonable rental value for the use and occupation of said premises or of such part thereof as may be in the possession of the mortgagor, and upon default in any such payment will vacate and surrender the possession of said premises to the mortgagee or to such receiver, and in default thereof may be evicted by summary proceedings.

14. That the whole of said principal sum and interest shall become due at the option of the mortgagee: (a) after failure to exhibit to the mortgagee, within ten days after demand, receipts showing payment of all taxes, water rates, sewer rents and assessments; or (b) after the actual or threatened alteration, demolition or

removal of any building on the premises without the written consent of the mortgagee and that in the event of such alteration, demolition or removal of any building the interest in the indebtedness secured by this mortgage shall be at the rate of six per centum per annum from the date of the commencement of such alteration, demolition or removal, if such interest rate at that time be less than six per centum per annum; or (c) after the assignment of the rents of the premises or any part thereof without the written consent of the mortgagee; or (d) if the buildings on said premises are not maintained in reasonably good repair after notice of the condition of the building is given to the mortgagor; or (e) after failure to comply with any requirement or order or notice of violation of law or ordinance issued by any governmental department claiming jurisdiction over the premises within three months from the issuance thereof; or (f) if on application of the mortgagee two or more fire insurance companies lawfully doing business in the State of New York refuse to issue policies insuring the buildings on the premises; or (g) in the event of the removal, demolition or destruction in whole or in part of any of the fixtures, chattels or articles of personal property covered hereby, unless the same are promptly replaced by similar fixtures, chattels and articles of personal property at least in quality and condition to those replaced, free from chattel mortgages or other encumbrances thereon and free from any reservation of title thereto; or (h) after thirty days' notice to the mortgagor, in the event of the passage of any law deducting from the value of land for the purposes of taxation any lien thereon, or changing in any way the taxation of mortgages or debts secured thereby for state or local purposes; or (i) if the mortgagor fails to keep, observe and perform any of the other covenants, conditions or agreements contained in this mortgage.

15. That the mortgagor will, in compliance with Section 13 of the Lien Law, receive the advances secured hereby and will hold the right to receive such advances as a trust fund to be applied for the purpose of paying the cost of the improvement and will apply the same first to the payment of the cost of the improvement before using any part of the total of the same for any other purpose.

16. This mortgage may not be changed or terminated orally. The covenants contained in this mortgage shall run with the land and bind the mortgagor, the heirs, successors and assigns of the mortgagor and all subsequent owners, encumbrances, tenants and subtenants of the premises and shall enure to the benefit of the mortgagee, the personal representatives, successors and assigns of the mortgagee and all subsequent holders of this mortgage. The word "mortgagor" shall be construed as if it read "mortgagors" and the word "mortgagee" shall be construed as if it read "mortgagees" when ever the sense of this mortgage so requires.

IN WITNESS WHEREOF this mortgage has been duly executed by the mortgagor.

IN THE PRESENCE OF:

ment Act of 1944, the Veterans Administration guarantees to qualified lenders a certain percentage of a mortgage loan to a veteran up to a maximum amount. The amount of maximum guarantee, rate of interest, and length of time of loan can be changed by act of Congress.

CONVENTIONAL MORTGAGE. The down payment on a purchase with a conventional loan is usually 20 to 30 per cent higher than on a G. I. or FHA mortgage, since the mortgage will fall between 50 and 80 per cent of appraised value. The market for conventional mortgages fluctuates less than G. I. or FHA mortgages because the interest rates are not fixed.

AMORTIZED MORTGAGE. In this type of mortgage the principal and interest are paid monthly or periodically to the end of the term.

BUDGET MORTGAGE. This type of mortgage provides not only for amortization of principal and interest, but also for the periodic amortization of insurance, water, and taxes.

PACKAGE MORTGAGE. This type of mortgage, a more complete budget mortgage, provides for the amortization of payments for mechanical equipment and appliances added in the home.

OPEN MORTGAGE. This is a mortgage which has become due but remains unpaid. The mortgagee can demand payment in full at any time.

BLANKET MORTGAGE. Used mainly by construction companies and developers, this mortgage covers more than one parcel of property. A partial release clause is usually incorporated, whereby the mortgagee agrees to release part of the premises upon payment of part of the loan.

OPEN END MORTGAGE. In this type of mortgage the borrower has an option during the term of the mortgage, whereby he may reborrow a sum up to the original amount of the mortgage on the same terms as the original mortgage.

PURCHASE MONEY MORTGAGE. This is a mortgage taken back by the seller as part of the consideration. It is ordinarily used to expedite the buyer's financing.

MORTGAGE OF A LEASE. If a lessee has a valuable lease, he may borrow money using the lease as security. If he defaults, the holder of the mortgage is entitled to an assignment of the lease.

MORTGAGE ON CROPS. One who has crops that have not as yet been harvested may borrow money in anticipation of the harvest and hypothecate its yield. The mortgagee, if unpaid, may sell the crops for reimbursement.

JUNIOR MORTGAGE. Any mortgage that has prior, superior liens ahead of it is referred to as a junior mortgage, i.e., a second, third, or fourth mortgage.

Foreclosure. A foreclosure proceeding is instituted to force a sale of property which has been mortgaged and which is in default in payments or covenants under the mortgage agreement. The action is regulated entirely by state statutes. The right to foreclose is vested in the real party in interest, that is, the party entitled to receive monies due and payable under the mortgage.

FORECLOSURE STEPS. Steps that are usually taken in a foreclosure by action and sale are the following:

A Title Search. The first step the mortgagee takes is to have a title search made or an abstract of title prepared. This is done to ascertain all the parties in interest.

The Action. A *lis pendens* is then filed in the county where the property is located and a summons and complaint are served on all interested parties. The suit, which is commenced in a court of competent jurisdiction, may be defended by the mortgagor or his grantee.

Default and Sale. If a default is declared, a decree is entered whereby the court determines the amount that is due on the mortgage debt and enters an order authorizing the sale of the mortgaged real estate. The plaintiff is now authorized to advertise and then sell the mortgaged premises at public auction. The sale is conducted in accordance with the statute and then reported to the court for confirmation. The court will confirm the sale unless there is proof of fraud, irregularity, or inadequate consideration. A deed is issued by the referee appointed by the court.

If the property is sold for less than the mortgage debt, the plaintiff may still have a deficiency judgment against the mortgagor. If there is a surplus, it is paid to junior lienors; if there are no other lienors, the surplus is returned to the mortgagor.

EQUITY OF REDEMPTION. In accordance with the law of the particular state, the mortgagor (property owner) has an equity of redemption. This means that within a period of time limited by the statute, usually up to the point of the actual sale by foreclosure, he may repay all monies that were the subject of his default, in addition to all costs and expenses of the foreclosure; he will then be entitled to the return of his property.

Financing Real Estate. The financing of real estate plays an important part in our economy. Years ago, mortgage moneylenders were apprehensive about lending money on real estate unless the mortgagor held a sizable equity in excess of the mortgage. The advent of government insured mortgages—FHA and VA—as well as a belief in real estate mortgages as a sound investment, resulted in lowering equity demands and increasing the ratio of mortgage to purchase price. The consequence has been the broadening of the base of the number of individuals who could become homeowners, opening the floodgates of enterprise in construction, banking, and related industries. In an average recent year more than 17,000,000 American firms and families owed over $280 billion in debts secured by mortgages. Newly written mortgages exceed four million per year. To supply this vast demand for credit more than 20,000 institutions, including commercial, savings, and mortgage banks, insurance companies, and savings and loan associations, in addition to countless individual mortgage moneylenders, are actually engaged in mortgage lending. Mortgage lending has traditionally paid among the highest rates of return of all major types of investment.

11

LIENS, EASEMENTS
AND OTHER ENCUMBRANCES

It is indeed rare that a parcel of real property may be owned in fee simple absolute without involving rights of third persons which in some manner encumber or diminish the total ownership —e.g., by statute, contract, custom, or agreement. Liens, easements, and encumbrances are vehicles for limiting complete ownership of realty.

LIENS

A lien is a right given by law to a creditor to have his debt or charge satisfied out of property belonging to the debtor. The debtor's consent is not required for satisfaction. Liens affect the possession and ownership of real property and may be either specific or general.

Specific Liens. Specific liens are those which affect only certain property of the debtor, examples being taxes, mortgages, mechanic's liens, vendor's liens, vendee's liens, surety bail bond liens, assessments and water rates, and attachments.

TAXES. Taxes are levied by the government, and property affected by a tax lien may be sold to satisfy a default in payment.

MORTGAGES. The mortgage, a prime example of a specific lien, has been discussed in Chapter 10.

MECHANIC'S LIENS. A mechanic's lien is a statutory remedy affording security to those who perform labor or furnish materials to improve real property. This remedy supplements the creditor's right to a personal action against the debtor.

Mechanic's lien laws vary among the states. Usually a notice of claim is filed with the county clerk in the county in which the property is located. The details of the claim are submitted under oath, and are required to be filed within a stipulated time (which varies according to the state from a time during which work was in progress to three to four months after completion). After labor has been performed (or materials furnished) and the mechanic's lien has been filed, the filing is usually good for one year, during which time action must be begun. However, the lien may be renewed for another year and would take precedence over all other liens recorded or filed afterward. A mechanic's lien may be filed by a contractor, a subcontractor, a materialman, a supply man, or others who have delivered material to, or performed labor on, the property.

Enforcement of Mechanic's Lien.   The enforcement of a mechanic's lien takes place through an action in foreclosure, i.e., the court issues a judgment of foreclosure after satisfactory proof of a valid claim has been submitted. The court will then order the sale of the property by an officer of the court, usually the sheriff. The proceeds of the sale are paid to the court and payment of all claims is then made in proper order of priority.

In New York State, all advances made by a mortgagee before liens are filed have priority over the mechanic's lien. Therefore, in case of default of the mortgage, the mortgagee may wipe out the mechanic's liens by foreclosure. Also in New York, all mortgage money advanced by the mortgagee is assigned to a trust fund for payments to contractors and materialmen under Section 13 of the Lien Law. This procedure is similarly followed in most of the other states.

The contractor must safeguard his rights by complying with the statute in filing his lien. He should recognize the rights of other lienors and act in conjunction with them to protect all parties concerned.

Discharge of Mechanic's Lien.   The mechanic's lien may be discharged in any of the following ways:

Expiration.   If there is no timely renewal of the lien or property foreclosure before action is begun, the lien expires according to statute.

Payment.   Receiving and filing of a satisfaction piece which attests that the lien has been paid in full constitutes a discharge of the lien.

Order of the Court.   If there is a failure to litigate the lien, the court, on the motion of the lienee, may order it cancelled. This is accomplished by action of the court which notifies the lienor to commence his action within a stated time; if he does not comply with the order, a final order of cancellation will follow. An owner can also have a disputed claim tried in court, and, upon justifying his defense, he may obtain an order of cancellation.

Filing of Bond Approved by Court. By providing a bond from personal sureties or a surety company, the owner may have the lien discharged. If the lienor is later successful in his action, he will be reimbursed by the surety.

Deposit of Money in Court. In this instance, the court is the stakeholder and if the lienor is successful in his action he will receive payment from the deposit; otherwise, it will be returned to the lienee.

Vendor's Liens. If a seller (vendor) conveys real property but does not receive the entire balance of the purchase price, he has a lien on the conveyed property for that unpaid balance. This lien is enforceable by foreclosure in addition to other remedies at law available to all creditors.

Vendee's Liens. If a seller defaults under a contract for the sale of real property, the purchaser (vendee) has a lien for the money he has paid under the contract. This lien includes all sums he has spent, if any, to improve the property. Unless so stipulated in the contract, it will not include fees for the title search. If this lien is not paid, it may be enforced by instituting foreclosure proceedings—subject, however, to the rights of prior recorded liens.

Surety Bail Bond Liens. In some states, bail, or an undertaking, guaranteeing the presence of a defendant at the date of trial may be a lien on real property. As such it must be filed with the county clerk or registrar of deeds. If the purpose of the bail is completed, a certificate of discharge is executed by the attorney general or the district attorney and this certificate may then be recorded to discharge the lien.

Assessments and Water Rates. Special assessments are used to enforce government levies to cover the cost of public improvements affecting specific realty. For example, water rates are charged for the use of water supplied to the owner of realty. Failure to pay creates a lien in favor of the government or in favor of the supervising agency.

Attachments. In some states the statutory privilege of attachment is granted to a creditor in an action for money damages before a judgment is procured. In effect the warrant of attachment ties up the property of the defendant so that, if the plaintiff is successful in his action, he may satisfy his judgment from the records of the sale of the property. This privilege is usually granted for a specific cause, as, for example, if the defendant is a non-resident or is about to remove property from the jurisdiction of the court, or if there is likelihood that a fraud will be perpetrated, or if the defendant is preparing to flee from the jurisdiction. The plaintiff is required to post a bond and to compensate the defendant for costs and damages in the event that the plaintiff is unsuccessful in his action. The warrant of attachment is filed in the same manner as a judgment. It has priority as of the day of its filing, and it terminates when the case is decided. If the defendant wishes to sell the property while the action is pending, he may file a surety bond equal to the plaintiff's claim plus costs, and then have the property discharged from the lien of the warrant of attachment. The proceeds of the surety bond are available to the plaintiff if he is successful in his action.

General Liens.   General liens are those which affect all the property of a debtor; these include judgments, decedent's debts, state transfer or inheritance tax liens, federal estate tax liens, corporation franchise tax liens, conditional bills of sale, and other encumbrances.

JUDGMENT.   A judgment is a legal determination by a court of competent jurisdiction of the rights of parties to an action. A judgment usually specifies payment of money and when it is properly recorded (docketed) it becomes a general lien on all property of the judgment debtor. A judgment is docketed in the county of the judgment debtor's residence, and the docket is arranged alphabetically by judgment debtor. In checking property, it is advisable to compare the names of former owners for the preceding twenty years with the judgment index, since a judgment is valid for that period of time.

A judgment is enforced by execution, i.e., a writ is issued directing the county sheriff to seize the judgment debtor's property and to sell as much of it as necessary to pay off the judgment plus expenses. Real or personal property may be seized; after proper advertisement, it may be sold at public auction to the highest bidder.

The lien of a judgment attaches to all land owned by a judgment debtor and remains in effect for a statutory period of time. Generally, a judgment of a court of record, properly docketed, is in effect for twenty years, and may be renewed. If the judgment is paid off, it may be discharged of record if a satisfaction piece is filed. If, after judgment, the case is appealed, the judgment debtor may file a bond or undertaking to free the property from the lien of the judgment, and the docket is then marked "suspended on appeal."

DECEDENT'S DEBTS. Although title to real property passes to the devisees or heirs immediately upon the death of the decedent, the title is subject to the existing debts left by the decedent. These debts are liens upon both the real and personal property. The personal property of the decedent must be used to pay off these debts before any proceeds from the real property can be applied for this purpose. In taking title to real property from an estate, or where property to be conveyed was recently owned by a deceased, it is imperative that the new owner secure satisfactory proof that the debts of the decedent have been fully liquidated.

STATE TRANSFER OR INHERITANCE TAX. This tax on the right to inherit from a decedent is borne by the recipient and not by the estate. However, the amount of the tax is an encumbrance upon the property of the estate until it is paid, and clear title cannot be given or conveyed until then. The state may enforce this lien by selling off enough of the assets of the inherited estate to pay the tax. The tax is computed as follows: An appraisal is made of the value of the interest of each beneficiary; the appraised value is reduced by the extent of the exemptions and deductions each beneficiary is entitled to; and the tax is levied on the basis of a percentage of the net appraised value.

FEDERAL ESTATE TAX. This is a tax on the transfer of the entire net estate of the decedent, and not on a particular share. The relationship of the beneficiary has no bearing on the amount of the tax. The estate may be taxed even though there is an escheat to the state because there are no heirs of the deceased. Credit is given for state estate taxes which have been paid, and the rate is progressive. This lien attaches to all the property of the estate and is good for ten years.

CORPORATION FRANCHISE TAX. This is a tax on the right of a corporation to do business in a state. It is usually based either upon the amount of capital stock of the corporation or upon its net income. It is a general lien which can be enforced against all the property of the corporation.

CONDITIONAL BILL OF SALE. A conditional bill of sale is not a true lien; rather, it arises out of a sale of personal property to improve the realty. The title to the personal property does not pass to the property owner until the purchase price of the goods is fully paid. The conditional bill of sale is filed in the county clerk's office at, or prior to, the delivery of the goods. When filed, it is valid against subsequent parties in interest to the real property, although the goods are affixed to the realty. Goods sold under a conditional bill of sale may include gas ranges, boilers, electric fixtures, screens, storm windows, and the like. The filing is good for one year and may be renewed.

Priority of Liens. The priority of a lien depends upon the order in time in which it is filed or recorded with the proper officials. However, a judgment is not good against the rights of those claiming under a deed or mortgage which is actually delivered prior to the date of the docketing of the judgment, even though the deed or mortgage is not recorded, if the mortgage or deed is for value and to an innocent person. This reasoning is justified since the mortgagee or grantee has relied on the record title when paying the money. Furthermore, the lien of a judgment is valid only against the property which the judgment debtor owned at the time when the judgment was docketed. If the deed or mortgage is executed to defraud creditors, it may be set aside, since legal recognition requires that it be made for value and in good faith.

The lien of a government agency for taxes and assessments is superior to every other lien regardless of the date of the recording. The relative priority of a lien, however, may be changed by agreement, as, for instance, in subordination.

EASEMENTS AND OTHER ENCUMBRANCES

Easements, restrictive covenants, and departmental violations and orders are not true liens; they are, however, charges against real property.

Easements. An easement is a right to use another's real property.

CLASSIFICATION OF EASEMENTS. Easements may be generally classified as easements appurtenant and easements in gross.

Easement Appurtenant. An easement appurtenant is the right of an owner of real property to use land adjacent for a particular purpose. The property benefited is referred to as the dominant estate, and the property affected as the subservient estate. This easement runs with the land and passes to subsequent grantees.

Easement in Gross.   An easement in gross is the right to use the land of another. This easement is personal and does not run with the land. There is no adjacent or dominant estate. Examples of easements in gross are: signs, bill boards, utility poles, and the like.

CREATION OF EASEMENTS.   Easements are created by express grant, implication, or prescription.

Express Grant.   A formal agreement between parties, which is properly recorded, may create an easement.

Implication or Necessity.   Where there is a clearly implied intent to create an easement, one is created. Also where it is strictly necessary to have an easement to provide access to a dominant land, or to support adjoining buildings or walls, or to use a party driveway, the courts will construe an easement.

Prescription.   If there is an open, exclusive, and continued use of land for a statutory period of time (usually a term of ten to twenty years) during which the true owner does not act or object to this use, an easement is acquired. An easement by prescription cannot be obtained against the federal or state government, or against an infant or insane person.

EXTINGUISHING EASEMENTS.   Easements are extinguished by express or implied release; merger of the dominant and servient estate; non-use beyond the statutory period; destruction of the servient tenement; wrongful or incompatible use; or expiration of purpose or necessity of the easement.

Restrictive Covenants.   Restrictions may arise from a covenant between two or more owners by agreement, which is usually recorded; examples are a stipulation in the deed given by a developer when he sells the property, and a declaration by a developer in a contract, made and recorded by him prior to sale.

In effect, restrictions limit the use of property. The covenants might specify the character, location, and use of buildings erected, or to be erected or maintained. The purpose of restrictions is to protect both the neighborhood and the property. The restrictions are uniformly applicable to all owners. Examples of governmental restrictions are found in zoning ordinances.

Departmental Violations and Orders.   The Building, Housing, Fire, Health and other departments of municipalities regulate the use and occupancy of buildings. Departmental orders issued are not liens. Non-compliance, however, may lead to an action in law against the property, and usually a *lis pendens* is filed if an action is commenced. Conviction for non-compliance will result in the imposition of a penalty. A departmental violation or order is an encumbrance that must be removed before the seller can convey a good and marketable title.

12

MISCELLANEOUS
REAL ESTATE INSTRUMENTS

In the practice of real estate, nearly all transactions are reduced to writing, a custom attributable largely to the Statute of Frauds. In order to facilitate transactions, various instruments have been developed, each with a high degree of uniformity according to the requirements of the particular situation.

Affidavit of Heirship. In selling the real property of a decedent who died intestate, the buyer may require the seller to execute an affidavit of heirship, which will set forth, under oath, a list of the heirs and distributees of the decedent. This is used as proof of the passing of title to the real estate to the individuals purporting to have the legal right to convey. In effect, this affidavit will tend to establish and identify the individuals who are entitled to an interest in the property by virtue of the intestacy.

Affidavit of Title. The affidavit of title is an instrument used to protect a purchaser further upon his taking title to real property. The commonly used form of affidavit of title recites, under oath, the following: a representation identifying the person signing the deed to be the owner of record; a representation, by the owner, that during the time that he owned the property, he never

Affidavit of Title

Title No...

STATE OF NEW YORK

COUNTY OF $\Big\}$ .ss:

each being duly sworn, says: I reside at

and am a citizen of the United States of America, over the age of twenty-one years, and am in every respect competent to convey (mortgage) the premises.

I am the owner in fee and in possession of said premises and the person described in and who executed a deed (mortgage) of said premises to

That said premises have been owned and held by me since
and that my ownership and possession have been peaceable, undisturbed, uninterrupted, continuous, actual,
open, notorious, hostile and adverse to all others and exclusive of the right or claim of any other persons.

The title to said premises has never been disputed, questioned or rejcted so far as I know, and I know
of no facts by reason of which said possession or title might be called in question, or by reason of which
any claim to any part of or interest in said premises adverse to me might be set up.

That no person has any contract for the purchase of, or claim to or against said premises for any reason whatsoever; that there is no suit or proceeding pending anywhere against me or affecting said
premises nor has any warrant of attachment been issued against said premises; that all bills and charges
for work, labor and services rendered and materials furnished in the improvement of said premises or any
part thereof have been paid and that no person or corporation has filed or has a right to file a mechanic's
lien therefor; that no conditional bills of sale or chattel mortgages have been filed against said premises
or against any personal property or fixtures attached to or used in connection with said premises; that
I am the owner of all personal property and fixtures attached to, appurtenant to or used in the operation
of said premises and that none of said personal property and fixtures aforesaid has been bought under an
agreement that title to them is not to vest until they are paid for; that said premises are now free and
clear of all taxes, mortgages, leases, assessments, water charges, sewer rents, liens, encumbrances and
charges of every nature or description, except

That there are no judgments against me unsatisfied of record in any court of this state or of the United
States, and that no proceedings in bankruptcy have ever been instituted by or against me, nor have I ever
made an assignment for the benefit of creditors.

That I,   , have not been known by any other name
during the past ten years, except

The premises are occupied as follows:

That the following judgments are not against me but are against other persons of a similar name:

That the buildings, retaining walls and fences on said premises shown on the survey thereof made by
                                        dated   have been
maintained in the same position and manner as they are shown on said survey since   ;
that no garage or other structure has been erected upon said premises and that no additions to or changes
in the exteriors of the buildings retaining walls and fences have been made during my ownership thereof
and that said buildings, retaining walls and fences now stand in the same positions as shown on said survey.

My wife, whose name is   , joins with me in the
                                        made by me, covering said premises. I have been married
to no other woman now living.

I am an unmarried man, having never been married to any woman now living.

We have never been married to any other person now living.

This affidavit is made to induce

and to induce Security Title and Guaranty Company to insure the same, well knowing that they will rely on the statements herein made.

Sworn to before me this

day of   19

heard of any other claim of title, lien of encumbrance, by anyone; a representation that the owner has created no other liens or encumbrances which may not appear of record; a representation, if the deed is executed by husband and wife, that the parties are actually married; and a statement that there are no outstanding judgments, except those of record (and if there are judgments recorded against a similar name, a statement that these judgments are not against the grantor).

The affidavit of title is signed and acknowledged by the seller and is retained by the buyer. It is not usually recorded.

Assignment of Mortgage. The bond and mortgage are personal property, or chattels real, and the assignor may transfer them by delivering them to the assignee. However, for the purposes of recording, or to negate the implication that the transferee's possession is by theft or fraud, a formal assignment of the mortgage is customarily executed.

The usual assignment of mortgage contains the following provisions: the date; identification of parties; consideration for the assignment (nominal consideration is adequate except in cases where the assignor is a fiduciary, such as an executor or administrator, when the actual, full consideration must be stated); description of the assigned mortgage, including date, parties, and amount of mortgage; statement regarding the bond or note, with interest, which is also assigned; amount of the unpaid principal and the date to which the interest was last paid; a statement that the assignment is made without recourse against any assignor; and the signature of the assignor, acknowledged or proved (if the assignors are the executors of an estate, then one signature is adequate; if there are two or more assignors, all must sign; and if the assignor is a guardian acting for an infant until the infant attains the age of 21, the guardian alone may sign, but, after the infant attains the age of 21, both must sign). The assignment should be recorded.

Assignment of Mortgage

KNOW that

assignor, in consideration of

dollars,

paid by

assignee, hereby assigns unto the assignee, a certain mortgage, made by

given to secure payment of the sum of

dollars

and interest, dated the   day of   19   ,

recorded on the   day of   in the office of the

of the County of   in Liber   of Mortgages, at page

covering premises

together with the bond   or

obligation   described in said mortgage   , and the moneys due and to grow due thereon with the interest.

TO HAVE AND TO HOLD the same unto the assignee, and to the successors, legal representatives and assigns of the assignee forever.

And the assignor covenants that there is now owing upon said mortgage   , without offset or defense of any kind, the principal sum of

dollars,

with interest thereon at   per centum per annum from the

day of   nineteen hundred and

IN WITNESS WHEREOF, the assignor has duly executed this assignment this

day of   , one thousand nine hundred and

IN THE PRESENCE OF:

Beam Right Agreement. If a property owner desires to erect a structure using an existing wall on an adjoining parcel of land, and the wall is strong enough to be a party wall, he may be able to secure a beam right agreement for a consideration from an agreeable owner of the existing wall. Thus, the expense of putting up a new wall will be avoided. The existing wall owner surrenders no rights in his land, as the wall is entirely on his property. However, the property is subject to an easement of support, i.e., the right of the dominant tenant to use the side of the building for that purpose as long as necessary. The right of the servient tenant to raze the building will require the consent of the dominant tenant.

Bill of Sale. When the sale of real property includes the incidental sale of personal property, a bill of sale is executed by the seller to the buyer. This document sets forth an inventory of the personalty included in the sale and a statement of the consideration therefor. It is signed by the seller.

Boundary Line Agreement. Where boundary lines between adjoining properties become uncertain, as when monuments have been obliterated, the property owners involved may, by agreement, fix a new boundary line. This document should be recorded. If there are prior mortgages, the mortgagee's consent is required for the agreement to be binding upon them.

Certificate of Reduction of Mortgage. When a mortgage is executed and recorded, only the original amount is a matter of record. Any reduction of the principal amount, by amortization or otherwise, is known usually only to the immediate parties thereto. Nowhere does a reduction of the mortgage debt appear as a matter of record. Therefore, when a mortgagor (owner) sells his property or assigns his interest therein, the grantee or assignee will require that the balance due on the mortgage be established. This he does by having the mortgagee execute a certificate of reduction of the mortgage.

The certificate of reduction of mortgage will contain the following provisions: the date; description of the mortgage; identification of the person executing the certificate; verification of the exact balance thereof; the current interest rate and the date to which interest has been paid; recitation of changes in mortgage provisions, if any; recitation of purpose of execution of the certificate (i.e., a statement that the property is being sold and that the purchaser will rely on the representation); and the signature of the mortgagee, acknowledged or proved, for purposes of recording.

Collateral Bond.   When the mortgagee desires additional security for his investment, which is in excess of the personal liability of the mortgagor and the value of the mortgaged property, he may require the mortgagor to have another person or persons guarantee the payment of the obligation in the event of default. This transaction is similar to the arrangement whereby a borrower provides a lending institution with a co-maker on a promissory note executed for the repayment of a loan.

Consolidation Agreement.   This form of agreement is executed for the purpose of having two or more mortgages on a parcel of real property, usually with a common mortgagee, united into one single lien. Thus, the consolidation agreement may set forth one set of terms for payment of principal and interest, and a uniform set of covenants. This agreement is signed by both the owner of the property and the mortgagee, and is recorded in the mortgage records.

Driveway Easement Agreement.   To avoid the waste of land between semi-detached buildings, a builder or two adjoining owners may wish to use a strip of land between the street and the rear of the property to provide access to a garage located there. One half of this strip of land will be on the land of each adjoining owner. This easement is usually created by being recited in each of the deeds, and it is usually made at the time the buildings are erected. Each parcel of land is both benefited and burdened by half of the land used as the driveway.

If the easement is to be created after the buildings have been erected, the adjoining owners will enter into a formal agreement reciting the mutual easements, and the agreement will then be recorded. If the properties are mortgaged at the time, the mortgagee's consent will have to be obtained in order to bind him to the terms of the easement agreement. If the easement is established by the common owner, it will be recited in the deed upon conveyance of the property; upon recording it will serve as notice to the world of the encumbrance upon the property.

Estoppel Certificate.   An estoppel certificate serves a purpose similar to that of a reduction certificate; that is, it establishes the balance of principal due on a mortgage and the rate of interest, but it differs from a reduction certificate in that it is executed by the mortgagor (owner of the property). It is used ordinarily by a mortgagee who seeks to sell or assign a mortgage and must establish the value of the mortgage to the satisfaction of the assignee or transferee. The mortgagor will certify that the mortgage principal has been reduced to a specified sum, which is a valid lien as of that date, and that he has no counterclaims, set-offs, or defenses to the mortgage. Subsequent to the execution of the estoppel certificate, the mortgagor may not dispute its authenticity as against the innocent party of the transaction. He would be "estopped" to deny its validity.

Extension Agreement.   An extension agreement is a contract between a mortgagor and a mortgagee and/or his assignee, whereby a mortgage which has not been amortized, and for which the principal debt is not overdue, is extended for an additional period of time, under the same or new terms.

Purpose of the Extension Agreement.   By using an extension agreement, the mortgagor avoids having the mortgagee call in the loan in a "tight" mortgage money market—that is, when there is little mortgage money available and he might experience difficulty in refinancing. Conversely, the mortgagee avoids having the mortgagor pay off the loan during a "loose" market—when, for instance, there are ample mortgage funds available and it might be financially unattractive for the mortgagee to re-invest, as the interest rate might be lower.

An extension agreement may be executed periodically to keep a mortgage from running open, i.e., past due. In these transactions the principal is usually not amortized and the interest represents a constant income. The renegotiations usually consider the re-appraisal value of the property and the condition of the mortgage market.

Contents of the Extension Agreement.   The usual form of extension agreement contains the following terms: date of agreement; parties, i.e., the present mortgagee (holder) and the present mortgagor (owner of the fee); description of the mortgage, which relates the date, amount, the parties, and the date, place, liber, and page of recording; date to which the mortgage is extended; rate of interest to be paid; amortization of principal, if any; balance of principal owed; date to which interest is paid; and standard mortgage clauses.

Under an extension agreement, the present owner becomes

primarily liable for payment of the mortgage debt and interest.

The original obligor on the bond is not completely absolved of his obligation thereon. Nevertheless he is not liable for any value that the property might lose after the signing of the extension agreement.

The original obligor is only liable for that part of the debt which exceeds the value of the property on the day the extension agreement is signed.

The extension agreement is usually prepared and executed in duplicate; it need not be recorded. However, the signatures of the parties, in case of foreclosure, must be proved by an acknowledgment or by deposition of the subscribing witness in order to be received as evidence in a legal proceeding.

Extension Agreement

THIS AGREEMENT, made the   day of   nineteen hundred and

BETWEEN

hereinafter designated as the party of the first part, and

hereinafter designated as the party of the second part,

WITNESSETH, that the party of the first part, the holder of the following mortgage   and of the bond or note   secured thereby:
Mortgage dated the   day of   , 19   , made by

to

in the principal sum of $ and recorded in Liber   of section
of Mortgages, page   , in the office of the   of the

now a   lien upon the premises situate

and on which bond   or note   there is now owing the sum of
                         dollars, with interest thereon, in consideration of one dollar paid by said

party of the second part, and other valuable consideration, the receipt whereof is hereby acknowledged, does hereby extend the time of payment of the principal indebtedness secured by said bond or note and mortgage so that the same shall be due and payable

PROVIDED, the party of the second part meanwhile pay interest on the amount owing on said bond or note from the   day of   , 19   , at the rate of

per centum per annum on the   day of   , 19 , next ensuing and thereafter,

and comply with all the other terms of said bond or note and mortgage as hereby modified.

The parties hereto certify that this instrument secures the same indebtedness secured by the said bond or note and mortgage hereinabove mentioned and secures no further or other indebtedness or obligation.

AND the party of the second part, in consideration of the above extension, does hereby assume, covenant and agree to pay said principal sum and interest as above set forth and not before the maturity thereof as the same s hereby extended, and to comply with the other terms of said bond or note and mortgage as hereby modified.

AND the party of the second part further covenants with the party of the first part as follows:

1. That the party of the second part will pay the indebtedness as hereinbefore provided.
2. That the party of the second part will keep the buildings on the premises insured against loss by fire for the benefit of the party of the first part; that he will assign and deliver the policies to the party of the first part; and that he will reimburse the party of the first part for any premiums paid for insurance made by the party of the first part on default of the party of the second part in so insuring the buildings or in so assigning and delivering the policies.
3. That no building on the premises shall be altered, removed or demolished without the consent of the party of the first part.
4. That the whole of said principal sum and interest shall become due at the option of the party of the first part: after default in the payment of any instalment of principal or of interest for fifteen days; or after default in the payment of any tax, water rate, sewer rent or assessment for thirty days after notice and demand; or after default after notice and demand either in assigning and delivering the policies insuring the buildings against loss by fire or in reimbursing the party of the first part for premiums paid on such insurance, as hereinbefore provided; or after default upon request in furnishing a statement of the amount due on the mortgage and whether any offsets or defenses exist against the mortgage debt, as hereinafter provided. An assessment which has been made payable in instalments at the application of the party of the second part or lessee of the premises shall nevertheless, for the purpose of this paragraph, be deemed due and payable in its entirety on the day the first instalment becomes due or payable or a lien.
5. That the holder of this mortgage, in any action to foreclose it, shall be entitled to the appointment of a receiver.
6. That the party of the second part will pay all taxes, assessments, sewer rents or water rates, and in default thereof, the party of the first part may pay the same.
7. That the party of the second part within five days upon request in person or within ten days upon request by mail will furnish a written statement duly acknowledged of the amount due on this mortgage and whether any offsets or defenses exist against the mortgage debt.
8. That notice and demand or request may be in writing and may be served in person or by mail.
9. That the party of the second part warrants the title to the premises.
10. That the fire insurance policies required by paragraph No. 2 above shall contain the usual extended coverage endorsement; that in addition thereto the party of the second part, within thirty days after notice and demand, will keep the premises insured against war risk and any other hazard that may reasonably be required by the party of the first part. All of the provisions of paragraphs No. 2 and No. 4 above relating to fire insurance and the provisions of Section 254 of the Real Property Law construing the same shall apply to the additional insurance required by this paragraph.
11. That in case of a foreclosure sale, said premises, or so much thereof as may be affected by said mortgage, may be sold in one parcel.
12. That if any action or proceeding be commenced (except an action to foreclose said mortgage or to collect the debt secured thereby), to which action or proceeding the party of the first part is made a party, or in which it becomes necessary to defend or uphold the lien of said mortgage, all sums paid by the party of the first part for the expense of any litigation to prosecute or defend the rights and lien created by said mortgage (including reasonable counsel fees), shall be paid by the party of the second part, together with interest thereon at the rate of six per cent. per annum, and any such sum and the interest thereon shall be a lien on said premises, prior to any right, or title to, interest in or claim upon said premises attaching or accruing subse-

quent to the lien of said mortgage, and shall be deemed to be secured by said mortgage. In any action or proceeding to foreclose said mortgage, or to recover or collect the debt secured thereby, the provisions of law respecting the recovering of costs, disbursements and allowances shall prevail unaffected by this covenant.

13.   That the party of the second part hereby assigns to the party of the first part the rents, issues and profits of the premises as further security for the payment of said indebtedness, and the party of the second part grants to the party of the first part the right to enter upon the premises for the purpose of collecting the same and to let the premises or any part thereof, and to apply the rents, issues and profits, after payment of all necessary charges and expenses, on account of said indebtedness. This assignment and grant shall continue in effect until said mortgage is paid.   The party of the first part hereby waives the right to enter upon said premises for the purpose of collecting said rents, issues and profits and the party of the second part shall be entitled to collect and receive said rents, issues and profits until default under any of the covenants, conditions or agreements contained in said mortgage, and agrees to use such rents, issues and profits in payment of principal and interest becoming due on said mortgage and in payment of taxes, assessments, sewer rents, water rates and carrying charges becoming due against said premises, but such right of the party of the second part may be revoked by the party of the first part upon any default, on five days' written notice. The party of the second part will not, without the written consent of the party of the first part, receive or collect rent from any tenant of said premises or any part thereof for a period of more than one month in advance, and in the event of any default under said mortgage will pay monthly in advance to the party of the first part, or to any receiver appointed to collect said rents, issues and profits, the fair and reasonable rental value for the use and occupation of said premises or of such part thereof as may be in the possession of the party of the second part, and upon default in any such payment will vacate and surrender the possession of said premises to the party of the first part or to such receiver, and in default thereof may be evicted by summary proceedings.

14.   That the whole of said principal sum and the interest shall become due at the option of the party of the first part: (a) after failure to exhibit to the party of the first part, within ten days after demand, receipts showing payment of all taxes, water rates, sewer rents and assessments; or (b) after the actual or threatened alteration, demolition or removal of any building on the premises without the written consent of the party of the first part; or (c) after the assignment of the rents of the premises or any part thereof without the written consent of the party of the first part; or (d) if the buildings on said premises are not maintained in reasonably good repair; or (e) after failure to comply with any requirement or order or notice of violation of law or ordinance issued by any governmental department claiming jurisdiction over the premises within three months from the issuance thereof; or (f) if on application of the party of the first part two or more fire insurance companies lawfully doing business in the State of New York refuse to issue policies insuring the buildings on the premises; or (g) in the event of the removal, demolition or destruction in whole or in part of any of the fixtures, chattels or articles of personal property covered hereby, unless the same are promptly replaced by similar fixtures, chattels and articles of personal property at least equal in quality and condition to those replaced, free from chattel mortgages or other encumbrances thereon and free from any reservation of title thereto; or (h) after thirty days' notice to the party of the second part, in the event of the passage of any law deducting from the value of land for the purposes of taxation any lien thereon, or changing in any way the taxation of mortgages or debts secured thereby for state or local purposes; or (i) if the party of the second part fails to keep, observe and perform any of the covenants, conditions or agreements contained in said mortgage or in this agreement.

15.   That the lien of said mortgage is hereby extended so as to cover all fixtures, chattels and articles of personal property now or hereafter attached to or used in connection with said premises, including but not limited to furnaces, boilers, oil burners, radiators and piping, coal stokers, plumbing and bathroom fixtures, refrigeration, air conditioning and sprinkler systems, wash-tubs, sinks, gas and electric fixtures, stoves, ranges, awnings, screens, window shades, elevators, motors, dynamos, refrigerators, kitchen cabinets, incinerators, plants and shrubbery and all other equipment and machinery, appliances, fittings, and fixtures of every kind in or used in the operation of the buildings standing on said premises, together with any and all replacements thereof and additions thereto.

16.   That the party of the second part does hereby assign to the party of the first part all awards heretofore and hereafter made to the party of the second part for taking by eminent domain the whole or any part of said premises or any easement therein, including any awards for changes of grade of streets, which said awards are hereby assigned to the party of the first part, who is hereby authorized to collect and receive the proceeds of such awards and to give proper receipts and acquittances therefor, and to apply the same toward the payment of the mortgage indebtedness, notwithstanding the fact that the amount owing thereon may not then be due and payable; and the said party of the second part hereby agrees, upon request, to make, execute and deliver any and all assignments and other instruments sufficient for the purpose of assigning said awards to the party of the first part, free, clear and discharged of any encumbrances of any kind or nature whatsoever.

17.   That the party of the second part is now the owner of the premises upon which said mortgage is a valid   lien for the amount above specified with interest thereon at the rate above set forth, and that there are no defenses or offsets to said mortgage or to the debt which it secures.

18.   That the principal and interest hereby agreed to be paid shall be a lien on the mortgaged premises and be secured by said bond or note and mortgage, and that when the terms and provisions contained in said bond or note and mortgage in any way conflict with the terms and provisions contained in this agreement, the terms and provisions herein contained shall prevail, and that as modified by this agreement the said bond or note and mortgage are hereby ratified and confirmed.

This agreement may not be changed or terminated orally. The covenants contained in this agreement shall run with the land and bind the party of the second part, the heirs, personal representatives, successors and assigns of the party of the second part and all subsequent owners, encumbrancers, tenants and sub-tenants of the premises, and shall enure to the benefit of the party of the first part, the personal representatives, successors and assigns of the party of the first part and all subsequent holders of this mortgage. The word "party" shall be construed as if it read "parties" whenever the sense of this agreement so requires.

IN WITNESS WHEREOF, this agreement has been duly executed by the parties hereto the day and year first above written.

IN PRESENCE OF:

Mortgage Participation Agreements. When it is the desire of the mortgagee to divide the mortgage interest of an existing mortgage (or sometimes at the extension of a new mortgage) among a group of participants, a mortgage participation agreement may be executed. This instrument divides the original interest of the mortgagee among several participating mortgagees, and sets forth the mortgage and the interests therein. Thus, if Abel held a $100,000 mortgage on Blake's property, and needed $75,000, he could raise the said amount by assigning quarter interests of $25,000 each to Davis, Edwards, and Fox. Abel, Davis, Edwards, and Fox would all become quarter owners in a $100,000 participation mortgage. The agreement would set forth the amount of the total mortgage; the various shares of the share owners; the priority of shares, if any; the method of collection and distribution of principal and interest as it is paid; and the administration of a foreclosure proceeding, if any is necessary.

Party Wall Agreements. If two people own adjoining parcels of land and desire to have buildings erected thereon with but one wall between them, these adjoining owners can accomplish their purpose by executing reciprocal party wall agreements. The wall to be erected will be half on one owner's land and half on the other owner's. The agreement will be in the nature of an easement of each owner in the other's land for the purpose of supporting the party wall. Thus, the title of each owner is encumbered to the extent of the easement thus created on the land covered by the party wall.

Party wall rights may also arise without agreement. One builder may erect two structures on a parcel of land he owns, and in construction use a common wall for both buildings. When he sells either or both buildings, the party wall status is in effect for the benefit of both adjoining owners. If one building burns down, for example, the owner can rebuild, using the existing wall.

Where the party wall agreement is executed by two adjoining owners, the instrument will recite the creation of the easements, reciprocally, in the land upon which the party wall stands; the instrument will be recorded as an easement against each parcel of property.

Power of Attorney. A power of attorney is a formal written instrument of agency, creating an "attorney in fact." This instrument sets forth the right, power, and authority of the agent to act, on behalf of his principal, in certain types of real estate transactions. Powers of attorney are generally used for delegating the right to execute, extend, or assign a mortgage, or for executing a deed or a lease. These acts may not ordinarily be consummated by an agent unless his power and status are established in accordance with the requirements of the Statute of Frauds.

Release of Mortgage. A release of mortgage is usually used where a blanket mortgage covers a large tract of land and the parties have agreed, in advance, that upon the payment of a stipulated sum, a portion of the premises will be released from the lien of the mortgage. This instrument is like a satisfaction of mortgage, except that it applies only to a part of the mortgaged premises. If the entirety of the mortgaged premises is to be released, then a satisfaction piece is required.

For example, a builder of many homes in a large subdivision may borrow money from a lending institution covering his needs for the entire project. By agreement, as each home is sold, and

Release of Mortgage

THIS INDENTURE, made the   day of   nineteen hundred **and**

BETWEEN

party of the first part, and

party of the second part,

WHEREAS, the party of the first part is the holder of the following **mortgage**   and of the bond   or note secured thereby:

Mortgage dated the   day of   , 19   , made by

to

in the principal sum of **$**   and recorded in the office of the
of the County   in liber   of section   of mortgages, page   , covering certain lands and tenements, of which the lands hereinafter described are
part,

AND WHEREAS, the party of the first part, at the request of the party of the second part, has agreed to
give up and surrender the lands hereinafter described unto the party of the second part, and to hold and
retain the residue of the mortgaged lands as security for the money remaining due on said
mortgage ,

NOW THIS INDENTURE WITNESSETH, that the party of the first part, in pursuance of said agreement and in consideration of

                                                                          Dollars,
lawful money of the United States,
paid by the party of the second part, does grant, release and quitclaim unto the party of the second part, all
that part of said mortgaged lands described as follows:

TOGETHER with all right, title and interest, if any, of the party of the first part of, in and to any streets and
roads abutting the above described premises to the center lines thereof and in and to any fixtures and articles
of personal property which are now contained in said premises and which may be covered by said mortgage.

TOGETHER with the hereditaments and appurtenances thereunto belonging, and all the right, title and interest
of the party of the first part, of, in and to the same, to the intent that the lands hereby released may be discharged from said   mortgage , and that the rest of the lands in said
        mortgage specified may remain to the party of the first part as heretofore.

TO HAVE AND TO HOLD the lands and premises hereby released and quitclaimed to the party of the
second part, and to the heirs, successors and assigns of the party of the second part forever, free, clear and
discharged of and from all lien and claim under and by virtue of said   mortgage
aforesaid.

IN WITNESS WHEREOF, the party of the first part has executed this release the day and year first above
written.

IN PRESENCE OF:

upon payment to the mortgagee of a stipulated sum, a specific lot is released from the lien of the mortgage. A release schedule of fees is usually agreed upon at the time of the execution of the mortgage.

Usually the release of mortgage contains the following provisions: date; parties thereto; recitation of mortgage in full; consideration paid for the release; description of the portion of the premises; a statement that the balance of the premises remains encumbered; and the signature of the mortgagee, acknowledged or proved so that the instrument may be recorded.

Restriction Agreements. It is common for a developer, in order to endeavor to retain and/or maintain the character and quality of the development, to impose certain restrictions on the properties which are in the best interests of all the home owners.

Such restrictions usually specify the number of families to occupy one home, the distance that each building is to be set back from the building line, covenants against objectionable uses of the property, and the like. In instances where a mortgagee's prior rights are involved, it is necessary to make the mortgagee a party to the agreement to make it completely binding. Several property owners may, by mutual agreement, impose reciprocal restrictions upon the use and/or occupation of their respective properties for the benefit of the entire group. Since restriction agreements burden the real property, they should be recorded.

Satisfaction of Mortgage. This document, commonly referred to as a satisfaction "piece," represents a formal acknowledgment by the mortgagee that the debt secured by the mortgage has been paid and that the mortgage may be discharged of record. It is good practice for the mortgagor, upon payment of the debt, to insist also that the original bond and mortgage be returned to him.

Since it is customary to record all mortgages, the payment of the mortgage debt does not cancel the mortgage as of record. It is incumbent upon the mortgagor, therefore, to record the satisfaction piece and thereby cancel the mortgage as of record. Thereupon, the lien of the mortgage is removed and no longer encumbers the property.

The satisfaction of mortgage is executed by the mortgagee. It further identifies the mortgagee, giving his name and address. It identifies the mortgage by reciting the date of its execution, the names of the mortgagor and mortgagee thereto, the principal sum thereof, the date of its recording, and the liber (book) number and page number of the book of mortgages where the mortgage was recorded in the office of the clerk of the county where the real property is located.

If the mortgage had subsequently been assigned, a recital of all assignments and the place of the recording will follow, together with a statement that the mortgage has not been further assigned as of record.

The signature of the mortgagee should be witnessed and the instrument acknowledged before a notary public.

Some states require the filing of the original mortgage, along with the satisfaction piece, to prevent forgery.

Spreading Agreement. The purpose of a spreading agreement is to enlarge the lien of the mortgage to include an additional property or other properties owned by the mortgagor. It is customarily used as the consideration to induce a mortgagee to continue or to renew his investment, and to provide additional security. This agreement is signed by both the mortgagor and the mortgagee, and is recorded.

Subordination Agreement. The priority of the lien of the mortgage is established according to the date of its recording, but sometimes a lender, in taking a mortgage, will agree in advance that his mortgage shall be subject and subordinate to a subsequently recorded mortgage. To change this order of priority, the parties will execute a subordination agreement. This type of transaction will ordinarily be used where the seller of land takes back a purchase money mortgage in partial or complete payment for his property. The buyer usually intends to improve the land and to develop the tract; his mortgage requirements, therefore, will far exceed the value of the land. Also, the mortgage requirements will be used to improve non-income producing land. In such a case the purchase money mortgagee will generally find it exceedingly advantageous to agree to subordinate his lien.

The subordination agreement will contain the following provisions: the date; parties; description of encumbered property; description of existing mortgage; statement regarding new mortgage to be placed on the property; consideration; statement by the present mortgagee that his lien is subject and subordinate to a new mortgage to be executed; and the signature of the parties, acknowledged and proved. The subordination agreement should also be recorded.

Subordination Agreement

AGREEMENT, made the   day of
one thousand nine hundred and   , between

hereinafter designated as the party of the first part, and

hereinafter designated as the party of the second part, WITNESSETH: that

WHEREAS, the said party of the first part now owns and holds a certain mortgage and the bond in said mortgage mentioned, made by

to

to secure the principal sum of

dollars

and interest, dated   19   , which said mortgage was recorded in the office of the Register of the County of   on   19   , in liber   of section   of mortgages at page   , and covers the premises hereinafter mentioned, and

WHEREAS
the present owner of the premises hereinafter mentioned   about to execute and deliver to said party of the second part, a bond and mortgage to secure the principal sum of

dollars

and interest, dated   19   , and covering premises

and more fully described in said last mentioned mortgage, and

WHEREAS, said party of the second part has refused to make said loan of

dollars

unless said first mentioned mortgage is subordinated in lien, to the lien of said mortgage about to be made to the party of the second part, and to all advances heretofore made, or which hereafter may be made to the extent of the last mentioned amount.

NOW THEREFORE, in consideration of the premises and to induce said party of the second part to make said loan, and of one dollar paid to said party of the first part by said party of the second part, the receipt whereof is hereby acknowledged, the said party of the first part hereby covenants and agrees with said party of the second part, that said mortgage held by said party of the first part is and shall continue to be subject and subordinate in lien to the lien of said mortgage for

dollars

about to be made to the party of the second part hereto, and to all advances heretofore made or which hereafter may be made to the extent of the last mentioned amount on the security of said mortgage secondly above described, and all such advances may be made without notice to the party of the first part.

THIS AGREEMENT shall be binding on, and enure to the benefit of the respective heirs, personal representatives, successors and assigns of the parties hereto.

IN WITNESS WHEREOF, the said party of the first part has signed and sealed these presents the day and year first above written.

13

TAXES AND ASSESSMENTS, VALUATION AND APPRAISAL

The taxation of real estate has long been a prime source of local government revenue. Of all the types of taxable assets real property, being the most difficult to hide, has always been the chief basis of taxation. In this chapter we shall be concerned with direct levies on real estate, i.e., general real estate taxes to provide income to the local political subdivision to carry on its functions; taxes imposed by special taxing authorities such as school or sanitary districts; and special direct assessments for the purpose of meeting the cost of a particular benefit to the property assessed, such as for streets, sidewalks, or sewers. In addition, we shall consider the basic principles pertaining to the valuation and appraisal of real estate.

TAXES AND ASSESSMENTS

Accepting the proposition that a human being cannot avoid death and taxes, we may note that, while alive, the only thing he cannot sidestep is taxes. Real property taxation is one of the most important limitations on the ownership of property. Taxes are charges levied by a taxing authority for the purpose of carrying out the functions of government. If taxes are not paid, the property may be forfeited to the taxing authority.

An assessment is the valuation of real property for tax purposes. In the taxation process, the first step is the assessment. A piece of property may be assessed once to cover all *ad valorem* (which means based on the value of the property) levies into one tax as in New York City, or it may be assessed by more than one unit of government for different tax purposes.

Direct Taxes. Direct taxes on real estate are of three basic types: (1) general property taxes imposed on real estate by the political subdivision to obtain revenue to carry out its function; (2) taxes levied by special taxing authorities, such as school and sanitary districts, to carry out their functions; and (3) special direct tax assessment for the purpose of meeting the cost of a particular benefit to the property assessed, such as the construction of sewers, sidewalks, or streets.

Real Property Taxes. These taxes are generally levied in proportion to the assessed value of the real property. Thus, they are considered *ad valorem* taxes. The measure of value for tax purposes is usually the assessed valuation, as distinguished from the actual market value.

The process of assessing the value of real property and the levying of the tax is administered by local government units such as the city, the town, the school district, the county, and the incorporated village.

The Assessor and Assessment Roll. The assessors or board of assessors are public officials charged with the duty of determining assessed valuation. The record of the assessment is known as the assessment roll, a record available for inspection by the public. Each year, following the appearance of the new assessment roll, a time period is granted for hearing the property owners who wish to object to, or protest, the assessment. The hearing is held for the purpose of determining whether there is to be a revision of an assessment.

Determination of the Tax Rates. After the assessment rolls have been completed, the local government unit can levy the tax. A determination of the tax rate can be arrived at by ascertaining the amount of revenue needed for the next tax year, which will be the total amount required by the budget, and by dividing the revenue by the total amount of assessed valuation of real property within the confines of the governmental unit requiring the taxes. A simple formula for arriving at the tax rate is:

$$\frac{\text{Budget}}{\text{Assessed Valuation}} = \text{Tax Rate}$$

This formula is, however, subject to the maximum tax rate limits imposed by law. Therefore, if the tax rate arrived at exceeds these maximum limits, there must be a roll-back in order to produce a rate not in excess of the maximum set by law.

School District Taxes. Variations in the procedure of levying the tax are found in the school districts. In Manhattan and Yonkers, New York, for instance, the budget for educational purposes is part of the overall city budget. All other school districts in New York State are fiscally independent. Under state law, they are units of government which can establish their own budget, levy their own taxes, and borrow money by floating a bond issue. These practices are similar to those of other states. The school district, as an entity, has the power to sue or be sued; it may buy property in its own name and be vested with title. The school budget is prepared by the local school board and upon approval by vote of the registered voters becomes effective. The school tax rate is then arrived at by a formula similar to that previously discussed:

$$\frac{\text{School Budget}}{\text{Assessed Valuation}} = \text{School Tax Rate}$$

Once the school budget has been approved, the tax rate arrived at must be put into effect by the city or town without change.

Tax Rolls, Collections, and Delinquencies.   The record of the tax levies is called the tax roll. After the tax roll has been prepared, the taxes are collected and the collections enforced. The individual property tax accounts are kept by section, block, and lot number. The owner of record, or his agent, of each piece of property is billed. It is the owner's responsibility to obtain a proper tax bill.

The payment of real property taxes is enforced by the imposition of penalties upon delinquents, usually by adding a fixed per cent of interest running from the day the tax becomes a lien. In New York City, for instance, after the payment of taxes has been in default for four years, the property is foreclosed in an *in rem* proceeding and sold to satisfy the obligation.

In Nassau County, New York, school tax rolls are sent to the county treasurer on May 31. County and town tax rolls are sent by August 31. Taxes which are unpaid by the third Monday in October are advertised for sale to the public once each week for three successive weeks immediately preceding the first Monday in December. Unpaid taxes thus advertised are sold by the county treasurer on the first Monday in December. After twenty-one months, the tax lien purchaser may file a notice to redeem the tax lien upon the affected or interested parties; thereupon, a statutory fee of twenty-five dollars is added to the lien. If then there is no redemption within ninety days (by redemption is meant payment in full of all unpaid taxes plus interest and charges), the tax lien holder may apply for a tax lien conveyance of the property. The aforementioned two procedures are generally in use in other cities and communities throughout the United States.

In New York City, the due dates for real estate taxes are October 1 and April 1. The City's fiscal year begins on July 1. The taxes are a lien as of October 1 and April 1. If the taxes are not paid within the calendar month in which they are due, interest at the rate of 7 per cent per annum from the due date is added.

In the three towns which constitute Nassau County, the town tax (which includes the county tax) is payable and becomes a lien in two installments, on January 1 and July 1. The fiscal year begins on January 1. The school tax in the towns is payable and becomes a lien in two installments, on October 1 and on April 1. The fiscal year begins on the preceding July 1. This method of fixing tax periods is in common use throughout the United States, except for the possible use of different calendar periods.

There is usually a grace period of a number of days for each installment of both the school and the town taxes, with a penalty usually about 1 per cent a month calculated from the due date, if the tax is not paid by the end of the grace period.

VALUATION AND APPRAISAL

Nearly every interest in real property is related, either directly or indirectly, to its value, and a host of questions involving valuation arises with respect to real estate. Value is involved in almost all real estate activity. For example, before a prospective buyer can make a reasonable offer, he must have some idea of the worth of the property he intends to buy. The broker's commission is almost always tied to the selling price of the property, which reflects value arrived at by the parties through negotiation; and the mortgage process involves the relationship of the amount of money to be loaned to a percentage of the value of the property to be encumbered. Real estate taxes are also basically *ad valorem*, that is, they are levied and assessed in proportion to the value of the property taxed.

Appraisal is the art of ascertaining the value of real property. It is an expression of opinion of value based upon the experience, judgment, and reputation of the appraiser. Values thus ascertained are, at best, estimates which depend greatly on the ability of the appraiser.

Value. What is value? In Southwestern Bell Telephone Co. *vs.* Public Service Commission (262 U.S. 276, p. 310), Justice Louis D. Brandeis said, "Value is a word of many meanings," and then went on to indicate that there are thirty or more criteria of value. Economists advance a more specific definition: value is the power of goods or things to command other goods or things in exchange or barter. Also, it is alleged that value is the present worth of future rights to income. The term value, as it pertains to real property, is usually interpreted as referring to market value.

MARKET VALUE. Market value may best be defined as the highest price of a commodity in terms of dollars, which a ready, willing, and able seller, not forced to sell, will accept from a ready, willing, and able buyer, not forced to buy—assuming that both parties are fully informed, act intelligently, and have sufficient time to deliberate fully.

For property to have market value, the following characteristics or determinants are usually prerequisite: *utility*, which is the power to render a service or fill a need; *scarcity*, which depends upon the law of supply and demand and upon the uses of property; *demand*, or the sum total of need plus purchasing power; and *transferability*, which implies that the property must be readily conveyable, without undue hardships, conditions, or impediments. The degree of presence of the aforementioned criteria will greatly affect value.

VALUE VS. PRICE AND COST. Value must be distinguished from price and cost. Value describes the barter relationship, while price is the measurement in terms of dollars of the commodity. Value may remain a constant, whereas price may fluctuate, depending upon the purchasing power of the dollar (as in an inflationary period, when prices tend to rise, or in a period of deflation, when prices tend to fall). Price may also be affected by the market conditions or by the terms of the sale.

Cost must be distinguished from value. Cost equals a measure of past expenditures, whereas value is equal to a measure of future rights. Value most closely approximates cost when real property and improvements are new; then cost is equal to the sum of the expenditures for land put to its highest and best use, plus the expenditures for improvements, plus the builder's profits. As the improvements grow older and depreciate, value may deviate from cost; also, the value of property may decrease in proportion to, or more rapidly than, the rate of depreciation or the rate of decrease in the value of the improvements. In the same way property values may as readily appreciate with the passage of time.

FACTORS AFFECTING VALUE. Although property itself is an important determinant of value, we must not overlook the fact that people *make* value. The environment or the setting in which we find property also determines value. Here social, economic, and political forces are instrumental in making or breaking property values.

Social and economic forces that affect value include population trends (births, marriages, and deaths), national income, saving and spending, the gross national product, taxes, climate, industry, credit, population characteristics, physical improvement or decay of neighborhoods, and the like. Political forces that influence value directly may be found in government participation in housing (e.g., subsidies for low- or middle-income housing construction), urban renewal projects, and government intervention which affects mortgage loans, insurance underwriting, slum clearance, land rehabilitation, and other ventures that may stimulate or retard the housing supply.

METHODS OF VALUATION. There are four methods of evaluating property: the cost approach, the market approach, the income approach, and the rule-of-thumb method.

The Cost Approach. This approach attempts to establish value by endeavoring to ascertain as closely as possible the amount of money it would take to replace the property in its present condition. The method is best expressed by the formula $V = C - D$—that is, actual cost value equals replacement cost less depreciation. Thus the replacement cost will be equal to the dollar outlay necessary to replace the land and improvements under existing conditions and current construction practices; the amount arrived at would be diminished by the amount of depreciation. There are three methods commonly used to estimate replacement cost: the quantity-survey method, the unit-in-place method, and the comparative method.

In the quantity-survey method, a detailed inventory of the cost of labor and materials to make up the improvement is ascertained. To this calculation are added the value of the raw land, the architect's fees, and the builder's overhead and profit. The gross total will be equal to the replacement cost.

The item cost process is the basis for the unit-in-place method. Here, the square footage of all the items that go into the total improvements is estimated, that is, the square footage of flooring, sheeting, roofing, plastering, and plumbing involved. Each figure for square footage is then multiplied by the item's unit cost-in-place factor. To this total are added the value of the raw land, the architect's fees, and the builder's overhead and profit. The gross total of these items will then be equal to the replacement cost.

Finally, in the comparative method, the cost per square foot or cubic foot of overall construction is multiplied by the total amount of square footage of property under appraisal. To this total are added the value of the raw land, the architect's fee, and the builder's overhead and profit. The sum total equals the replacement cost.

The quantity-survey method and the unit-in-place method are more costly and time-consuming than the comparative method; the former are frequently used in bidding on new construction, whereas the comparative method, used extensively by appraisers in evaluating property already built, is fairly accurate, expeditious, and most generally used. Regardless of the method used, if the site is an old one, there will be deducted the amount of depreciation that may arise from ordinary wear and tear, action of the elements, functional obsolescence resulting from the changes in design, and economic obsolescence resulting from a change in demand in the area under consideration.

The Market Approach. In the market approach to valuation, an estimate of value is arrived at by gathering price data from similar properties recently sold in the vicinity of the property being evaluated. One must use due care to analyze properties which are comparable in condition, size, construction, and location. When the real estate market is active and there are many comparisons available, the results will be highly satisfactory. Price data may be obtained from financial news services, abstract and title companies, county clerks' offices, real estate boards, and the experience records tabulated by individual brokers.

The Income Approach. The income approach to valuation is feasible where income-producing properties are being evaluated. Also, it may be used where there is a complete absence of market sales data, and where an estimate of the reproduction costs of the facilities is not feasible. The validity of this approach is based upon the theory that value equals the present worth of anticipated future income. To determine the income value of property one starts with the gross estimated income revenues. From this amount are subtracted the anticipated losses expected from vacancies and failure to pay rent. The remainder constitutes gross income. The stabilized operating costs must be subtracted from this amount in order to ascertain the net income. Net income can then be capitalized by being discounted at the market rate of interest (also called capitalization rate) to arrive at the income value.

This method has the advantage that it is usually difficult to forecast with a great degree of accuracy the future income or service life of a parcel of real property. The problem is simplified if the income is tied to long-term secured leaseholds. Also, the extent of future income may fluctuate radically, depending upon the management.

The Rule-of-Thumb Approach. Another common method used by investors and speculators may be described, for want of a better name, as the rule-of-thumb method. Here the value is determined by multiplying the gross annual income by a predetermined factor, or number, depending upon the particular type of occupancy. This factor or number is one which is generally accepted by custom and usage, and is therefore based upon the experience of the profession. Experience has indicated that this method is, in many instances, as valid or accurate as any of the other methods used.

An example of the rule-of-thumb method is as follows: the multiple factor, in purchasing multi-family apartment houses in a particular area, is established as seven times the gross annual rent roll. Therefore, the value of a specific apartment house which develops an annual rent roll of $100,000 is $700,000.

Appraisers and Appraising. The appraisal practice as a profession is of recent vintage, having developed in this country only since 1932. This profession was an infant born of the Great Depression of the 1930's. The American Institute of Real Estate Appraisers was founded in 1932 as an affiliate of the National Association of Real Estate Boards (NAREB). It is a professional organization dedicated to the furtherance of the art of appraising.

Among other activities, it publishes a textbook entitled *The Appraisal of Real Estate*. It also publishes for its members a magazine issued quarterly: *The Appraisal Journal*.

The Society of Residential Appraisers was founded in 1935. This society was sponsored by member organizations of the United States Savings and Loan League, which was primarily interested in mortgage loans made on residential properties.

Both the American Institute of Real Estate Appraisers and the Society of Residential Appraisers are national in scope and international in affiliation. The need for these organizations was accentuated by calamitous experiences encountered by lending institutions during the Great Depression. The tremendous number of mortgage foreclosures pointed up sharply the need for more qualified and professional personnel to serve as appraisers to evaluate property offered as security for mortgage loans made by large lending institutions.

TRAINING AND QUALIFICATIONS. In England upon satisfactory completion of two years of university training in special courses in real estate principles, or suitable corresponding courses given by leading appraisal societies, the applicant is usually apprenticed to a broker or appraiser for a period of two years for further on-the-job study, after which he must take and pass a searching examination to be eligible for employment with an appraisal firm. When he has been accepted for membership in one of the appraisal societies, he gains public recognition as an appraiser.

In America, the American Institute of Real Estate Appraisers, in order to perfect the practice of real estate appraisal and also to safeguard the public against incompetent practitioners, grants its membership designation (M.A.I. or Member of the Appraising Institute) to candiates who acquire a minimum of 120 points. These points may be accumulated partially by fulfilling the following basic requirements: an applicant must be at least thirty years of age, have had at least five years of appraisal experience, and have completed a high-school education; he must submit three adequate narrative appraisal reports covering different classes of property and then must also pass two eight-hour written examinations answering questions pertaining to the theory of valuation. The balance of points may be accumulated by a combination of the following: completion of a college education, more than five years of appraisal practice and experience, preparation of additional narrative appraisal reports, and passing of additional examinations.

THE REAL ESTATE APPRAISER AND HIS OFFICE.   The basic tools of a competent real estate appraiser consist of his broad experience, mature judgment, acceptable educational background, and use of an efficient appraisal office. He must also be aware of the geographical limitations of the profession, since the art of appraising pertains to the local characteristics and nature of real property.

Although education, experience, and judgment are highly instrumental in opening the door of the profession to a worthy applicant, a vital ingredient of success is a properly maintained "appraisal plant" or office. Such an office should contain the following:

1. City or subdivision tax maps which are current, since these data provide property locations, lot dimensions, street identification, and locations.

2. City or county utility maps which identify the existence of, and the area serviced by, different utilities, such as underground power lines, sewage systems, water and gas mains, electric and telephone service, fire alarm boxes, and fire hydrants.

3. Current zoning maps which contain information regarding restrictions and reservations. These are useful in forecasting trends in land usage.

4. Community statistics which contain information regarding retail sales, bank clearances, savings bank deposits, employment trends, apartment house and commercial property rentals and vacancies, public utility connects and disconnects, transportation routes, costs and insurance rates, bankruptcy records, mortgage foreclosure rates, new building construction activity, restorations and renovations, conveyances and encumbrances recorded, and other pertinent information.

5. Sales transaction records which contain information relevant to executed sales and listings.

6. Essential reference books and various professional services, such as periodicals, brochures, governmental agency

releases, reports on new ideas about appraisal, court decisions on the rights and values of property, and government statistics relating to housing, construction, and mortgages.

THE APPRAISAL PROCESS. The appraisal process is an orderly plan of action designed to reach a sound conclusion or estimate of value of a parcel of real property. The following are the usual steps in the appraisal process:

1. Appraisal Data to Be Obtained. The appraiser is looking primarily for a determination of value.
2. Determining the Purpose of the Appraisal. At the outset, the appraiser should be aware of the purpose of the appraisal in order to eliminate possible future misunderstandings between the appraiser and his client. The appraisal approach varies with the purpose. For example, if the purpose of the report is to assist a buy and sell deal, different considerations will be taken into account than would be the case for an insurance loss, a tax matter, or a mortgage transaction.
3. Securing an Accurate Description of the Property. A description of the premises assists identification and also reveals the scope of the project.
4. Planning the Appraisal. This step includes actual planning, allocating the work, and organizing the data for the job.
5. Estimating the Cost of the Appraisal Assignment. Appraisal costs can be estimated by projecting costs of time and labor, plus miscellaneous expense.
6. Study of the Appraisal Data. Through an analysis of all the pertinent data, a determination of the value can be arrived at by use of procedures, such as the rule-of-thumb, income, or cost approaches.
7. Investigating Economic, Social, and Political Factors. Since the study may affect the value of the property being appraised, it should be considered an important step in the appraisal process.
8. Writing a Final Report. A final report will correlate all value findings, and will present a sound outline of the analysis and include a concluding statement.

14

PROPERTY MANAGEMENT

Property management consists of the operation, supervision, and execution of management policies pertaining to real estate. Basically, its purpose is to secure for the property owner the maximum continuous net return on his investment and to maintain the physical aspects of the property for optimum efficiency and economy. Property management is one of the newest areas of activity in the real estate business. This field has been developed, and is still developing further, as an art requiring special training. The broker who specializes in property management deserves the title of "professional."

Development of Property Management. In the early stages of property management the manager was probably the janitor or custodian employed by the owner to perform such tasks as supplying heat and hot water, making incidental repairs, and keeping the area clean. In addition to these menial duties, in the owner's absence he collected rents, leased apartments, and took care of tenants' complaints. With the trend toward the larger multi-family apartment house and the skyscraper office building, there was a commensurate increase in the duties of the janitor or custodian. The multiplicity of duties and areas of responsibility required the delegation of authority to persons competent in each particular phase of the landlord-tenant relationship.

The need for a professional approach was accentuated by the trend toward urbanization and growth of larger cities, construction of larger buildings, technological developments in building construction, increased interest and participation in syndications, and absentee corporate and individual ownership. The perfection of the art of property management was the natural result, therefore, of the realization by property owners that it would be both more expeditious and sound to delegate the performance of these services to those best qualified by reason of education, experience, or ability.

Property management as a profession has been developed primarily by real estate brokers, who recognized the need for setting up special departments in their offices to provide this service; by lending institutions such as banks, insurance companies, and other mortgage money lenders, who, because of mortgage foreclosures, largely the result of the Great Depression, became extensive property holders, and for purposes of protecting their equities were obligated to maintain the properties until they could be sold; and by organizations and institutions that purchase or build properties to derive a net return on their investment.

Real property management as a profession was organized in 1933 by real estate brokers who were members of the National Association of Real Estate Boards. In that year they founded the Institute of Real Estate Management as a division of NAREB. The Institute publishes the *Quarterly Journal of Property Management,* conducts courses of study for members, and grants the designation of C.P.M. (Certified Property Manager) to duly qualified members.

The Property Manager. The property manager assumes responsibility for administrative functions and makes executive decisions for the owner; thus, he performs a creative function in carrying out his assigned task. The successful property manager must, therefore, possess skills not often found among the ranks of property owners. Property management involves something more than merely renting apartments, offices, or other space.*

TYPES OF PROPERTY MANAGERS. Since the field of property management is as diverse as there are properties, areas of specialization have been developed. These specialized services are provided for residential buildings; retail and commercial buildings; manufacturing and loft properties; public and semi-public buildings; and agricultural and farm lands.

FUNCTIONS OF A PROPERTY MANAGER. It may be assumed that a property manager is concerned primarily with the responsibility for the administration of real property which is actually in exist-

---

* We must not confuse the collection of rent with property management, although the former plays an integral role in the latter. When a broker or agent serves a principal as a rent collector, and only for that purpose, and the principal reserves the power to make all the decisions regarding the property, it is not technically correct to say that the broker is engaged in property management.

ence and represents a going business. In this widely accepted sense, the manager will be concerned with rendering a service to the tenants as well as to the owner; hearing and determining tenants' complaints; buying supplies; hiring and training employees; authorizing and supervising repairs; paying bills; arranging adequate insurance coverage; scrutinizing taxes and assessments; analyzing depreciation deductions; collecting rent; and maintaining and preparing records.

The services of a property manager may also be extremely helpful during the pre-construction phase. He may perform any of the following functions: making surveys of trends of the area where a building is to be located; preparing an analysis of the best type of building to be erected to improve a site; devising projected rental schedules based on cost of investment, competitive rentals, area experience, and projected expenses; and assisting in promotional activities in behalf of the new building, by helping to establish policy regarding advertising, selling space, selection of tenants, and leasing of premises.

SELECTION OF PROPERTY MANAGER. In selecting a property manager the employer usually considers the services to be performed and the qualifications of the applicant—especially his experience, education, past record, sales ability and character, personality, and qualities of tact and diplomacy.

In many instances the property manager may reverse the process and select his employer by convincing him that he can bring the highest net return from the capital investment.

THE MANAGER'S FEES. The fees of the property manager are usually set forth in a contract between the parties, and they vary with the type of service provided. For instance, the fee for management may be a flat percentage of the gross rentals received from the operation; the fee for leasing may be based upon the value of new leases negotiated; the fee for supervising repairs may be a percentage of the gross cost of labor and services entailed in making the repairs; and the fee for selling may be a commission amounting to a percentage of the value of the transaction.

THE CREATIVE MANAGER. We have indicated that a flair for creativity should be among the attributes of a property manager. It is difficult to localize and generalize regarding this function since each assignment is unique. However, the creative manager has often contributed effectively to property salvage operations so that slum properties have been razed and replaced by new construction, and obsolete industrial areas and plants have been revived. Ingenuity must be applied to the never-ending problems of keeping older properties competitive with the newer ones.

15

LEASES: LANDLORD AND TENANT

A lease is a contract between an owner or a person with an interest in real property (landlord, lessor) and another person (tenant, lessee), stating the conditions under which the lessee may use and occupy the property, and the responsibilities of the lessor. It is an agreement or conveyance, for the hire of real property, whereby the tenant takes possession for a stipulated term and undertakes to pay a stipulated amount of money (rent) therefor. The contract of lease, voluntarily entered into between the parties, largely determines the law by which the parties are to be governed.

Ordinarily a lease is not required to be in any particular form: it may be oral or in writing. However, in many jurisdictions, as in New York State, a contract which cannot be performed within a year must be in writing. Thus, a lease for a term in excess of one year must be in writing to be enforceable. In some states oral leases are valid for as long as three years.

Requirements of a Lease.   The following elements are present in a majority of valid leases: (1) a lessee and lessor both possessing contractual capacity, (2) an agreement to take and let, (3) a description of the premises, (4) the term of the lease, (5) the consideration or rent to be paid, (6) execution of the lease in accordance with statute, (7) covenants and conditions, and (8) delivery and acceptance.

The omission of a covenant to pay rent, or the failure to fix the term, does not invalidate the lease, since these clauses may be omitted for reasons best known to the parties. If no consideration is mentioned, the courts will conclude that a reasonable value is intended. If no term is mentioned, then the tenancy is from month to month.

A lease becomes effective when it is executed and delivered to the lessee or his agent.

Term of Lease.   Generally speaking, there are no limitations upon the duration of a lease. It may be for a day, a month, a year, ninety-nine years, life, or whatever term is desired. However, it cannot be forever.

The right of a tenant to use and occupy real property under a lease is a *chattel real*—i.e., personal property—and is called a "leasehold."

Rent.   Rent is a "definite periodic return for the use of property." Rent may be payable in money, goods, produce of the land, services, and the like. Although rent need not necessarily be fixed, it should be determinable.

If the rent is a stipulated percentage of crops at harvest, or a percentage of gross volume of sales over a fixed minimum, the lease is known as a *percentage lease*. If the rent is to be uniform for the entire term, the lease is a *fixed* or *straight rental lease*. If the rent is to be graduated upward during the term, the lease is an *escalator lease*. Where the rent for the first term is fixed or graduated, and upon renewal the rent is based upon a fixed percentage of the value of the property, the lease is a *reappraisal lease*. And finally, where the rent includes payment of all the fixed costs of the property, except (usually) amortization of the principal and interest of a mortgage, the lease is a *net lease*.

Types of Tenancies.   There are two main types of tenancies under a lease: fixed or definite term, and indefinite tenancies.

FIXED OR DEFINITE TERM.   Under this type there are the following general categories:

Monthly.   If the tenant holds over at the expiration of the agreed upon term, whether it is for a month, two years, or whatever, and the landlord continues to accept the rent, the lease continues for another month; if so continued, it becomes a month-to-month tenancy. In New York State, if a landlord wishes to terminate a month-to-month tenancy, he is obligated to give the tenant thirty-days' notice to vacate.

Yearly.   This lease for a year or for more than a year must be in writing to be enforceable and ends on the last day of the term, without notice to the tenant. If the tenant holds over, the landlord may exercise any of the following options: dispossess the tenant, hold the tenant to the lease for another year, or hold the tenant on a month-to-month basis.

Many leases contain automatic renewal clauses requiring the tenant to give the landlord notice of intent to vacate within a designated period of time prior to the termination of his lease; otherwise, his lease is automatically renewed upon the same terms and conditions. In New York State, these automatic renewal clauses are enforceable only if the landlord, prior to the time the tenant is required to notify him of his intentions, gives the tenant notice of this obligation under the terms of his lease. The time within which the landlord must give the tenant notice is usually equal to the time during which the tenant must notify the landlord. This time period is stated as part of the automatic renewal elapse.

INDEFINITE TENANCIES.   These are tenancies of indefinite duration and arise by (1) *agreement* between the parties that the lease is to run from period to period subject to termination upon notice, (2) *holding over* and continuing to pay rent under an expired lease, thus giving rise to a month-to-month tenancy, which may be terminated by either party on thirty-days' notice, and (3) *entering* upon the property and paying rent under a void lease for years. This situation creates a month-to-month tenancy. In all these cases, at least thirty-days' notice must be given by either party to terminate the tenancy effectively.

Tenancy at Will.   This tenancy arises by agreement or implication, but it may be terminated at the option of either party. Notice of termination is necessary, but the details of this requirement vary in the several states.

Statutory Tenancy.   This type of tenancy arose from emergency legislation enacted to deal with the housing shortage when the demands of World War II blocked nearly all housing construction during the war period. Rent control was instituted to prevent victimization of tenants and to limit war profiteering. Restrictions were placed upon the traditional rights of landlords in certain aspects of their operations. The landlord could no longer expel a tenant from the premises, despite expiration of the lease, if the tenant continued to pay a reasonable rent. This restriction remains in force in many states and local communities which have not repealed their rent control legislation.

Tenancy by Sufferance.   This tenancy arises if a tenant remains in wrongful possession of property after the expiration of the term for legal possession, as when a lawful lease has ended. The tenant cannot be treated as a trespasser and may remain in possession until the landlord evicts him. In New York State, a tenant by sufferance must be given thirty-days' notice to vacate.

Long-Term Leases. An apartment lease for more than three years, a store or commercial lease for more than ten years, or a ground lease for more than twenty years are generally referred to as long-term leases. In many instances they are net leases, and are usually recorded.

Ground Leases. In a ground lease arrangement, the tenant rents unimproved land for a term of years, and he is permitted to erect a building or buildings thereon. Through a stipulation in the lease, the parties usually come to an agreement regarding the disposition of the building at the end of the term; otherwise, it becomes part of the real property upon erection and belongs to the owner of the fee, unless otherwise provided for. The tenant is usually allowed to amortize the cost of the building during the term of the lease and the fee owner owns the improvement outright upon termination of the lease. In some instances the lease may provide that the landlord pay the tenant the appraised value of the improvement upon termination. The ground rent is generally based upon a percentage of the value of the land. In addition, the tenant usually pays all the taxes and fixed costs, and the landlord receives a net rent. The ground lease may also provide for the reappraisal of the land value and the ground rent upon each term renewal. The specific terms in this type of lease vary with the needs of the parties.

The tenant takes the following items into consideration in order to compute the rental value of a ground lease: ground rent; taxes and assessments; insurance premiums (fire, liability); charges for water, electricity, heat, gas, and power; costs of labor, repairs, service, and maintenance; amortization of the cost of the building during the term of the lease; compensation for leaseholders' services and the risk involved in the enterprise; and provisions for losses due to vacancies and bad debts.

Covenants and Conditions of a Lease. In most leases there are certain covenants and conditions which may be express or implied.

LANDLORD-TENANT COVENANTS. In the usual lease the landlord covenants, specifically, to give the tenant peaceful and quiet enjoyment of the premises for the term of the lease. Impliedly he covenants that the tenant will occupy the premises to the exclusion of everyone else, including the landlord, and that the premises are fit for the use described in the lease. If the land-lord wants the right to enter the premises for the purpose of re-letting the property, before the expiration of the lease, he must reserve that right in the lease. Also, the landlord must reserve the right to enter the premises to make alterations and repairs, or to comply with orders of governmental authorities, whenever neces-sary.

The tenant covenants to pay the rent, to use the property in accordance with the terms of the lease, and to abide by all the conditions of the lease.

OPTION FOR RENEWAL. If the privilege is to be given to the tenant to renew the lease at the expiration of his term, the provi-sion for exercising this option must be clearly stated in the lease at the time of its execution.

IMPROVEMENTS. All permant improvements of the building become the property of the landlord when they are made, except those otherwise provided for. Improvements of trade fixtures and machinery remain personal property and may be removed by the tenant at, or prior to, the expiration of the lease. Alterations and improvements of the building usually require the landlord's con-sent.

REPAIRS. The tenant is obligated to return the premises to the landlord in the same condition as he receives it, except for reason-able wear and tear. Therefore, the tenant is obligated to make *all* repairs except the following: repairs which the landlord obligates himself to make under the terms of the lease; repairs necessary to keep the building tenantable; repairs required by statute to be made by the landlord; repairs of a portion of the premises, over which the landlord has exclusive control; and repairs of a struc-tural nature.

The destruction of the entire building ends the lease. Neither party is required to rebuild, unless this obligation is expressly stated in the lease.

LIENS. If a tenant makes repairs or alterations with the con-sent of the landlord and does not pay the suppliers or the laborers, these creditors may file mechanic's liens against the premises, which are enforceable against the property. The landlord protects himself against this eventuality by inserting a term in the lease granting him the privilege to pay the amount of the lien and add it to the next installment of rent when due. Failure to pay the full rent is a breach of the lease and the landlord may then evict the tenant. The landlord may also require, as a condition to securing his consent, that the tenant post a surety bond to guarantee the payment of the costs of the repairs, alterations, or construction. The latter method is the best protection in instances where the lease calls for extensive repairs.

SECURITY. To guarantee the performance of the terms of the lease, the tenant is usually required to post with the landlord a sum of money, or securities, or a bond. The amount required is usually either a multiple of a month's rent or a percentage of the value of the lease. With cash security, the landlord is not obligated to pay interest to the tenant unless the lease so provides. This security is not regarded as liquidated damages, or a stipulation thereof, but rather a fund from which the landlord may retain damages that accrue to him as the result of the tenant's breach of the lease. Any excess remaining with the landlord must be returned to the tenant. If the parties agree that the security is to be treated as liquidated damages, then the amount required must not be excessive; otherwise it will be regarded as a penalty. (Since our courts abhor penalties, arrangements for excessive security constitute poor practice.) The lessor is personally liable for the return of the security, unless the lease permits its transfer to some other party.

ADDITIONAL CHARGES PAID BY THE TENANT. Depending upon the terms of the lease, some or all of the carrying charges of the property may be assumed by the tenant. These include taxes, assessments, water rates, insurance premiums, and costs of heat, utilities, and the like. If all of these charges are borne by the tenant, the lease is a *net lease*. Where a tenant agrees to pay certain charges, the lease usually grants the privilege to the landlord, upon the tenant's default, to make the payment, and then to add that amount to the next installment of rent. If the charge is unpaid, there is a breach of the lease for which the tenant may be evicted.

FIRE CLAUSE. The lease usually provides that a tenant must notify the landlord at once of any loss by fire. The landlord is obligated to repair the property as quickly as possible. If the tenant remains in possession after a fire, he remains liable for the rent. If the premises become untenantable and the tenant must move, the rent ceases until the premises are restored to their former condition. If there is a total destruction by the fire, the lease is terminated and the rent is payable only to the date of the fire.

SALES CLAUSE.   Since a lease is in the nature of an encumbrance upon real property, a landlord might find it difficult to sell his property subject to an existing lease. To protect himself a landlord may insert a clause in the lease making the leasehold subject and subordinate to a future sale. Thus he can terminate the lease upon a sale. The lessee, who must take the lease containing such a clause, may protect his leasehold interest by including a "first right of refusal" clause. This clause affords the tenant the right to have the premises first offered to him in case of sale. If he refuses to buy, then the premises may be sold and the lease terminated.

MORTGAGING THE LEASE.   A tenant may give his lease as security for the payment of money borrowed unless this practice is prohibited by the lease. Mortgaging of a lease usually requires the consent of the landlord. The mortgage is recorded in the same manner as a mortgage of real property. Some states regard this transaction as a chattel mortgage. In case of doubt, it is advisable to record the mortgage in both ways.

ASSIGNMENT AND SUBLETTING.   In an assignment of a lease, the original tenant transfers *all* of his rights under a lease to another, and the relationship of landlord and tenant arises between the lessor and the assignee. The obligation of the assignor of the lease depends on the terms of the agreement.

The tenant may assign his lease unless this is forbidden by the terms thereof. The usual covenant in a lease requires the landlord's consent, since the lease is written on the basis of the tenant's financial stability. A lease that has been assigned with the consent of the landlord, or by his ratification, becomes freely assignable. The landlord may protect himself against this eventuality by inserting the following clause in the lease: "the landlord's failure to insist upon strict performance constitutes no waiver of a future breach." The landlord's consent to an assignment does not relieve the original lessee of the obligation to pay the rent even though the new assignee is in possession, unless there is an agreement to the contrary, i.e., by a novation. The landlord has the right to receive rent from an assignee in possession, for the use and occupation of the premises, unless the assignee has bound himself to pay a stipulated rent. The value of the use and occupation may be the rent as stipulated in the lease, or a reasonable value thereof. If the rent received from the assignee is less than the rent called for by the lease, the assignor is liable for the deficiency.

In a subletting, the tenant lets all or part of his tenancy of the premises to a subtenant and establishes a landlord-tenant relationship with the sub-tenant, while still maintaining his tenancy under the original lease. The letting may be for all or part of the premises, and for all or part of the term. Most leases require the landlord's consent to a subletting, in order to protect the landlord's right to prevent an undesirable occupancy.

USE OF THE PREMISES. If there are no specific restrictions in the lease, the premises may be used in any legal manner that does not interfere with the rights of other tenants. If there is an illegal use stipulated in the lease, the lease is void and cannot be enforced by either party. If there are to be any limitations on the use of the leased premises, the lease should clearly stipulate the restrictions. Broad, general restrictions are undesirable as they are subject to more than one interpretation.

ORDERS OF LOCAL GOVERNMENT AUTHORITIES. Observance of the rules of the fire, health, building, labor, and other government departments is a responsibility of the landlord. In instances where a major part of the control over the building passes to the tenant, the landlord, in order to protect himself against violations, should require the tenant, at his own expense, to comply with all orders issued by local authorities. (It is only reasonable that the tenant should assume responsibility for compliance to these orders, coextensive with his degree of possession.)

TENANT'S LIABILITY AFTER REENTRY. The lease should stipulate that if the tenant is dispossessed, or abandons the property, and the landlord then reenters and takes possession, the landlord has the option of holding the tenant liable to the end of the term of the lease. The landlord may then relet the premises as agent for the tenant and credit the rent received against the tenant's obligation. Thus, a termination of the lease occasioned by the landlord's reentry and/or summary proceedings is avoided.

RIGHT OF REDEMPTION. Some states provide that in a long-term lease, one usually running for more than five years, the tenant may reenter after having been dispossessed, pay his arrears, and repossess the property. To negate this possibility, the landlord may require, at the execution of the lease, that the tenant waive his right of redemption. Thus, the landlord may completely protect himself against undesirable tenants.

GUARANTORS AND SURETIES. In order to secure adequately the obligations of the tenant, the landlord may require that a third party or a surety company guarantee the faithful performance of all the terms of the lease. This must be in writing, signed by the guarantor, and may either be executed by separate instrument or endorsed on the lease. Thus, there is compliance with the provisions of the Statute of Frauds, which requires that a contract to pay for the debt, default, or miscarriage of another be in writing.

INDEMNIFICATION AGAINST DAMAGES. In order to protect the landlord, the lease should contain a "hold harmless" clause, whereby the tenant assumes liability for all personal injury and property damage occasioned by his use and possession. Liability for personal injury and property damage generally depends upon who has care, custody, and control of the premises. The tenant of an entire building assumes complete responsibility if he has total possession and control of the premises. The tenant of a portion of the building, such as an apartment or office space, accepts responsibility for his particular use and occupancy. The landlord is usually responsible for those parts of the building which are used in common by all tenants.

To place liability upon either the landlord or the tenant, it must be established that (1) there was actual, implied, or constructive notice of the condition of the premises, (2) there was negligence, and (3) the injured party was free from contributory negligence.

In most jurisdictions, the landlord who leases out an entire building retains responsibility for conditions that existed at the time of the leasing. The landlord is responsible for inherent defects in construction or for renting the premises for a dangerous or illegal purpose. Both the landlord and the tenant are liable if the landlord creates a nuisance and the tenant continues it.

SUBORDINATION. All leases are subordinate to a mortgage which encumbers the property at the time of the leasing. To protect himself against future mortgages, the tenant should record his lease and thus give notice of his rights. A tenant may be required to take a lease subject to future mortgages. This request can be accomplished by having the tenant agree in advance, by executing a *subordination* agreement, to make his lease subordinate to a future mortgage. Existing leases are of extreme importance to a new lessee since they may adversely affect his use and possession of the premises. Existing leases are important to new mortgagees since they limit the extent of the security. A lease may also be made subject to a mortgage, or mortgages, up to a certain stipulated amount. Any lessee who would be bound, to a degree, by subsequently executed mortgages, can be required to execute a subordination agreement for the benefit of such mortgagee or mortgagees.

Termination of a Lease. A lease may terminate in any of the following ways:

EXPIRATION. If a lease for years expires, no notice of termination is necessary. In a month-to-month tenancy, thirty-days' notice is required.

AGREEMENT. Prior to the expiration of the lease, the tenant may surrender the premises, and the landlord may accept them, by mutual consent, without liability to either party. This mutual agreement may be oral or in writing. However, if the lease was recorded, then the parties should execute a surrender agreement, in writing, which should be duly signed, acknowledged, and recorded.

BREACH. The landlord is entitled to institute summary (dispossess) proceedings if a breach of a condition of the lease is occasioned by the following: non-payment of rent; a holdover at the end of the term; an illegal use of the premises; non-payment of taxes or assessment, if the tenant has obligated himself to pay same; or the tenant's bankruptcy or act of insolvency, if these are stated in the lease. (If this last stipulation is omitted in a lease, the landlord can proceed only with an action in ejectment, which is lengthy and expensive.)

A well-drawn lease places conditions and covenants into a class for which summary proceedings can be instituted. For instance, all charges which are payable by the tenant may be treated as additional rent, after the landlord has exercised the option to pay them himself; non-payment will allow the landlord to institute summary proceedings. The landlord may also place a conditional limitation on the term of the lease. Therefore, unless the tenant fulfills all the covenants of the lease, the landlord reserves the right to accelerate the term of the lease. By exercising this option, the term is ended, and the tenant then assumes the status of a holdover. The landlord can then obtain the possession of the premises by dispossession of the tenant.

ACTUAL EVICTION. The lease is terminated if the tenant is ousted from all or part of the premises by the landlord, or by any other person holding paramount title.

CONSTRUCTIVE EVICTION. If the leased premises are in such condition, because of an act or omission to act by the landlord, that the premises can no longer be occupied by the tenant for the purpose intended, there is a constructive eviction. To make this claim, the tenant must vacate the premises while the condition persists. If the tenant moves and can substantiate his claim, the lease is terminated. The tenant may also recover for any damages he has sustained by instituting an action against the landlord because the latter has breached the covenant of quiet enjoyment.

There may also be a constructive eviction from a part of the premises. The tenant may consider the lease as an entire contract and vacate all the premises, or he may remain in the unaffected portion and refuse to pay rent until restored to complete possession.

Constructive eviction is based upon an act or omission of the landlord which deprives the tenant of the use of the property for the purpose intended in the lease. The following have been held to be adequate grounds to sustain a claim of constructive eviction: failing to furnish heat or other agreed services; failing to allow proper access to the premises; allowing excessive vermin or rodents; and failing to suppress a nuisance which is within the landlord's control.

The courts have uniformly held that a diminution of light, air, or access is not a constructive eviction.

EMINENT DOMAIN. If the state, by condemnation (eminent domain) proceedings, takes over the property of the lessor for a public purpose, the lease is terminated. However, the tenant is entitled to a condemnation award for the reasonable value of the unexpired term.

DESTRUCTION OF THE PROPERTY. If the entire property is destroyed, the lease is terminated.

BANKRUPTCY. Most leases provide that bankruptcy of the tenant will terminate the lease. If no such provision is made, the lease is part of the bankrupt's estate. If the lease is rejected by the trustee in bankruptcy, the landlord may enter a claim for the value of the future rents. The trustee may treat the lease as an asset and continue under it until expiration.

PARAMOUNT LIEN. If the lease is subsequent and subordinate to a mortgage or lien, a foreclosure will terminate the lease if the lessee is made a party to the foreclosure proceedings.

Dispossess Proceedings. The most common method used by a landlord to recover possession of his premises from a tenant is by summary or dispossess proceedings. This action is begun by filing and serving a precept and petition reciting the tenancy and the basis of the action, and then requesting that a dispossess be served on the tenant. On the return day (usually seven days later) the tenant must appear to answer and defend the action. If the tenant fails to appear and answer, or if there is a judgment for the landlord, a warrant of dispossess is issued. This warrant, if there is extreme distress or hardship, may be stayed by the court for a reasonable length of time. If, after the warrant has been issued, the tenant does not move out, then he may be forcibly evicted from the premises by a marshal or similar public official.

The right to dispossess has been greatly restricted in rent-control areas, where it is granted only in cases involving non-payment of rent; even then, if there is extreme hardship, long stays of eviction are granted.

16

SUBDIVISIONS AND DEVELOPMENTS

When the layman talks of subdivisions and developments he usually uses the terms interchangeably, as though they meant one and the same thing; however, in technical real estate usage these terms have entirely different connotations and meanings. Reference to subdivision of land means the process of breaking up large tracts of raw land into smaller plots or sites which will be offered for sale to persons interested in further development thereon. Reference to the development of land means a process involving the field actions which take place to further the subdivision plans, including all the expenditures made to provide the essential site facilities.

SUBDIVISIONS

Of prime importance in this phase of real estate activity is the application of the concept of putting the land to the *highest and best use*. The subdivider, in breaking up his large tract of land, must be cognizant of the local zoning and building code regulations. Subdividing involves purchasing and surveying the raw land tract, staking out the plat or site boundaries, and obtaining local governmental approval of the surveyor's plat of the subdivision. Platting property does not necessarily require that physical changes be made. The plat will usually contain the subdivision name; the block, lot and street designations, and dimensions; and the proposed easements and rights of way to be dedicated to public use.

After the local government approves the plat, it may become a matter of public record, usually upon filing with the office of the county clerk where the property is located. At this point the proposal is a "paper subdivision"—the filing of a notice of intent to effectuate a land change in the community. The filing of the plat is not irrevocably binding upon a subsequent purchaser. If the land is bought in its entirety, the new buyer may use it as platted or, if he feels that he can subdivide the land to a higher and better use, he may file a new plat indicating the changes. As long as the changes do not violate local restrictions, obtaining approval will present no problem.

It is the goal of the subdivider to make a profit based on the difference between the value of the land in its raw state and its value in a platted state.

DEVELOPMENTS

In developing land, the developer progresses from the paper subdivision to the stage of providing the land with site facilities. This phase of activity is extensive and requires substantial expenditures above and beyond the purchase price of the land. The developer takes into consideration community space requirements, community growth and population trends, the number of new sites which can be sold, and local real estate trends. This phase of developing requires extensive experience in the field of land utilization.

Classification of Developments. Developments may be classified as urban, suburban, and rururban.

URBAN DEVELOPMENT. In urban development we are concerned with land within an area where the community growth pattern has been established. Since most urban areas have reached the saturation point of land available for developments, the land utilized will in most instances be on the fringe or borderline of the area. However, it will also involve land taken over for slum clearance and urban renewal.

This type of development usually follows established patterns, since the land utilization has already been defined and the street service and utility patterns have been formed. Since the ground work of development is thus predetermined, there is a decided cost advantage. The disadvantage lies in the fact that the developer is severely restricted in trying to supply new ideas, and he has less latitude in his planning and less control of the entire pattern of development.

SUBURBAN DEVELOPMENT. As in rururban development (discussed below), the developer of land in outlying districts just beyond the borders of established cities has greater latitude in planning. According to his purpose, he can select the type of development that best utilizes the topographical nature of the land, or he can establish winding roads to secure maximum privacy and vary his plot sizes, subject of course to zoning and requirements. He may even decide to create a self-contained community of residential units with adequate provision for shopping facilities, schools, churches, and transportation.

RURURBAN DEVELOPMENT. This type of development is of recent vintage. The land is used for small farms, ranches, and the like, located usually at a considerable distance from urban centers. Recent strides in providing modern and swift transportation facilities have made this type of development practical, feasible, and financially sound.

Development Costs. Development costs are an important factor in establishing the spread between the cost of the raw land per acre and the price of the developed land per plot or lot. The average development site must, to be a profitable venture, yield a price that represents at least three to four times the cost of the raw land. This ratio will vary depending upon the location of the property, the amount and kind of expenditures incurred, the type and sizes of lots, the population density, the kind and number of available services, and the types of improvements made.

Some of the more usual items that make up the development cost, in addition to the price of the raw land, include water mains, sewers, street grading and paving, curbs and gutters, legal and clerical expenses, filing fees, survey costs, brokerage fees, sales and overhead costs, plus an allowance for a profit on the venture and for the risk assumed. Other factors that may be included in costs are the public facilities: sidewalk installations, gas mains, electric power lines, telephone lines, and the like.

The planning of an urban or suburban development requires the close cooperation of the developer with planning commissions, architects, engineers, lawyers, real estate consultants, financial institutions, and government agencies.

After he has improved the subdivision with streets, utilities, and other facilities, the developer may decide to offer building sites for sale, or he may try to sell the entire development to a builder for mass construction of houses, or he may build the houses himself, usually starting with model homes to attract customers.

Development Financing. The developer usually purchases the raw land for a development outright and uses his equity in the land to finance the project. The raw land often represents about 5 per cent of the total development costs. If the developer decides not to use his own funds for the early stage of developing, he can borrow short-term improvement funds, using his equity to acquire a blanket mortgage that will cover all the land and the improvements. This blanket mortgage is ordinarily subject to a release of lien agreement which will provide for the release of individual sites from their proportionate liability in the blanket mortgage, upon payment of a previously agreed sum of money. Thus, sites may be sold free and clear of the mortgage. The proceeds of the sale will be adequate to cover the amount needed to secure the release of lien, plus a profit. If the builder proceeds to build the houses, he will increase the blanket mortgage to obtain construction funds. When he sells a house, the developer will pay a predetermined sum for the release of the lien; the new purchaser will finance his purchase by using his mortgage to pay back the construction loan plus a profit to the builder.

17

CURRENT TRENDS IN REAL ESTATE

During the past decade many new developments have had an impact on the real estate business. Those that we shall consider in this chapter are sale and lease-back; real estate syndications; cooperatives; condominiums; real estate investment trusts; urban renewal; city planning; zoning; and property insurance.

SALE AND LEASE-BACK

The sale and lease-back is perhaps the most outstanding of recent developments in the real estate business. In this transaction a property owner sells a building he uses in his business and then leases it back from his grantee.

This situation is advantageous for the buyer, since he obtains an income (rent) therefrom; he also gets a tax advantage and he can start depreciating the property all over again. It is advantageous to the seller, who now becomes the lessee, because it puts him in a stronger cash position. He receives ready cash to work with and a new tax advantage represented by the rent that he is obligated to pay.

The sale and lease-back opens the door to many attractive real estate deals. In this way a property owner can turn dormant situations into highly profitable transactions.

REAL ESTATE SYNDICATIONS

A real estate syndication is basically a plan whereby a group of people join together to purchase real property.

History of Syndications. Prior to 1940, the syndication of real estate was limited to groups of wealthy private investors who joined in the purchase of a parcel of real estate either because the investment required was beyond the means of a single individual or because the participants wished to avoid risking too much money in any one piece of property. Investors with limited capital usually confined their holdings to two- or four-family houses or small apartment houses. Inflationary prices for land, rising costs of labor and materials, and the trend toward the construction of multi-million dollar rental and commercial buildings required substantial initial investments. Further, the fact that tax increases were counteracted to some extent by allowances for depreciation and other costs vastly increased the attractiveness of real estate ownership to the investor, who was interested in the potential income coupled with these tax benefits. Consequently, many small investors welcomed real estate syndications as a highly profitable method of securing better returns on their investment than those available in other fields. The trend toward increasing popularity increased participation in syndications until late in 1964 when a reversal set in as the result of the collapse of some highly respectable syndications. Poor management, questionable administration, even fraud and embezzlement, led to unexpected losses and bankruptcies, and the public became apprehensive and cautious. It became apparent that the degree of success of a syndication depends upon the efficiency and morality of its management. In many areas, confidence in this form of investment will have to be re-established, and government supervision and control imposed. Obviously, for the cautious investor there is no real substitute for thorough knowledge about the managers and property.

The Syndicator.   The syndicator of real property can be compared best with a promoter who attempts to organize or underwrite a business corporation. He investigates, locates, and inspects properties that are available and amenable to syndication; he also buys outright or on option, or enters into a contract for the sale and purchase of such property, primarily for the purpose of forming a syndicate in which the public may invest. He then solicits investment by the general public. Often, after he acquires the property on behalf of the syndicate, he takes charge of the management of the property on behalf of the investor. Depending upon the size and needs of the venture, the syndicator will surround himself with people who are highly qualified to assist him —attorneys who are expert in real property, real estate management, and tax problems; accountants; management specialists; engineers; architects; contractors; labor and personnel specialists; and sales and leasing brokers. The syndicator and his organization will therefore possess skills and talents rarely found in any individual investor, and will be in a better position to assure the success of the syndication venture.

The Syndicate Investor.   It should always be borne in mind that there is an ever present element of risk in practically every business venture. Thus, as in all good investment practices, one should only use those funds which are in excess of forseeable needs. Since participation in a syndicate allows the small investor to share with others in a project ordinarily beyond his limited individual means, it opens an avenue of possible profitable investment heretofore reserved only for the large investor. On the other hand, the large investor is now in a position to limit and diversify his investments and still retain certain tax advantages. Generally, syndications are organized as limited partnerships, with the attendant benefits of that form of business organization. However, many syndications have been organized as general partnerships, trusts, or corporations—depending on the nature of the venture. Legally, therefore, an investor is in a position to limit his liability solely to the extent of his investment. Federal and state laws govern the sale of syndicate offerings and the eligibility of investors. If an offering has been registered with the Securities and Exchange Commission it may be purchased by an investor in any state in which all applicable laws have been complied with. If an offering is registered in one state only, then it is limited to the residents of that state.

Investment and Return.   Syndications are usually presented for investment in the form of syndication units. Each unit represents a specified sum of money, ranging from $1,000 to $5,000 per unit. The return on the unit investment will vary with each syndicate; however, the rate of return is usually higher than that from mutual funds, stocks, bonds, savings bank accounts, and the like.

Tax Benefits.   The syndicate investor enjoys a tax shelter in that portion of the net cash distribution which does not represent distribution income. His taxable income will not be equal to his total net cash profit received, but will be that sum plus mortgage amortization, less depreciation. For example, Jones invests $1,000 in the XYZ syndicate which is capitalized at $100,000: the syndicate property costs $150,000 and is subject to a mortgage of $50,000. If we assume that the property has a life of twenty-five years, the annual depreciation is $6,000 per year. The annual amortization of the mortgage is $2,000 per year. If the annual net income is $13,000 after the $2,000 is paid for amortization, $11,000 will be available for distribution. Mr. Jones as a 1 per cent owner receives $110 or an eleven per cent return on his investment. However, for income tax purposes $6,000 is deducted from the $13,000 leaving $7,000 as taxable income. Jones will therefore pay income tax on $70 rather than the $110. The $40 is not part of Jones's taxable income.

Alienation of Syndicate Interest. A syndicate interest may be sold, transferred, or assigned; in the event of death it may be passed under the terms of a will or the laws of intestacy. There is usually a market for syndicate units, and the value fluctuates according to the character of the property and the earnings experience. Depending upon the syndication agreement, the units will be salable to other members of the syndicate or to the general public. There are also specialty brokers who handle such resales, usually for a 5 per cent commission paid by the seller.

Regulation of Syndications. The public offerings of syndications are regulated by both state and federal statutes. Also, there is a self-regulating body, the Association of Real Estate Syndicators, to which most of the reputable syndicators belong. The members of the organization subscribe to a code of ethics formulated to serve the best interests of the investing public.

Advantages and Disadvantages of Syndications. There are several advantages and disadvantages of syndications. Among the advantages is that syndication acts as a hedge against inflation, for real estate values and income generally keep pace with the rise in the cost of living. Moreover, real estate values and earnings have greater stability than stock and bond prices. Excess proceeds for mortgage refinancing are also available to the investor, and upon complete amortization of the mortgage he can obtain higher returns. Finally, if property is sold at a profit, the investor will receive a pro rata share of profits in addition to recouping his capital share.

Among the disadvantages of syndication are the loss of rentals that may reduce, or even eliminate, future income, and the poor marketability of shares in less successful syndications. Many syndications are so complex and intricate that investors require skilled counsel for comprehension. Inadequate regulation of syndications has increased the incidence of fraudulent and dishonest plans. The recent trend toward syndications of business—such as bowling alleys and motels, as well as traditional income-producing properties—has increased the risk in these types of investment.

COOPERATIVES

In a cooperative, the residents own shares in a corporation controlling their building. The amount of shares held by each tenant owner depends upon the amount of equity he invests, which, in turn, is governed by the size of the apartment he purchases. Instead of paying rent, the tenant owner pays a monthly carrying charge calculated on a per room basis. The monthly charge pays for taxes, debt service, building maintenance, care of grounds, and the upkeep of any other facility that is jointly serviced.

That portion of the monthly charge that represents taxes and interest may be deducted by the tenant owner as an expense on his individual income tax return, whereas a tenant who pays rent monthly under a lease merely accumulates twelve rent receipts by the end of the year, for he cannot apply any portion of the landlord's tax or interest burden to his own tax benefit. Further, in a cooperative the tenant-owner's equity as represented by his share ownership has value. If his cooperative agreement allows him to sell without the consent of the operators, the value is equal to the market value; otherwise, the value of the shares may be stipulated in the cooperative agreement.

Cooperatives may be regarded as a compromise between two extremes: owning an individual dwelling unit with attendant responsibilities and upkeep; and renting an apartment managed by a landlord to make a profit. (The condominium, to be discussed below, is a modified form of cooperative retaining some features of individual ownership.)

Appraisal of the Cooperative. In the cooperative, each co-operator is sold shares representing an interest in the land and building, with the right to occupy one apartment exclusively and to occupy certain areas in common with others. Covenants for maintenance and repair are set forth in the separate deeds, and these covenants are intended to bind successors and assigns. Conditions may be attached to the covenants providing for forfeiture or reversion of title. Under such an arrangement the laws of the state where the property is located should be examined to ascertain that the estates or interests in the individual apartment are susceptible of separate ownership, sale, and/or mortgaging and that the related instruments are legally entitled to be recorded. Also, the investor should ascertain whether the covenants are of the kind which legally can run with the land. If not, then the project is subject to doubt. If the provisions relating to forfeiture or reversion are necessary to the enforcement of the covenants, as to either the initial or subsequent owners of apartments, then the apartments would not be acceptable security for institutional mortgages even though other requirements were met. Must an owner, desiring to sell, find a buyer who is acceptable as a member of a club or a similar group, or one who must be first approved by a committee? Such restrictions are generally unacceptable to institutional lenders. None of these restrictions is found in the condominium.

CONDOMINIUMS

The term "condominium" has only recently joined the vocabulary of the real estate broker, investor, and attorney. The word comes from the French (condominium) but the idea itself dates back to the ancient Romans. The condominium is the newest twist in housing: it is a cross between a cooperative apartment and a private home. In the next ten years condominium projects are expected to revolutionize the building industry in the United States, and they have been referred to as "the new frontier of the housing industry."

The Statutory Condominium. A condominium is a statutory system of ownership in fee of individual units in multiple-unit buildings with common elements. It has also been referred to as a "statutory cooperative." The condominium is concerned with the concept of the division of the ownership of real estate into horizontal layers, as opposed to the concept of ownership of real property in fee as vertical ownership of the property from the center of the earth to the highest attainable point in Heaven.

The concepts behind condominiums are new to American law; but with the rapid development of multiple-unit housing in this country, it has become an exceedingly important factor, and there is a good deal of excitement about this new mode of urban living. In Puerto Rico there are several condominium apartment buildings, and new condominiums have already been constructed in several cities in the United States where state enabling legislation has been enacted. Some of the more elaborate condominiums are located in New York City, Tucson, Arizona, and Miami, Florida.

The Horizontal Property Act.   Puerto Rico was the first place within United States jurisdiction to enact enabling legislation pertaining to condominiums. The Horizontal Property Act became law in September, 1958, and was patterned very closely after the Cuban Horizontal Property Act. Under the Puerto Rican Horizontal Property Act, the individual unit is defined as an "apartment"—the term "apartment" designating a unit of property to be used for a residence, office, business, or industry.

Under the Horizontal Property Act the apartment may be freely and separately sold or mortgaged, with the deeds and mortgages being recordable. In fact, the "apartment" may be the object of ownership or possession and of all types of juridic acts *inter vivos* or *causa mortis*, irrespective of the building of which it forms a part. Further, each apartment is separately assessed for tax purposes. The apartment owner also has an undivided estate in common with the other apartment owners in the common elements of the building, such as the land, foundations, main walls, halls, lobby, stairs, elevators, and utility services. The proportion of this interest is set forth at the time the condominium is established, and it determines the share of the apartment owner in the profits and expenses of the building. This share is permanent and not subject to change, nor may the common elements be mortgaged, except with the unanimous consent of the apartment owners. The common elements remain undivided and may not be the object of a sale or an action in partition.

The Horizontal Property Act establishes minimum rules governing the use of apartments and provides for by-laws covering the minimum requirements governing the administration, maintenance, and repair of the common elements. Decisions are adopted on the basis of majority vote; however, any change in the system of administering the building requires a three-fourths vote, and such a change must be filed with the same formality as a deed. Strict compliance with rules and by-laws, subject to legal action, is required of every apartment owner.

Each apartment owner must contribute proportionately toward the administration, repair, and maintenance of the common elements. He may waive or abandon the use or the enjoyment of the common elements, but this does not relieve him from his responsibility to contribute his proportionate share.

If an apartment is sold, the seller and the purchaser are both liable for any contributions which are in effect at the time of the sale. If the purchaser must pay, he has a right of recoupment from the seller. The building administration is given a prior claim against apartment owners for their contributions, subject only to taxes for three years, insurance premiums for two years, and recorded mortgages. The building administration must also keep detailed books of account and make them available for inspection by apartment owners at reasonable and convenient times.

The apartment owners may, upon approval by a majority, insure the building without prejudice to the right of each apartment owner to insure his apartment for his own benefit. The insurance proceeds are applied to reconstruction, but this is not compulsory if the damage comprises more than three-quarters of the building. In the latter case, unless unanimously agreed upon to the contrary, the proceeds are shared *pro rata* by all the apartment owners. If a building is not insured or if the insurance proceeds are inadequate to recover repair and restoration, such costs are borne proportionately by the apartment owners affected directly by the damage.

The Horizontal Property Act details the method whereby the property may be accorded the advantage of the provisions established by the Act. A deed describing the property and the various apartments is signed by the owner or owners of the property and to it is attached a copy of the plans of the building certified by the Secretary of the Planning Board of the Commonwealth and a copy of the by-laws governing its administration. The deed also describes the common elements and establishes the undivided interest pertaining to each apartment in the proportion which the value of the apartment bears to the value of the building as a whole. The property may not thereafter be withdrawn from the Act without the consent of the owners of all of the apartments. When individual apartments are mortgaged or sold, a copy of the plan of the apartment is attached to each deed or mortgage. The condominium thus has a strong statutory basis which governs the creation of estates and the recording of titles, and the relationship of the apartment owner to his apartment, to the common elements, to the administration of the building, and to the owners of the other apartments. The covenants for administration, maintenance, and repair are made binding by statute on all original owners and subsequent owners of apartments.

Hawaii was the first state in the United States to adopt a Horizontal Property Act. Approved in 1961, the Hawaiian Act is modeled substantially on the Puerto Rican Act. The Hawaiian Act provides that condominiums may be established on a leasehold estate. The reason for this provision is that much of the land in Hawaii available for residence is subject to ground leases. In these cases, the apartment owner, instead of having a fee, has a subleasehold estate, or a leasehold estate if the master lease can be divided into separate leases for each apartment.

Condominium Mortgages. In 1961, the National Housing Act was amended to authorize FHA insurance of mortgages on condominium apartments. This authorization extends to leasehold as well as fee interests. The authorization is by its terms limited: where "the structure is or has been covered by a mortgage insured under another section of the Act, where the structure is subject to an FHA mortgage." The family unit sold will be released from the lien of the mortgage. The structure may be new, existing, or rehabilitated. This provision makes certain that all of the structures have been built or rehabilitated in accordance with FHA minimum requirements, inspections, and appraisals.

This amendment was intended to assist in making high-ratio mortgage financing available to purchasers of condominium apartments and therefore to make the construction of these projects feasible for middle- and low-income groups. It should be noted, however, that the amendment states that its purpose is "to provide an additional means of increasing the supply of privately owned dwelling units where, under the law of the state in which the property is located, real property title and ownership are established with respect to a one-family unit which is part of a multi-family structure."

Advantages of Condominiums over Individual Homes. The advantages of condominiums are numerous. For example, they make for more economical use of costly land. In Puerto Rico, it has been estimated that a $10,000 condominium unit compares favorably with a $17,000 single-family residence on a lot measuring 60 x 100 feet. Government officials in Puerto Rico acclaim the great savings to be secured from reductions in necessary services and in the number of workers supplying such services, such as street maintenance, public lighting, garbage collection, police and fire department functions, schools, and transportation.

Advantages of Condominiums over Cooperatives. Since the condominium owner pays a monthly maintenance charge only for his share of maintaining the common elements, this charge is considerably less than the monthly bill in a cooperative which includes taxes and mortgage interest on the building as a whole. The condominium owner pays separate interest charges on his own mortgage, and the real estate taxes on his apartment are assessed individually. In both instances, of course, taxes and interest are deductible for income tax purposes.

Since the condominium owner buys his own apartment, he has freedom to negotiate his own mortgage terms, perhaps with a large down payment to reduce interest charges. Or he can choose to speed up the payments and retire the mortgage early. In a cooperative there is no such flexibility.

Another advantage is that the condominium owner does not have to worry about shouldering a share of the charges for any vacant apartments in the building—sometimes a burden in a cooperative during a recession.

The most significant advantage of a condominium, however, is that it is a concrete piece of real estate which is salable on the open market at a possible profit and at a substantially improved equity position; making a profit on a cooperative, however, is often difficult, since the corporation usually has first choice at the original sales price, or reserves the right to approve of the buyer. In addition, outright ownership of an apartment gives the condominium owner complete freedom to do what he wants with it, without a nod from all of the neighbors. A cooperative dweller is still largely a tenant, under a proprietary lease, owning shares in the building corporation.

REAL ESTATE INVESTMENT TRUST

In September, 1960, the Congress of the United States enacted legislation encompassing the Real Estate Investment Trust Act of 1960. This Act affords a small investor the opportunity to invest in real estate in the same manner that he would invest in stocks and bonds by buying mutual funds. Theoretically, the Real Estate Investment Trust Act legally sanctions mutual funds for real estate. These trusts are similar to the Massachusetts trust or business trust, and although they were never forbidden prior to September, 1960, they were treated as associations and taxed as corporations.

The Act provided that if the trust distributes 90 per cent or more of its ordinary income to shareholders, there will be no tax to the trust on distributed earnings. The shareholder pays the normal income tax on his income from the trust and receives favorable capital gains. Thus, the former disadvantage of double taxation of profits and gains was eliminated by the Act.

The trust generally provides for freely transferable certificates of beneficial interest, centralized control in trustees who are a continuing body, and limited liability of the shareholders. To prevent the use of investment activities not contemplated by the legislature, certain safeguards were built into the Act. Among these are:

1. Management must be vested in one or more trustees.
2. The beneficial ownership is evidenced by transferable certificates of beneficial interest.
3. Property may not be held primarily for sale to customers in the ordinary course of trade or business.
4. There must be at least one hundred shareholders.
5. More than 50 per cent of the shares may not be owned by five or fewer than five individuals.
6. At least 90 per cent of the gross income must come from traditional investment sources.
7. At least 75 per cent of the gross income must come from real estate sources.
8. Not more than 30 per cent of gross income may be derived from the sales of stock or securities held six months or less, or real property held less than four years.
9. At least 75 per cent of the assets of the trust must be in real estate, cash, cash items, and government securities.
10. Not more than 25 per cent of the assets of the trust may be in securities other than those listed in (9) above.

The Treasury Department of the United States formulated a list of rules governing the real estate investment trusts formed in accordance with the Act. These new regulations cleared up much of the confusion that followed the enactment of the law. The

Treasury Department clearly set forth the powers of the trustees, the duties of the independent contractors, and the methods by which trust assets must be determined for purposes of qualifying as a trust. Although not all of the important legislative questions were settled by the issuance of the rules, at least a forward step was thus taken to clarify policy.

Advantages and Disadvantages of the Real Estate Investment Trust. It is too soon to predict the public's attitude toward the real estate investment trust as an area for investment. However, the advantages created by the Act are apparent. Removing this form of realty investment from the realm of corporate ownership eliminated the "bogie" of double taxation. The small investor gained an opportunity to participate in large-scale realty investments. Further, it was the intent of Congress to eliminate not only many disadvantages of owning real estate in the corporate form, but certain disadvantages of the limited partnership form as well. Quite apart from the investment trust, there has recently been an increase in syndicated realty investments, indicating that the public feels that syndication in the limited partnership form is acceptable. However, recent syndicate scandals may alter this point of view.

The Real Estate Investment Trust Law has some real disadvantages. It is not possible to own property in trust form and create a tax loss, which is sometimes a prime factor in a projected investment, and tax problems are bound to arise. Also, title insurance companies may have difficulty ascertaining the validity and legality of the trust. This difficulty may have a strong bearing on insurability and may require extensive examination of the statutes and the case law of each state wherein the trust is created and operates. Such an inquiry is an extremely hazardous task at best. The extent of control to be granted to the shareholders, the effect of claims against shareholders, and the necessity of the joinder of one or more shareholders in conveyancing out of the trust are matters requiring careful consideration. How much power may be given to shareholders to amend the trust agreement, or to remove or replace trustees? Improvident trust agreements would nullify the desired effects of the Act.

Only time and experience will disclose the degree of acceptability of this form of real estate investment.

URBAN RENEWAL

The Federal Housing Act of 1949 declared that the general welfare and security of the nation and the health and living standards of its people require housing production and related community development sufficient to remedy the severe housing shortage, to eliminate substandard and other inadequate housing through the clearance of slums and blighted areas, and to achieve as soon as feasible the goal of a decent home and a suitable environment for every American family. The Urban Renewal programs throughout the United States further the objectives of this Act.

Urban Renewal Legislation from 1949 to 1961. Title I of the Housing Act of 1949, as amended, is the principal federal law authorizing federal assistance for slum clearance and urban renewal. The Housing Act of 1954 broadened the provisions of Title I to authorize federal assistance in the prevention of the spread of slums and urban blight areas through the rehabilitation and conservation of blighted and deteriorating areas, in addition to the clearance and redevelopment of slums. It also provided that communities carrying out slum clearance and urban redevelopment projects prior to the enactment of the 1954 law would be permitted to complete such projects under the provisions of Title I of the Housing Act of 1949.

The Housing Act of 1956 again liberalized Title I of the Housing Act of 1949 by authorizing, among others, payments to individuals, families, and business concerns for moving expenses and losses of property resulting from their displacement from an urban renewal project, and the provision of federal advances for the preparation of "General Neighborhood Renewal Plans."

The Housing Act of 1959, in addition to other changes made in the law, again increased the authorization in Title I of the 1949 Act for federal financial assistance to urban renewal, and included new provisions for federal grants to "Community Renewal Programs." Moreover, relocation payments were increased, and relocation payments were authorized to be made when displacement from an urban renewal area resulted from acquisition of real property by the urban renewal agency or any other public body in an urban renewal area, or from code enforcement in connection with an urban renewal project, or from programs of voluntary repair and rehabilitation in accordance with an urban renewal plan.

Title I was again amended by the Housing Act of 1961, which increased the authorization for federal grants to two billion dollars and also increased from two-thirds to three-fourths the federal contribution to urban renewal in any municipality with a population of 50,000 or less (150,000 or less for a municipality in an economically distressed area). Among other amendments made by the 1961 Act to Title I, local agencies engaged in urban renewal were authorized to pool their surplus local grant-in-aid credits between projects on the two-thirds basis and projects on the three-fourths basis. The local urban renewal agencies were also authorized to carry out rehabilitation demonstrations in urban renewal areas. In addition, the Small Business Administration was authorized to make loans on special terms to displaced small business firms.

Miscellaneous Urban Renewal Legislation. The Housing Act of 1954 provided federal grants to assist in developing, testing, and demonstrating activities for urban renewal, and federal grants to assist urban planning.

The National Housing Act passed by the Seventy-third Congress authorized special Federal Housing Administration (FHA) loan and mortgage insurance programs to aid the financing of the construction and rehabilitation of housing in urban renewal areas and those families displaced by urban renewal activities or other governmental action. The provisions of the National Housing Act provide assistance in the form of loans for the modernization and repair of homes; mortgages for the rehabilitation of multi-family housing; mortgages for the purchase of existing housing; and "open end" mortgages whereby property owners may obtain additional funds for modernization or basic improvements and repay them as part of an existing mortgage without the expense of complete refinancing.

Under Title III of the National Housing Act (the Federal National Mortgage Association Charter Act), the Federal National Mortgage Association (Fannie Mae) assists in the provision of credit for FHA urban renewal and for relocation housing by purchasing the mortgages from lenders and giving advance commitments to make such purchases.

The provisions of the United States Housing Act of 1937 passed by the Seventy-fifth Congress required that in the admission of families to low-rent public housing preference be given to those displaced by urban renewal activities, and further required the elimination of a number of slum dwellings equal to the number of low-rent public housing units provided with federal assistance in a community.

Administration of Urban Renewal Assistance. Most of the provisions of the Housing and Home Finance Administration with respect to federal assistance to slum clearance and urban renewal are administered by the Urban Renewal Administration, a constituent of the Housing and Home Finance Agency. The mortgage insurance provisions for urban renewal housing is administered by the FHA, and Fannie Mae provides a secondary market for the mortgages. The latter two are also constituent agencies of the Housing and Home Finance Agency. The low-rent public housing program is assisted by the Public Housing Administration, another constituent agency, with housing owned and operated by the local public housing agencies.

CITY PLANNING

The planning of cities is as old as cities themselves. However, many of the plans that have been put into effect in the past are now considered obsolete in the light of present needs, desires, and purposes. It should be obvious that no plan however ingenious will be universally accepted or approved.

City planning is concerned primarily with the remaking of present metropolitan areas which for one reason or another do not conform to ideas of a desirable city pattern. It is much simpler to plan areas which are either undeveloped or in the early stages of development; but older, established sections need replanning and this is a more difficult task. City planning must necessarily be affected by the extent of public interest displayed, the cooperation of property owners, and the extent to which this interest and cooperation can be translated into a program that meets with the approval of the courts and the legislative and administrative bodies of the city.

The City Planning Job. The task of city planning assigned to a duly authorized commission is immensely complex and formidable. It requires the preparation and adoption of a master plan subject to final approval by the municipal authorities; the preparation of platting regulations; the formulation of zoning regulations; and the preparation of a new official city map. Further, constant study is necessary in regard to population trends and their effect on future needs; water and sewerage requirements; transit and transportation problems; public utilities and their expansion; recreation facilities; public building expansion; land needs for business, industrial, and residential uses; and methods of improving the appearance of the city itself.

The problems involved in the creation of a city plan are summarized in Thomas Adams' *Outlines of Town and City Planning* (Russell Sage Foundation, New York, pages 297–98):

1. Ways of communication
    a. Railroad extensions and terminals; harbors and waterfronts; airplane landing fields; transit lines and street railroads.
    b. New highways, speedways, parkways, and streets; improvement of alignment, width, and connections of existing highways and streets; approaches to and from the center of towns and from railroad terminals; bridges and subways; by-pass roads; treatment of intersections of main thoroughfares.
    c. Coordination of transportation, transit, and traffic facilities.
2. Zoning and land uses
    a. Designation of areas for different uses such as residence, industry, business, and open development uses (agriculture, and so forth).
    b. Designation of parts of residential areas for different types of dwelling such as single-family (detached), two-family (semidetached or one above the other), groups or rows, and apartment buildings.
    c. Restrictions affecting heights and densities of buildings, degrees of coverage (area of occupancy) of lots, building setbacks and court space, and position of building lines.
3. Open spaces and preservation of amenities
    a. Designation of areas for regional and city parks, athletic fields, playgrounds and other open spaces, public and private.
    b. Preservation of historic buildings and places of natural beauty and proposals for architectural control.
    c. Regulation of the erection of temporary structures, including billboards and gasoline filling stations.

4. Control of land subdivision and determination of sites for civic centers and other local developments.
   a. Restrictions affecting the subdivision of land into streets, blocks, and lots.
   b. Selection of sites for supplementary planning as neighborhood units or residential estates and civic or transportation centers.
   c. Proposals for the development of satellite communities.

ZONING

The general purpose of zoning is to control and order the future growth of an area in accordance with a comprehensive plan. The legality of zoning regulations is based upon the police power of the state, i.e., the right of the sovereign to protect the welfare of the public.

Principles in Zoning. The police power, which is an inherent attribute of sovereignty, must be implemented by constitutional provision or by an act of the legislature. It may be delegated by the legislative branch of government to the political subdivisions of the state. It may also be exercised through regulations designed to promote the public order, health, safety, and morals, or the general welfare of the community. For instance, the zoning of a municipal subdivision into use districts is a constitutional exercise of police power, provided that it be neither arbitrary nor unreasonable.

Two further principles of zoning should be noted: zoning regulations cannot have a retroactive effect; and compensation for the diminution of property values is not required.

Types of Zoning Control. Zoning ordinances accomplish their purpose by dividing property into districts and specifying or limiting the use to which the property in those districts can be put and by setting restrictions and requirements concerning the improvement and use of the land.

There are three basic types of control, as follows:

1. Control of use—which refers to the activity carried on in building on or improving the real property, such as residential (single or multi-family), commercial, light manufacturing, industrial, and similar enterprises.
2. Control of height and area—which refers to the control of

the number of stories permitted or the height permitted, or both; fixing of the minimum front, side, and rear yard setback of buildings; limiting of the portion of a lot that may be covered by a building; fixing of the minimum size of a dwelling; and limiting of the relationship of the height of the building to the width of the street.

3. Control of population density—which refers to specifying the maximum number of families per acre; a minimum lot area for a family to be housed; the number of square feet of open space required; and a maximum number of families that may be permitted to occupy a given area.

Variances. A variance is an *exceptional permit* which a local board of appeals issues to grant an exception to a zoning ordinance if an undue hardship not created by the owner exists or if a unique situation with respect to a particular parcel of property can be demonstrated.

Undue hardship may arise, for instance, if the owner of an odd-shaped parcel of property could not use it for any purpose permissible under the zoning ordinance, even though the proposed use would not seriously impair the purpose of the zoning ordinance. A unique situation could be demonstrated, for example, by an owner of a vacant parcel of land which is completely surrounded by properties with legal non-conforming uses, so that his land could not reasonably be put to the use for which it is zoned.

Wherever zoning restrictions destroy the ability of the owners to obtain either a reasonable use of their land, or a fair return from it, and the hardship is special to a particular property owner and its alleviation would not impair the character of the zoning district, there is a fair chance of obtaining a variance.

PROPERTY INSURANCE

The purpose of property insurance is to provide for reimbursement against hazards causing loss or damage to the real property. Fundamentally, insurance involves a pooling or sharing of a risk, namely, the risk of possible financial loss. The insurance contract provides for a transfer of the risk to the insurance carrier.

The most common policies for the protection of real property are the following: fire, extended coverage, additional extended coverage, indirect loss coverage, legal liability, employers liability and workmen's compensation, miscellaneous damage to the realty, and multiple line coverage.

Analysis of the Basic Insurance Coverages. Most owners or managers of real property will carry one or more of the following coverages to protect themselves against a possible risk of loss.

FIRE. Few persons owning property want to be without the protection afforded by a fire insurance contract. The purpose of fire insurance is to indemnify a named insured should the property be damaged or destroyed by fire or lightning. Whether one is an owner in fee simple, or a tenant, or a mortgagee, or in any manner has an insurable interest in real property, he can protect himself against the risk of losing or diminishing that interest by obtaining this basic protection.

EXTENDED COVERAGE. One of the most comprehensive extensions of the fire insurance contract is the extended coverage endorsement. When added to a fire policy this endorsement extends the hazards covered to include the following additional perils: windstorm, civil commotion, smoke damage, hail, aircraft damage, vehicle damage, explosion, riot, and riot attending a strike. The cost of the additional premium for the attachment of an extended coverage endorsement is quite nominal and is commonly purchased with a fire insurance policy. Most banks and other lending institutions will not provide mortgage money on real property unless the mortgagor purchases, at his expense, a fire and extended coverage policy protecting the mortgagee's interest.

ADDITIONAL EXTENDED COVERAGE. Another widely used endorsement available to owners and tenants is the additional extended coverage endorsement. This endorsement broadens the coverage of a fire and extended coverage policy to include the following additional perils: water damage from plumbing and heating systems, rupture or bursting of steam or hot water systems, vandalism or malicious mischief, damage from vehicles owned or operated by the insured or a tenant, falling trees, falling objects, freezing of plumbing, collapse of buildings, landslide, and glass breakage. In some states (New York included) the additional extended coverage endorsement can be purchased only under a Homeowners Contract (see Multiple Line coverage, page 187).

SPECIAL AND ALLIED FIRE LINES. A number of other miscellaneous perils are associated with fire insurance to provide coverage for special situations not covered by the policies previously discussed. These include: sprinkler leakage insurance for damage caused by accidental discharge of water from automatic sprinklers in a building; builders risk insurance, a special contract available for changing values and ownership interests during construction; and crop insurance, for damage to crops by weather, insects, and disease.

INDIRECT LOSS COVERAGE. Although the need for insurance against direct loss to property is obvious to most property owners, what is much less understood and recognized is the seriousness of indirect losses to real property. These include losses which result from interruption of business caused by damage to the insured's property; contingent losses from business interruption; loss of income from rents or rental value; extra expense incurred to conduct business or maintain a home; and loss of leasehold or excess rental value due to the cancellation of a lease following the destruction of the leased property. The policies written to provide coverage against these risks are usually titled according to the perils insured against, namely, business interruption insurance, contingent business interruption insurance, rents and rental value insurance, extra expense insurance, and leasehold interest insurance.

LEGAL LIABILITY. The ownership, purchase, or interest in real property involves significant legal consequences arising out of liability claims based upon negligence. To protect against this hazard, the liability policy shifts to the insurance company the responsibility to pay on behalf of the insured all claims arising out of legal liability to others for damages. This coverage is extremely important since it is possible that liability claims may far exceed the capital invested in the property. Further, it may take a substantial sum of money to prove that there is no liability when a groundless claim is litigated. The sense of security afforded by this coverage is obvious.

EMPLOYERS' LIABILITY AND WORKMEN'S COMPENSATION. Most states have enacted legislation to provide for the coverage of employees who are injured, or get sick, or die, without regard to negligence, as the result of accidents or occurrences arising out of and in the course of employment. In New York, as in most states, this coverage is mandatory and anyone in that state who owns real property and employs individuals in connection therewith is legally obligated to carry this form of insurance and provide health, disability, and death benefits for his employees.

MISCELLANEOUS DAMAGE TO THE REALTY. Insurance coverages for damage caused by various crimes and miscellaneous causes provide for reimbursement to an insured for the actual cash value of the damaged property or the cost to repair or replace the damaged property when the loss arises out of the peril insured against. For example, robbery and theft policies include coverage for damages to the realty resulting from the commission of the crime.

MULTIPLE LINE COVERAGE. One of the most significant recent developments in insurance has been the trend toward the combination of insurance coverages which previously had been treated as separate and distinct parts of the insurance business.

The multiple lines policy combines the traditional basic types of coverages in fire and casualty insurance. Homeowners policies are today the best known of multiple lines coverages. These policies provide coverage, in varying degrees depending on the type purchased, against loss by fire or lightning, extended coverages, additional extended coverages, loss from theft or vandalism, and liability for injury to others on the premises. Also, these policies provide against loss of contents of the building, as well as damage to garages and appurtenances, and they pay for related medical services and for additional living expenses.

REAL ESTATE LICENSE LAWS

All states have enacted laws for the licensing of brokers and salesmen. Although individually enacted, these laws have a thread of uniformity. An understanding of the New York, California, and Florida State laws will therefore reflect many of the regulations to be found throughout the United States.

New York State

The business of real estate brokerage in New York State is regulated by Article XII A of the Real Property Law of New York, which is also known as the Real Estate Broker's and Salesmen's License Law. No person can act as a broker or salesman until a license has been officially issued to him, and all applicants must establish their competence by passing written examinations. Forms, applications, and study materials are supplied by the Division of Licenses, Department of State, Albany, New York.

Anyone who is not a duly licensed broker or salesman is forbidden to negotiate any form of real estate transaction for another and for compensation of any kind in the State of New York. These transactions include negotiation of mortgages, making leases, sales, or collecting rents, and the like. (There is one exception: Licensing statutes do not apply to public officers while they are performing official duties, persons acting under an order of the court, or attorneys at law. But, if an attorney wishes to employ a real estate salesman, he must obtain a broker's license.)

The commission of a felony bars the licensing of a broker or salesman unless he has subsequently been pardoned, or has received a certificate of good conduct from his parole board.

Broker's License. In New York State, brokers' licenses are granted to citizens of the United States or persons who have declared their intention to become citizens and are over the age of twenty-one. The applicant must (1) have worked as a real estate salesman for two years, or have had equivalent real estate experience for two years, or have worked as a salesman for a real estate broker for one year and have attended and successfully completed a real estate course of at least forty-five hours that has been approved by the Secretary of the State of New York, and (2) have passed a written examination which is given by the state once a month. Beginning in September, 1971, every applicant for a broker's license will be required to attend and successfully complete a real etate course that has been approved by the Secretary of State of New York.

A non-resident broker who lives in, and has his office in, another state may be licensed to conduct negotiations in New York State, but he must first authorize the Secretary of the State of New York to accept the service of process on him, and he must pass a written examination in New York State, *unless* New York real estate brokers may be licensed in his state without taking a written examination. (The latter arrangement is known as reciprocity.)

A licensed broker may not employ an unlicensed person to assist in the negotiation of a real estate transaction. If he does, he forfeits his commission, commits a misdemeanor, and may have his license suspended or revoked.

A real estate broker must have and maintain a principal place of business, and he may maintain such branch offices as he desires, paying one-half of the license fee for each branch office. The license must be conspicuously displayed in his principal place of business and branch offices at all times. He may not display expired licenses, and need not display his salesmen's licenses. A real estate broker must also post a sign, containing his name and the words "licensed real estate broker," on the outside of his place of business; the sign must be readable from the sidewalk. If he has an office in a commercial building, apartment house, or hotel, the sign must be posted in a space provided in the lobby, other than the mailbox. He must also post a similar sign at each branch office, if applicable. If a broker operates from his home and is restricted against posting a sign because of local zoning regulations, he must move his office or surrender his license.

Salesman's License. An applicant for salesman must pass a written examination that will satisfy the department as to his character and general intelligence. The salesman's examination is held on Monday of each week throughout the year, but if Monday is a legal holiday, it is held on Tuesday. There is no education or experience requirement, citizenship is not a factor, and the minimum age is eighteen years.

A salesman's license is mailed to, and kept in, the custody of the broker with whom the salesman is employed. During the salesman's employment the pocket license cards are mailed to the broker and delivered by him to the salesman as soon as received. A person cannot act as a broker and a salesman at the same time.

Upon the termination of a salesman's employment, his license must be returned by the broker to the Division of Licenses. If the salesman is discharged for cause, the broker must submit a sworn statement attesting to the reason for the dismissal. The broker cannot withhold the return of the salesman's license for an overdrawn account. The salesman should act promptly to have his broker expedite the reissuance of his license to his new broker.

Salesmen are not required to post a sign, nor can they advertise as real estate agents, unless they clearly indicate that they are acting as salesmen for licensed real estate brokers.

A salesman may not demand or receive compensation from any person except a duly licensed real estate broker. A client who pays a commission to a salesman is still liable to the broker for the services rendered by the salesman.

Term of License. Effective November 1, 1961, the license term, which previously had been for one year, was increased to two years. The license term begins on November 1 and ends on October 31 two years later. The license fee for the two years is fifty dollars for a broker and ten dollars for a salesman. The real estate broker's license is issued directly to the licensee. If changes are to be made in the address or the business, the broker must return the license so that it can be endorsed and reissued to show the new address or the present status. Pocket licenses must accompany the returned license.

A person who has been issued a license, and who does not apply for renewal within a year after the expiration of the previously issued license, must take and pass a new written examination in order to remain eligible to conduct real estate transactions.

If corporations or co-partnerships engage in the real estate business, each corporate officer or each co-partner must be licensed as a real estate broker.

Split Fees. A broker may not pay any part of his fee, commission, or other compensation received by him to any person who has rendered service, help, or aid unless such person is a licensed real estate salesman employed by the broker, or is a licensed real estate broker in New York, or is in the real estate brokerage business in another state, or is exempt from the license law. Nor may he engage in "kick-backs" to a party to the transaction.

Controversies. Controversies between brokers and clients, between brokers and salesmen, or between brokers are decided by the courts and not by the licensing authorities.

Penalty Provisions. A violation of Article XII A of the Real Property Law is a misdemeanor, punishable upon conviction by a fine of not more than $500 or imprisonment for a term of not more than one year, or both.

Any person who receives a commission or any money in consequence of committing an offense is also liable to a civil penalty equal to four times the amount received, payable to the aggrieved person.

Grounds for Suspension or Revocation of License. The license of a broker or salesman may be suspended pending a hearing or may be suspended or revoked after a hearing and conviction under the following circumstances: (1) the licensee is guilty of a violation of the license law, or (2) the licensee has made a material misstatement in his application for his license, or (3) the licensee is guilty of fraud or fraudulent practices, or the use of dishonest or misleading advertising, or (4) the licensee has demonstrated untrustworthiness to act as a real estate broker or salesman.

If the license of a broker is suspended or revoked, this action automatically suspends the licenses of his salesmen pending change of employer.

If the license of a broker is revoked, or if the license of a salesman is revoked, he is ineligible for relicensing for a period of at least one year after the revocation.

A real estate broker may not draw legal documents or give legal advice. If he does he may lose his commissions as well as his license. In addition, he may also assume legal liability for damages and penalties.

The Secretary of State enforces Article XII A. His office may investigate complaints of persons against licensed brokers or salesmen, or he may act on his own initiative to investigate violations of Article XII A. He may investigate the business, business practices, and business methods of anyone holding a real estate license. He also has the power to subpoena persons and/or their books.

California

Regulation of Licensing of Brokers and Salesmen. The regulatory agency for the California Real Estate Law is the Division of Real Estate which is in the Department of Investment. The Division of Real Estate is administered by a Real Estate Commission, consisting of a Real Estate Commissioner and six other members, all of whom are appointed by the Governor for a term of four years, and hold office until the appointment and qualification of their successors. The principal office of the Commission is located at 1015 L Street, Sacramento, California. District offices are located at Fresno, Los Angeles, Oakland, Sacramento, San Diego, and San Francisco.

Original and Renewal Licenses. It is unlawful for any person to engage in the business, act in the capacity of, advertise, or assume to act as a real estate broker or real estate salesman without first obtaining a real estate license from the Division. Every applicant for an *original* real estate broker's license must be over twenty-one years of age, a citizen of the United States, and have his fingerprints on file with the Division. He must either have been actively engaged as a real estate salesman for at least two years during the five years immediately preceding the application, or prove to the satisfaction of the Real Estate Commission that he has had the general real estate experience which would be the equivalent of two years of full time experience as a salesman. As an alternate means of qualification, he may show graduation from a four year university or college course, which course included specialization in real estate subjects. The broker applicant must submit the recommendations of two real estate owners certifying his honesty, truthfulness, and good reputation. After his experience or educational qualifications are approved, the applicant must pass a written examination. An applicant for an original real estate salesman's license must be at least eighteen years of age. His application must be accompanied by the recommendation of the broker who is to be his employer, certifying that the applicant is honest, truthful, and of good reputation. He must also pass a written examination. All applications must be accompanied by the appropriate license fee. The original license fee for a broker is twenty-five dollars; for a salesman, ten dollars. The original license is valid for one year. A renewal license examination is taken before the original license expires. The fee for the broker is ten dollars; for the salesman, five dollars. Upon successfully passing the renewal license examination, an applicant receives a renewal license for a four year period. The renewal license fee for a broker is fifty dollars; for a salesman, thirty dollars.

Written Examination. The written examination endeavors to ascertain whether an applicant has: (1) appropriate knowledge of the English language and of elementary arithmetic, (2) a fair understanding of the rudimentary principles of real estate conveyancing, and (3) a general and fair understanding of the obligations between principal and agent, the principles of real estate practice, and the canons of business ethics pertaining thereto.

Exemptions from Licensing. The following are exempt from license requirements: (1) a property owner, or one holding a duly executed power of attorney from an owner, or officers of a corporation selling corporate property without compensation; (2) an attorney at law rendering services while performing his duties as an attorney at law; (3) any receiver, trustee in bankruptcy, or any person acting under order of any court; or (4) any trustee selling under a deed of trust or a will.

Licenses and Signs. The real estate licenses of the broker and salesmen are required to be prominently displayed in the office of the real estate broker. The real estate license of a salesman remains in the possession of the licensed broker employer until canceled, or until the salesman leaves the broker's employ. Each real estate broker must erect and maintain a sign in a conspicuous place on his premises, clearly indicating his name and that he is a licensed real estate broker. The sign must be displayed in the broker's office so that it shall be readily apparent from the exterior of the office to anyone entering the premises from the main entrance. The minimum size of the lettering on the sign shall be one-half inch in height.

Suspension or Revocation of License. The Commissioner may suspend or revoke a real estate license at anytime where a licensee in the performance of his acts in the real estate business has been guilty of: (1) making any substantial misrepresentation; (2) making any false promise of a character likely to influence, persuade, or induce; (3) a continued and flagrant course of misrepresentation, or making of false promises through real estate agents or salesmen; (4) acting for more than one party in a transaction without the knowledge or consent of all parties thereto; (5) commingling with his own money or property the money or property of others which is received and held by him; (6) consummating an exclusive listing agreement that does not contain a specified date of final and complete termination; (7) taking a secret profit, commission, or fee; (8) combining an agency to sell with an option of the licensee to purchase the property unless there is full disclosure of the licensee's profit and written approval by the principal; or (9) any other conduct which constitutes fraud or dishonest dealing.

The Commissioner may suspend or revoke the real estate license of a licensee or refuse to issue a license to an applicant who has: (1) procured or attempted to procure a real estate license for himself or any salesman by fraud, misrepresentation, deceit, or by making any material misrepresentation of fact in an application for a real estate license; (2) been guilty of a felony or a crime involving moral turpitude; (3) knowingly falsely advertised concerning his business or any land or subdivision offered for sale; (4) wilfully disregarded or violated any provision of the Real Estate Law; (5) wilfully used the term "Realtor" on any trade name or insignia of membership in any Real Estate organization of which the licensee is not a member; (6) acted or conducted himself in a manner that would have warranted the denial of his application for a real estate license; (7) demonstrated negligence or incompetence in performing any act for which he is required to hold a license; (8) as a broker licensee, failed to exercise reasonable supervision over the activities of a salesman; (9) used his employment by a governmental agency to violate the confidential nature of records to which he has access; (10) been guilty of any other conduct constituting fraud or dishonest dealing; or who has (11) violated terms, conditions, restrictions, and limitations in a restricted license. The Commissioner may also suspend or revoke the license of a real estate licensee or refuse to issue a license to an applicant who is committed or adjudged insane, mentally ill, or incompetent by any court of competent jurisdiction.

All applications for an original or renewal license must be on a form furnished by the Division. The appropriate fee must accompany the application. A personal appearance of an applicant at an office of the Division for an interview may be required. The Commissioner may refuse to issue a license under an individual, partnership, or corporate

name if said name is the same as that of any person whose license has
been suspended or revoked.

Partnership and Corporate Licenses. Partnerships and corporations may transact a brokerage business under the Real Estate Law
if licensed through officers of the corporation or members of the partnership who qualify as brokers, provided the corporation or partnership
applies for and secures licenses for each such active officer or member.
The license issued for a corporation or partnership entitles the qualified
officer or member to transact business only for and on behalf of the
corporation or partnership. A separate license must be secured to enable
the individual to transact business as an individual or for another
firm. No member of a partnership or officer of a corporation shall be
issued a salesman's license to act on behalf of a partnership or a corporation.

Limited and Restricted Real Estate Licenses. The California
Real Estate License Law provides also for the issuance of limited as
well as restricted real estate licenses. The *Limited Real Estate Salesman
License* is issued for a period of not more than one hundred and twenty
days. The limited real estate salesman cannot transfer from one employing broker to another without the Commissioner's consent. The
license cannot be extended or renewed, nor can an applicant obtain a
second limited license. Limited licenses may be revoked without a hearing at any time. The limited real estate salesman license examination is
the least difficult given by the Division of Real Estate. A limited licensee is not permitted to sign any contract or agreement on behalf of
his employing broker.

The Commissioner may issue a *restricted* license to a person who has
been licensed and found, after a hearing, to have violated the law,
where such violation would justify suspension or revocation of license.
Or it may be issued to a person applying for a regular license, who has
met the examination and experience requirements, but who has been
found by the Commissioner, after a hearing, to have failed to make a
satisfactory showing that he meets all of the other requirements for the
license applied for. The restrictions may apply to: (1) the term of the
license, (2) employment by a particular broker, if a salesman, and (3)
conditions to be observed in the exercise of privileges granted. These
restrictions are within the discretion of the Commissioner as he deems
advisable in the public interest. The Commissioner may require the
filing of a surety bond by the restricted licensee to protect the public.
The issuance of the restricted license grants no property right to the
licensee, nor does he have the right to its renewal. This license may be
suspended without a hearing pending a final determination made after
a formal hearing.

Florida

Florida Real Estate Commission.   All brokers and salesmen engaged in the real estate business in the State of Florida must be registered with the Florida Real Estate Commission. The Florida Real Estate Commission is appointed by the Governor, and consists of three resident citizens of the state, each of whose vocation for at least ten years prior to appointment was that of a real estate broker. Their term of office is three years; that of one member expiring each year. The Commission selects from its number a chairman to act as executive officer and a secretary. Two members constitute a quorum.

Qualifications.   All applicants for registration must be at least twenty-one years of age, citizens of the United States, honest, trustworthy, of good character, and good reputation for fair dealing. Also they must be qualified and competent to make real estate transactions and conduct negotiations therefor with safety to investors and to those with whom they may undertake a relationship of trust and confidence. An applicant for *salesman's* registration must have been a bona fide resident of the state for at least six months unless the applicant had been a duly licensed real estate broker or salesman in another state for two years prior to filing his application. An applicant for *broker's* registration must show that he has been a bona fide resident of the state for one year immediately prior to filing his application. In addition, the applicant for broker's registration must show that he served an apprenticeship of at least twelve consecutive months under the guidance and instruction of a Florida real estate broker. This apprenticeship is established by affidavits filed by the salesman and his sponsoring broker with the Florida Real Estate Commission on a form supplied by the Commission.

Fees.   The fee for application for registration as a real estate broker is twenty-five dollars; for a real estate salesman, fifteen dollars. The annual fee for certificates of registration for a broker is ten dollars; for a salesman, five dollars. Said license periods may be staggered by the Commission, but in no event may exceed twenty-four months. Certificates for license periods exceeding twelve months pay a pro rata fee. Every certificate expires at the end of the license period. Certificates for the next succeeding license period are issued upon written request on a form provided by the Commission, if accompanied by the required fee, and if such request is made while registration is in force. If so made, such request may not be denied or unreasonably delayed.

Exemptions.   The following are exempt from the registration requirements of the law: (a) an owner or part-owner of property who receives from his proceeds only his pro rata share of investment, unless excess has no relation to his services as a broker; (b) a president of a corporation selling corporate property without compensation; (c) one holding power of attorney authorizing execution of contracts or conveyances; (d) an attorney at law within the scope of his duties as such; (e) executors and court appointed officers, such as receivers, administrators, trustees, or masters; and (f) a trustee under a deed of trust or trust agreement.

Examination. After the application for registration has been approved for experience and qualification, the applicant must take and pass a written examination to establish his competence.

Signs. Every registered broker must maintain a sign on or about the entrance of his principal office and all branch offices, which sign can be easily observed and read by any person about to enter the office. Said sign must contain the name of the broker together with his trade name, if any, and if a partnership or corporation, the name of the firm or corporation, and all the names of the active partners or all active officers of the corporation, beneath which shall be the words "Registered Real Estate Broker (or Brokers)," all in letters not less than one inch in height. The names of salesmen may be placed on the sign at the broker's option, separate from those of the brokers, and captioned with "Salesmen, Associates," or any other word clearly indicating that they are not brokers.

Disciplinary Grounds. The registration of a registrant may be suspended for a period not exceeding two years upon a finding of facts showing the registrant has been guilty of: (a) fraud, misrepresentation, concealment, false promises, false pretenses, dishonest dealing, trick, scheme or device, culpable negligence, or breach of trust; (b) false advertising; (c) failure to account for personal property entrusted to him; (d) violation of provisions of the Real Estate License Law; (e) a crime against the laws of the State of Florida, or of any other state, or of the United States involving moral turpitude or dishonest dealing; (f) sharing a commission or fee with an unregistered person; (g) becoming temporarily incapacitated to act as a broker or falseman with safety to investors or those in a fiduciary relation with him because of drunkenness, use of drugs, or temporary mental derangement (suspension in these cases is for the period of incapacity); (h) rendering an opinion that title to property is good or merchantable except if correctly based upon an attorney at law's opinion, or failing to advise a prospective purchaser to consult an attorney on the merchantability of title, or to purchase title insurance; or of (i) failure to separate client's funds from his own in accordance with the law.

The registration of a registrant may be *revoked* if: (a) a registration certificate was obtained by fraud, misrepresentation, or concealment; (b) the registrant has become a non-resident of the state; (c) the registrant is confined to any state or federal prison, or insane asylum, or through mental disease or deterioration he can no longer safely be entrusted to deal with the public in a confidential capacity; (d) a registration certificate was issued through mistake or inadvertence of the Commission; (e) the registrant has been found guilty, for the second time, of any misconduct that warrants suspension; or if (f) the registrant has been found guilty of a course of conduct or practices which show that he is so incompetent, negligent, dishonest, or untruthful that the money, property transactions, and rights of investors, or those with whom he may sustain a confidential relation may not be safely entrusted to him.

Additionally, brokers may be disciplined by the Commission if guilty of: (a) employing a salesman who is non-licensed or whose license has been suspended or revoked; (b) converting any contract, deed, note, mortgage, or abstract of title; (c) failure to disclose any information or produce day records when requested by the Commission; (d) failure to maintain an office as required by law; (e) continuing to operate according to any plan of selling after objection thereto by the Commission.

REVIEW QUESTIONS AND ANSWERS

THE REAL ESTATE BUSINESS AND THE MARKET

Short questions

1. Define real property, generally.
2. Enumerate some of the main areas of the real estate business.
3. Indicate briefly, the role played by the National Association of Real Estate Boards (NAREB) in the real estate business.
4. How is the real estate market created?
5. Classify the real estate market according to income and use.
6. How does the mortgage affect the real estate market?
7. What is the effect of supply and demand on the real estate market, and what forces influence supply and demand?

Answers

1. Real property consists of land together with its appurtenances and improvements.
2. Brokerage, marketing, property management, financing, construction and appraisal.
3. NAREB endeavors to promote high professional standards of practice, provide educational facilities and publications, administer a code of ethics, and regulate relationships between the realtors and the public.
4. The market is created as buyers and sellers find the means to translate their wishes to buy and sell into action.
5. The real estate market may either be classified according to whether the property is income producing or not, or whether the property is commercial, residential, industrial, or agricultural.
6. The availability of mortgage funds is a decided factor in the real estate market. When such funds are loose or readily available they broaden the base of prospective buyers and volume of business increases. A tight mortgage market cuts down the number of potential buyers and restricts the volume of business.
7. The effect is considerable. The number of housing units available, the size and income of the population, local business conditions, the tempo of construction, government controls, and costs of land and labor are forces that influence the supply and demand of real estate.

True or False

1. The National Association of Real Estate Boards is a government administered agency.
2. More people are engaged in brokerage than in any other phase of the real estate business.
3. Building construction is not a phase of the real estate business.
4. Government insured mortgages are an effective support of the real estate market.
5. The demand for housing is in no way related to the size or income level of the population.
6. The real estate market is created by the real estate brokers and salesmen.
7. Income-producing properties on the real estate market include any properties from modest two-family houses to multi-million dollar developments.
8. An income-producing apartment house is an example of commercial real estate.
9. Industrial property is real estate used in connection with the manufacture of industrial and consumer goods.
10. The demand for dwelling space depends to a large extent upon the formation of the household.

Answers

1. F.   2. T.   3. F.   4. T.   5. F.   6. F.   7. T.   8. F.   9. T.   10. T.

PROPERTY RIGHTS AND INTERESTS

Short questions

1. Distinguish between a freehold estate in land and an estate less than freehold.
2. List some examples of freehold estates and of estates less than freehold.
3. Distinguish between dower and curtesy.
4. What is community property, how does it differ from separate property?
5. Define briefly: (a) tenancy at will, (b) tenancy by sufferance (c) statutory tenant.
6. Distinguish between a reversion and a remainder.
7. Distinguish between a fee, fee simple, and fee simple absolute.
8. What are the prime differences between a tenancy in common and a joint tenancy?
9. List the methods by which real property may be alienated, (a) voluntarily, (b) involuntarily.
10. How may title be acquired by adverse possession?

Answers

1. In a freehold estate ownership is either forever or for life. The right to the property for any other period would be an estate less than freehold.

2. Freehold estate—fee simple, fee tail, life estate. Less than freehold—tenancy for years, tenancy at will, tenancy by sufferance, monthly tenancy.

3. In dower, if there has been a valid marriage and the husband who owned real property during the married life dies, the surviving wife receives a life estate in one-third of the real property so owned by the deceased husband. In curtesy, if there has been a valid marriage and a child born thereof and the wife who owned property dies, the surviving husband receives a life estate in all the real property.

4. Community property is that property accumulated through the joint efforts of a husband and wife living together, whereas separate property is property acquired by either spouse prior to the marriage or received either by gift or divorce after the marriage.

5. (a) In a tenancy at will the tenant has a license to use or occupy the premises at the will of the owner. (b) In a tenancy by sufferance the tenant who has been on the premises under a claim of right stays on wrongfully. (c) A statutory tenant is one whose lease has expired but cannot be removed by the landlord as long as he continues to pay rent.

6. Both are expectant estates whose benefits can only be enjoyed at a future time. The remainder is the residue of an estate left to a third person by a grantor after the expiration of an intermediate estate granted out by him.

7. There is no difference in these estates. They are synonymous and represent the highest estate in real property.

8. A tenancy in common represents divisible ownership in land by two or more persons wherein there is no right of survivorship, and upon the death of one of the owners, his interest passes to his estate, heirs, or devisees. In a joint tenancy there is an undivided ownership of real property with a right of survivorship. Upon the death of one of the owners the surviving owner acquires the interest of the deceased.

9. (a) By sale, gift or devise, mortgage, lease dedication, and descent. (b) By judicial process, adverse possession, erosion, eminent domain, escheat, and confiscation.

10. Title to real property may be acquired by an occupant against a true owner if he comes on the land under a claim of right and actually and hostilely holds it in an open and notorious fashion,

exclusively, continuously, and uninterruptedly for a period of time as provided by the statute of the particular state.

True or False

1. Any two people may own real property in a tenancy by the entirety.
2. In a tenancy in common there is no right of survivorship.
3. A 50 year lease is real property.
4. Property taken by the state under the right of eminent domain, the property owner is not compensated therefore.
5. By escheat is meant the reversion of property to the state due to the lack of heirs capable of inheriting the property.
6. If a person is not as yet born at the time a remainder estate is created there is a vested remainder.
7. In a lease, the lessor has an estate in reversion after the lease is terminated.
8. By accretion is meant the acquisition of title to land which gradually and imperceptibly attaches to the property by the operation of natural causes.
9. Squatters are people who obtain title to land by virtue of long time adverse possession.
10. An owner in common may acquire title to the property by adverse possession against his co-owner.

Answers

1. F.   2. T.   3. F.   4. F.   5. T.   6. F.   7. T.   8. T.   9. F.   10. F.

AGENCY AND BROKERAGE

Short questions

1. Broker Trout secures an oral listing from seller, Atalay, to sell his house for $17,500; agreement to terminate in 30 days, commission to be 6 per cent. Trout secures a buyer for the property of $17,500. The owner refused to permit broker to complete sale and completes it himself. Trout demands his commission. Can he recover?
2. A broker is employed by a wife to sell her real estate; he secures a buyer on her terms; the husband refuses to sign the contract of sale and the deal falls through. Is the broker entitled to a commission from the wife?
3. An owner gives an exclusive listing to broker Doyle for a six-months period. During the exclusive period, he gives a non-exclusive listing to Bienstock who produces a buyer. What is the owner's liability for commission?
4. A salesman is assisted in a deal by another salesman employed by another broker. The first salesman pays one-half of his commission to the salesman who assisted him. Is this legal?

5. Why does an exclusive right to sell listing contract afford the broker more protection than an exclusive listing?

6. Assuming you are a broker and discover you have obtained an Exclusive Right to Sell contract from a property owner who is incompetent. What are your rights in enforcing this contract?

7. If you have a property listed for sale and find a prospect who is willing to take an option on the same at the terms offered, are you entitled to your commission?

8. Brower owns a small farm and no other real estate. He gave broker Donohoe a written listing for 90 days on January 3, 1963 at a sales price of $10,500, commission 6 per cent. The description portion of the listing contract reads: "The place of John Brower." Is this a sufficient description?

9. George Gelston is a personal friend of Joseph Kalt, broker. In the presence of witnesses Gelston orally authorized Kalt to sell his home for $15,000 cash. In response to Kalt's advertisement a buyer paid $15,000 direct to Gelston who conveyed the property. Kalt sued Gelston for a commission. Can he recover?

10. If you listed a house for sale, which had wall-to-wall carpeting in the living room and hall, would you make reference to the carpeting in your listing?

11. Name at least five methods by which an agency may be terminated.

12. A broker is employed by the son of A and B, husband and wife, to sell the parents' real property. The mother has authorized the son to list the property but the father has not. The broker secures a buyer on the exact terms of the listing; the father refuses to sign an agreement of sale and the deal falls through. Can the broker recover a commission?

13. A broker claimed a commission for procuring a purchaser for an owner's property. He obtained a buyer. When the deal was closed, title was taken in the name of the father of the purchaser and the property leased to the son. Can the broker recover a commission?

14. Haucke, a broker, had an exclusive listing on Kaplan's home, which expired on August 30, 1956. Before the listing expired, Haucke procured Klavins as a prospect. On August 15, 1956, Kaplan leased the property to Klavins for six months and on December 6, signed an agreement to sell him the property. Is Haucke entitled to a commission?

15. A broker is employed by a wife to sell her real estate; he secures a buyer on the exact terms of the listing; the husband refuses to sign a deed and the deal falls through. Is the broker entitled to a commission from the wife?

16. Where A lists property for sale with broker, B, who procures a

purchaser, C, can B collect a commission if the agreements are made between A and D, the father-in-law of C?

17. Nowak lists property for sale with Rockmore, a broker, at $6,000. Rockmore purchases the property in Liebowitz's name and sells it to Johnson for $7,500. Rockmore collects a commission from Nowak of $300. Later Nowak discovers the real facts. What redress does he have?

18. Seller lists property for sale with Jones, a broker, at $8,000, the broker to receive a commission of 5 per cent. Jones procures a buyer who refuses to pay more than $7,500. Two months later the deal is made at $7,500 and Jones claims $375 as commission. Seller refuses to pay claiming the listing was at $8,000. Can Jones recover?

19. Bruskin, a broker, was employed by Bellow to sell three lots for him. It was not an exclusive agency. Bruskin procured Mrs. Morgan who was acting for herself and her husband. Each purchased one lot, as did Holm, whom Mrs. Morgan had informed that the lots in question were for sale. Bruskin sued Bellow for a commission on the sale of all three lots. Can he recover?

20. The plaintiff broker, Blake "worked upon" one Murphy and induced him to look at property owned by Person, listed with Blake for sale. Murphy finally decided not to buy himself; but upon Murphy's advice, Murphy's brother bought directly from the owner, Person. Is Blake entitled to a commission on the sale?

21. Hoxie gave Demar an exclusive right to share listing upon his property at $9,000. The agreement was for a term of 3 months at 5 per cent commission. The agreement provided for termination after the term upon 30 days' written notice from the owner. "In default of such notice, this exclusive contract shall renew itself from term to term as an exclusive contract . . . until notice herein provided shall be given to terminate." The agreement was dated November 28, 1959. Notice of termination was given on May 16, 1960. The property was sold by the owner, Hoxie, on July 26, 1960. Is the broker entitled to his commission?

22. A, a minor, employs B to sell a piece of real estate which he owns. B, dubious as to A's age, makes inquiry. A misrepresents his age to be 25 years. After B sells the property, A disaffirms that contract of employment and refuses to pay B any commission. Can B recover?

23. Owner wrote to broker, "You might proceed to sell the entire 13 houses separately for $50,000 net cash to me. Your commission of 3 per cent to come out of the last sale made." The houses were sold by broker for an aggregate amount of $50,000. Owner refuses to pay any commission. Can broker recover?

24. The plaintiff broker claimed a commission for procuring a purchaser

for defendant owner's property. He arranged for the sale and the price. When the transaction was closed, title was taken in the name of the purchaser's wife and the property leased to the husband. Can the broker collect?

25. On March 28, 1961, broker was employed by the defendant, Roth, to negotiate certain investment real estate for $72,000. The price of the property was held at $76,000. The owner, Ames, has listed the property for sale with broker at the latter figure. Broker testified that he did not expect a commission from owner, Ames, and had not received any commission. Can broker recover from the purchaser Roth?

26. On October 2, 1959, A listed a property for sale with B at $15,000 and agreed to pay B a commission of 5 per cent. On December 27, 1959, B notified A that an Albert Ross had inspected the property that day and B was going immediately to Ross's house to try to close the deal with him if it was satisfactory to A, and A was not going to give the tenant of the property the first opportunity to buy it. A replied that Ross could buy the property if B could make a deal with him. On the same day Ross agreed to buy the property and paid $500 earnest money. The next day B went to A to tell him about the sale, but, before he had an opportunity to speak, A said, "The house is sold; the tenant bought it." Is the broker entitled to a commission?

27. DiGangi negotiated a lease with Crane, in behalf of Alder, owner, for a 5-year term at $250 monthly with a 5-year option at $300. The owner agreed, in writing, to pay DiGangi a commission of 5 per cent of the total rentals received during term "and any renewal thereof." During the original term, the tenant, Crane, persuaded Alder to reduce the rental from time to time, and Alder paid DiGangi commission upon the rents actually received. Crane did not exercise his option, but before the expiration of the lease, renewed for 1 year at a monthly rental of $150. Is DiGangi entitled to commission upon a new lease?

Answers

1. Yes, unless state law requires listing to be in writing (not in N. Y.).
2. Yes, he has fully earned his commission of employment since he produced a buyer who is ready, willing, and able to buy. However, if the broker had good reason to believe that the husband would not join, the decision would be different.
3. He must pay a double commission to Doyle and Bienstock.
4. No, a salesman has no right to recognize anyone other than his employing broker. The latter should deal and recognize the other broker and not his salesman.

5. Full commission is assured to the broker even if the owner sells during the term of the listing.

6. None, as the contract is voidable.

7. No, an option does not bond the optioner to buy, and the broker is entitled to his commission only if he produces a ready buyer.

8. Yes, insofar as the listing contract is concerned. This is not considered good practice to use in real estate contracts.

9. Yes, in states where oral listings are enforceable.

10. Yes, if it is the owner's agreement to include it with the realty. Thus later arguments and possible loss of sale is avoided.

11. (a) Agreement. (b) Expiration of term. (c) Extinction of subject matter. (d) Death of principal or agent. (e) Incapacity of principal or agent. (f) Renunciation by either principal or agent.

12. Yes, from the mother, as the son was her agent, from the son, if he held himself out to be the father's agent. No right of commission from the father.

13. Yes, the manner in which title was conveyed is immaterial.

14. Yes, as it appears that the lease was an arrangement to circumvent the claim for commission and the parties thereto did not act in good faith.

15. Yes, because he has produced a buyer ready, willing, and able to buy.

16. Yes, if C is the real purchaser and takes possession of the premises. It is immaterial that title is taken in D's name or even whether he furnishes the money. It is assumed that A knew or should have known the relationship between C and D.

17. Recover $1,500 profit + $300 commission. Broker forfeits commission and secret profits because of duplicity.

18. Yes, in this case, as the courts will not permit an owner to take advantage of the broker's efforts. The agent was the efficient and procuring cause of the sale.

19. Only for the two lots sold to Mrs. Morgan and her husband, since the broker was not directly connected to the sale to Holm. The law recognizes only proximate and not remote causes.

20. No, in the absence of collusion. The broker was not the procuring cause of the sale.

21. Yes, the notice of May 16th was too late to terminate the contract during the term in which it was given. It operated to terminate the listing as of Aug. 28, 1960, as property sold July 26, 1960, commissions payable to broker.

22. No, infant may avoid his contract because he misrepresented age. B should end the infant in tort (deceit) as infant is liable for torts.

23. No, as deal was a net listing, nothing over amount left for broker.

24. Yes, the broker clearly made this "deal" and the subterfuge should not prevent collection.
25. No, since broker was already employed by seller, he cannot collect a commission from the buyer; a servant cannot serve two masters.
26. Yes, although the broker did not have an exclusive agency, he was entitled to a reasonable time within which to conclude his deal with Ross since A agreed to same. The owner (A) did not have the right to use broker's efforts as a means of making the sale to tenant and avoid paying a commission.
27. Yes, the intention of the parties was that DiGangi should receive commissions as long as Crane continued to be an occupant of the building as a tenant. The word "renewal" included a new lease between Alder and Crane.

Short questions

1. Define an agent.
2. List at least five ways by which an agency may be terminated.
3. Outline the duties that an agent owes to a principal.
4. List the more important duties of a principal to his agent.
5. Under what circumstances is an agent personally liable to third persons.
6. You are a broker who has obtained an exclusive listing from an incompetent property owner, may you enforce this contract?
7. You are a broker who has an open listing on a parcel or property. You secure a prospect who is ready, willing, and able to take an option to purchase the property at the seller's terms. Have you earned a commission?
8. Describe five commonly used types of listing contracts and specify which one is not to be used in New York.
9. A broker has an open listing to sell three houses for a property owner. He sells two houses to a brother and sister, the latter recommends a friend to the seller who purchases the third house. To what commission is the broker entitled?
10. A broker has listing reciting that commission will only be paid after title is conveyed. He procures a buyer ready, willing, and able to purchase at the seller's terms who enters into a contract of sale. Arbitrarily, thereafter, the seller refuses to consummate the transaction. Is the broker entitled to a commission although title has not passed?

Answers

1. An agent is any person who represents another (principal) from whom he has derived his authority.

2. (a) By agreement of the parties. (b) By the terms of the agency contract. (c) By the death or incapacity of either party. (d) By the destruction of the subject matter of the agency. (e) By renunciation of either party. (f) By the insolvency or bankruptcy of the principal. (g) By operation of law.

3. The agent owes to his principal the duty of loyalty and good faith in the performance of the agency; to be obedient to the principal's orders; to use the degree of skill, care, and diligence commensurate with the performance of the task, and to faithfully account for all funds of the principal coming into his possession.

4. Unless there is a contract to the contrary, the principal is obligated to: (a) compensate the agent, (b) reimburse the agent for his expenses, (c) to indemnify the agent against risks, (d) to pay damages for breach of the agency contract.

5. If an agent breaches a duty common to all persons, or acts for an incompetent, non-existent, or undisclosed principal, or mis-represents the scope of his authority, or receives money wrongfully, or commits a tort, he is personally responsible for the damages accruing as the result of his acts.

6. No. The listing contract is voidable at the option of the home-owner.

7. No. An option is not the same as an unequivocal offer to buy as it does not obligate the purchaser unless he exercises his option since the broker has not produced a buyer who is ready, willing, and able to buy he has not earned his commission.

8. (a) Open listing—one given to several brokers. The first to sell is not entitled to commission and the listing is terminated. (b) Multiple listing—an open listing which is circulated among and made available to all the brokers belonging to a bureau, providing for a commission-sharing plan. (c) Net listing—the broker can only receive his commission from the amount of money exceeding the listed price that the seller will accept. The net listing cannot be used in New York. (d) Exclusive agency listing—the listing broker carries the listing to the exclusion of all other brokers. Sale of the property by anyone except the owner requires payment of a commission to the broker. (e) Exclusive right to sell listing—the listing broker receives the exclusive right to sell the property. A sale made by the owner himself would require the payment of a commission to the broker.

9. Commission for the sale of two houses only, since he was not the sole procuring cause of the third sale.

10. Yes, because the seller arbitrarily refused to go through with the deal.

True or False

1. The rate of commission to be received by a licensed real estate broker is fixed by law.
2. Generally, a broker earns his commission when he has produced a purchaser who is ready, willing, and able to comply with the terms fixed by the owner.
3. It is legal for the broker and the owner to agree that no commission is earned until the title is actually conveyed.
4. In a listing contract, the owner is the principal.
5. A broker may represent both the owner and the purchaser without their knowledge or consent.
6. A listing contract is terminated if the property is destroyed by fire.
7. An exclusive agency listing is more desirable than an exclusive right to sell listing.
8. In most states, a listing contract must be in writing to be valid.
9. It is not necessary for a real estate broker to understand the law of agency.
10. The term "Realtor" can only be used by a person engaged in the real estate business who is a Board Member or Individual Member of the National Association of Real Estate Boards and observes its standards of ethical conduct.

Answers

1. F. 2. T. 3. T. 4. T. 5. F. 6. T. 7. F. 8. F. 9. F. 10. T.

THE REAL ESTATE OFFICE AND OPERATIONS

Short questions

1. A broker sued for $1500 commission in connection with the sale he negotiated of a one-family house. He failed to plead that he was a licensed real estate broker. What effect does this have on his claim?
2. List at least three forms of organization a broker may use in setting up his real estate business.
3. Define the term realtor.
4. Enumerate the service commonly provided by a real estate office.
5. You are opening a new real estate office. How would you obtain listings?

Answers

1. This omission is fatal to the broker's action and he cannot recover.
2. (a) Individual proprietorship. (b) Partnership. (c) Corporation.

3. A realtor is a licensed real estate broker who is a member of a local real estate board that is affiliated with the National Association of Real Estate Boards.

4. Sales, exchanges, financing, management leasing, appraisal, and subdivisions and developments.

5. By personal contact with owners; advertising in newspapers or direct mail; contact with financial institutions; following up on properties listed and advertised for sale by other brokers; checking back on news items of persons leaving the area; through other brokers; and membership in a multiple listing bureau.

True or False

1. A real estate listing is a written list of improvements on the land.
2. The relationship of a licensed real estate broker to his principal is that of a fiduciary.
3. The rate of commission that a broker may charge on the sale of improved property is not limited by law but may be any rate agreed upon between the broker and the owner.
4. The charging of an exorbitant rate of commission by a broker is usury.
5. A real estate broker, as part of the services he renders, may render an opinion as to the validity of title to real estate.
6. It is perfectly valid for two licensed real estate brokers to agree to split a commission.
7. So long as his broker consents, a real estate salesman may split his commission with a real estate salesman of another broker.
8. A real estate broker may employ an unlicensed person, on a salary basis, to solicit listings.
9. If a broker is not paid his commission he may file a mechanics' lien against the property.
10. It is improper for a broker to purchase a property listed with him, unless he so notifies the owner and secures his consent.

Answers

1. F. 2. T. 3. T. 4. F. 5. F. 6. T. 7. F. 8. F. 9. F. 10. T.

SALESMANSHIP AND ADVERTISING

True or False

1. One of the most successful methods of securing listings is by canvassing in the community and speaking directly to the owners.
2. An important selling rule that should be remembered by a real estate salesman is never to argue, he may win the argument and lose the sale.

3. The largest group of property buyers numerically are income-producing property buyers.
4. Most real estate advertising is by radio and television.
5. In placing a property to the public a real estate broker uses institutional advertising.
6. The best day of the week to run a real estate advertisement is on Saturday.
7. One cannot consider the business stationery used by a real estate broker as a form of advertising.
8. The manner and actions of the personnel in a real estate broker's office is a phase of advertising.
9. The first principle of advertising is to secure action to buy.
10. Emphasizing pride of ownership, security, saving, and prestige are important factors in advertising.

Answers

1. T.   2. T.   3. F.   4. F.   5. F.   6. F.   7. F.   8. T.   9. F.   10. T.

Short questions

1. Name the elements that make up the AIDA formula in advertising.
2. Distinguish between name, institutional, and specific advertising.
3. List and describe some methods a broker may use in advertising in a newspaper.
4. What are the most generally used advertising media?

Answers

1. Attract attention, arouse interest, create desire, and obtain action.
2. In name advertising the purpose is to present the advertiser's name before the public; in institutional advertising the aim is to create good will and confidence in the real estate profession; specific advertising advertises a particular parcel or property.
3. (a) News notices—to keep the broker's name before the public and emphasize his expertise in the profession. (b) Classified advertising—these are relatively inexpensive and can be focalized on a particular parcel of property. (c) Display advertising—more expensive and larger than classified usually for presenting developments or large transactions.
4. Newspaper, magazine, radio, television, billboards, car cards, calendars, blotters, pens and pencils, pamphlets, brochures, and circulars.

LEGAL ASPECTS OF REAL ESTATE TRANSACTIONS

Short questions

1. List the essential elements of a valid contract.
2. Why is it necessary for a contract for the sale of real property to be in writing?
3. When may an offer be revoked?
4. How may an offer be revoked?
5. What factors may affect the realty of consent to a contract?
6. Distinguish between an express, an implied, and quasi-contract.
7. If a contract stipulates that "time is of the essence," what is the effect thereof?
8. Define "tender of performance."
9. Distinguish between general, special, liquidated, and nominal damages.
10. What is a "binder"?

Answers

1. (a) Mutuality of consent, i.e., offer and acceptance. (b) Capacity of the parties. (c) Consideration. (d) Legality of purpose. (e) Form in accordance with law.
2. Under the Statute of Frauds, a contract that transfers an interest in real property must be in writing.
3. At any time prior to acceptance provided that there is no option or special interest involved.
4. By agreement, by lapse of a reasonable period of time, by the death or insanity of the offeror, by the destruction of the subject matter of the offer, or by operation of law.
5. Fraud, misrepresentation, mistake, duress, and undue influence.
6. An express contract is one that is expressed in words either oral or written, whereas an implied contract arises from the acts and conduct of the parties, and a quasi-contract arises by operation of law.
7. The parties have agreed that the time of performance is an element of particular importance, and if one party fails to perform within the prescribed time, the contractual obligation of the other is discharged.
8. A tender of performance is an offer by a party to the contract to do what he had promised to do but is prevented from so doing by the acts of the other party.
9. General damages are those which may accrue to any person so injured; special damages are those that did in fact accrue to the particular party by reason of the particular circumstances involved;

liquidated damages are those which the parties have agreed upon beforehand, to be paid in case of breach or default; nominal damages are awarded when a wrong is established but no real damages are proved.

10. A binder is a temporary instrument usually containing a deposit, executed by a buyer and a seller relating to a projected sale of real property, contemplating a more formal contract therein.

True or False

1. An agreement whereby the owner holds his property off the market in return for a consideration is called an option.
2. If the purchase fails to go through with the contract to purchase real property, his down payment becomes the property of the broker.
3. A contract must be witnessed by at least one person.
4. An oral contract for the sale of real estate is unenforceable.
5. If a person takes an option to purchase real property he is obligated to consumate the purchase.
6. There is no difference between satisfactory performance and substantial performance as they mean the same thing.
7. The bankruptcy of the seller discharges his obligation under the contract of sale of real property.
8. By the parol evidence rule is meant that once parties have reduced an agreement to writing, they are bound thereby and cannot offer proof of an oral agreement contradicting the terms of the writing.
9. The force and effect of the seal in contracts is rapidly becoming obsolete.
10. A unilateral contract embodies the exchange of a promise for an act.

Answers

1. T. 2. F. 3. F. 4. T. 5. F. 6. F. 7. T. 8. T. 9. T. 10. T.

THE CONTRACT OF SALE

Short questions

1. List the essential elements to be included in a contract of sale of real property.
2. What are the items that are usually apportioned or adjusted in a sale of real estate?
3. What are the most commonly used methods for describing real property?
4. Indicate briefly the most common items that a parcel of real property may be sold "subject to."
5. What is the purpose of the personal property clause in a contract of sale of real property?

6. Generally, how are assessments provided for in a contract of sale?
7. If the contract of sale provides that the buyer assume an existing mortgage, how is he protected as to the amount of the exact balance thereof?
8. Is it necessary for the contract of sale to be acknowledged before a notary public?

Answers

1. Identity of the parties, description of the property, terms of sale, conditions of sale, apportionment clause, personal property clause, type of deed to be delivered, date and place of closing, signatures of the parties.
2. Rents, taxes and water rates, interest, insurance, fuel, and escrow account, if any.
3. Metes and bounds, section block and lot number, government or geodetic survey, and monuments.
4. Prior existing mortgages, covenants and restrictions, leases and tenancies, implied warranties, easements and licenses.
5. Since the contract primarily conveys real property and incidental personal property, any confusion or misunderstanding regarding the nature and the extent of the personal property included in the sale is specifically clarified by the personal property clause.
6. If, at the time of the delivery of the deed, the property is affected by an assessment which is a lien thereon and not as yet fully paid, the balance is due and payable by the seller to the buyer upon the delivery of the deed.
7. The buyer is entitled to receive proof of the exact status of the mortgage on the day that title is conveyed. The seller must present either a letter or a reduction certificate from the mortgagee, duly executed, and verifying the unpaid balance of principal and interest, the rate of interest, and the date of maturity of the mortgage.
8. Usually not. Since it is not customary to record a contract of sale, no acknowledgment of the signature is required. However, if the buyer intends to record it, then he would require an acknowledgment so that the instrument would be accepted by the county clerk for recording.

True or False

1. The purchaser under a contract of sale is known as the vendor.
2. A contract of sale, in order to be binding, must be entered into by competent parties.
3. Upon the sale of real property all existing insurance policies are immediately cancelled and new policies written.
4. If, after the execution of a contract of sale, the buyer refuses to go

through with the transaction, he is liable to the broker for the commission.

5. If the parties enter into an oral contract for the purchase and sale of real estate, that contract is not void, but unenforceable.
6. Where property is held in tenancy by the entirety, both the husband and wife must sign the contract of sale.
7. An option differs from a contract of sale in that an option requires no consideration.
8. Where the buyer defaults, the deposit or earnest money belongs to the seller.
9. The seller of real estate is referred to as the vendor, and the buyer as the vendee.
10. The primary reason for obtaining a deposit on the sale of real property is to insure the buyer's good faith and ability to go through with the transaction.

Answers

1. F.   2. T.   3. F.   4. F.   5. T.   6. T.   7. F.   8. T.   9. T.   10. T.

DEEDS

Short questions

1. Outline the essential elements of a valid deed.
2. What is a deed?
3. List the most commonly used types of deeds.
4. List some of the types of deeds that are used to convey real property, other than those in question 3.
5. Is it necessary to secure the acknowledgment of the grantor's signature on the deed? Why?
6. What are the warranties that are found in a full covenant and warranty deed?
7. What covenant is contained in the bargain and sale deed with covenant against grantor's acts?
8. What is the purpose of the Labendum clause?
9. In the event that there is an inconsistency between the estate conveyed by the granting clause and that conveyed by the Labendum clause, which controls?
10. What is the purpose of a quitclaim deed?

Answers

1. Names of grantor and grantee, the description of the premises conveyed, the granting clause, the consideration, the interest conveyed, the Labendum clause, proper execution and acknowledgment, delivery and acceptance.

2. A deed is a carefully drawn and executed instrument, in writing, whereby one party, known as the grantor, conveys real property or an interest therein to another party, known as the grantee.

3. The full covenant and warranty, the bargain and sale with covenant against grantor's acts, the bargain and sale and the quitclaim deed.

4. Executor's deed, administrator's deed, guardian's deed, referee's deed, deed of release, deed of surrender, cession deed, committee's deed.

5. Yes, since the deed is to be recorded, the recording office will not accept it for that purpose unless there is an acknowledgment before a notary public of the grantor's signature.

6. Grantor's seizin and right to convey; grantee will receive quiet enjoyment of the premises; there are no encumbrances other than those expressed; further assurance and the grantor forever continues to warrant title.

7. That the title is good and the grantor has done nothing to encumber it.

8. It describes the estate conveyed by the grantor to the grantee.

9. The estate conveyed by the granting clause.

10. It conveys any title held by the grantor to the grantee without binding him to any warranty.

True or False

1. By a coveyance, is meant the passing of title to real estate or any interest therein from one person to another.

2. A deed restriction may be enforced by any member of the community.

3. Good and marketable title is ordinarily conveyed by a quitclaim deed.

4. One of the best legal descriptions that can be used in a deed is the house number, name of street, city and state where the property is located.

5. An oral deed is void.

6. It is legal to deed real estate to a minor.

7. The consideration for a deed may only be expressed in money.

8. The granting clause is an essential element of a deed.

9. If a deed is forged, it is void and does not convey any good title under any circumstances.

10. A deed has no legal effect until it is delivered by the grantor to the grantee, who accepts it.

Answers

1. T. 2. F. 3. F. 4. F. 5. T. 6. T. 7. F. 8. T. 9. T. 10. T.

TITLE SEARCH AND INSURANCE, CLOSINGS AND RECORDINGS

Short questions

1. Smith sells his property to Jones, who does not record the deed. Later, Smith sells the same property to Brown, an innocent purchaser, in good faith and for value who records his deed and takes possession of the property. What are the rights of Brown and Jones?

2. A sells his property to B for $15,000. B pays A a deposit of $1,000 and agrees to pay him an additional $4,000 on closing and take the property subject to an existing mortgage of $10,000. The mortgage interest is 6 per cent per annum payable quarterly. The last interest payment was made on March 31, 1966. The closing is to take place May 1, 1966. Taxes and insurance are to be apportioned as of the date of closing—the annual taxes, based on the calendar year, are $240 and are unpaid. The insurance is for three years and the premium of $54, covering the period Nov. 1, 1964–Nov. 1, 1967, is paid. Prepare a closing statement showing how much money the buyer will have to give the seller on the date of closing to be entitled to the delivery of the deed.

3. Explain who pays the following expenses incurred in the closing of title. (a) Mortgage brokerage commission. (b) Deed stamp tax. (c) Mortgage stamp tax. (d) Fee for drawing the deed. (e) Fee for drawing the mortgage. (f) Real estate taxes. (g) Fee for recording the deed.

4. What is the danger in not recording a deed promptly?

Answers

1. Brown being the first to record his deed is recognized by law as the owner of the property and retains ownership and possession. Since Jones failed to record his deed expeditiously, he has no rights in the property; however, he may sue Smith for fraud.

2.

Buyer		Seller	
Cash deposit	$ 1,000.00	Sale price	$15,000.00
Mortgage assumed	$10,000.00	Prepaid Insurance	
Unpaid taxes		(5/1/66–11/1/67)	
4 mos.	$ 80.00	18 mos.	$ 27.00
Unpaid interest			$15,027.00
1 mo.	$ 50.00		$11,130.00
	$11,130.00	Answer:	$ 3,897.00

3. (a) The mortgagor, i.e., the new buyer. (b) The seller. (c) The mortgagor, i.e., the new buyer. (d) The buyer. (e) The mortgagor, i.e., the new buyer. (f) Apportioned between buyer and seller as responsibility is indicated. (g) The buyer.

4. Judgments against the previous owner may be filed against the property. The previous owner may sell or mortgage the property to someone else.

True or False

1. If a contract of sales does not make "time of the essence" the parties may take as much time as they wish to close the transaction.
2. After having negotiated the terms of the sale, the most important requirement on the purchaser's part is to have the title searched.
3. If an encumbrance is not listed or specifically waived by the buyer in the contract of sale, it must be accepted by the buyer.
4. It is the seller's duty to clear up all encumbrances revealed by the title search, except those previously disposed of by the parties.
5. The title search is a summary of the operative parts of all instruments of conveyance affecting the land, title, or interest therein, together with a statement of all liens, charges, and encumbrances to which the property is subject.
6. The cost of the title search is a proper expense to the seller.
7. In making a mortgage loan the lender pays for the cost of the title search to insure his loan.
8. The Federal Internal Revenue Stamp tax on the deed amounts to 55¢ for each $500 of equity the seller receives, or fraction thereof.
9. The tax stamp on a deed is paid for by the buyer.
10. The usual time lapse between a contract of sale and the closing is from four to six weeks.
11. The recording fees for the deed and the mortgage is paid for by the seller.

Answers

1. F. 2. T. 3. F. 4. T. 5. T. 6. F. 7. F. 8. T. 9. F. 10. T.
11. F.

BONDS AND MORTGAGES

Short questions

1. Distinguish between a bond and a mortgage.
2. Outline the essential elements of a mortgage.
3. What is the purpose of an acceleration clause in a mortgage?
4. Define the following: (a) Amortized mortgage, (b) Budget mortgage, (c) Package mortgage, (d) Open mortgage, (e) Open end mortgage, (f) Blanket mortgage, (g) Purchase money mortgage.

Answers

1. The bond is the personal obligation assumed by the borrower to pay the mortgage loan. The mortgage is a security transaction creating a lien on the property so that it can be sold and the proceeds used for the repayment of the debt.

2. Parties with contractual capacity, description of mortgaged property or interest therein, mortgage clause, purpose of mortgage, mortgagor's covenant, proper execution, delivery and acceptance.

3. If the mortgagor defaults in his mortgage agreement, the mortgagee at his option may thereupon demand full payment of the unpaid balance of the principal.

4. (a) An amortized mortgage is one in which the principal and interest are repaid in regular periodic payments to the end of the mortgage period. (b) A budget mortgage is one in which the mortgagee amortizes for taxes, insurance, and water charges in addition to principal and interest. (c) A package mortgage, in addition to providing for amortization of expenses found in a budget mortgage, also provides for amortization of payment for appliances and equipment added to the property. (d) An open mortgage is one that is past due and allowed to remain unpaid by the mortgagee, who reserves the right to call it in upon demand. (e) An open end mortgage is one that stipulates, in advance, an amount to which the mortgagor may reborrow upon the property during the term of the mortgage. (f) A blanket mortgage is one mortgage secured by two or more parcels of real property. (g) A purchase money mortgage is one wherein the seller agrees to lend part of the purchase price to the buyer, with the property as security thereof, in order to expedite the transaction.

True or False

1. In a bond and mortgage transaction the mortgagor is also the obligor.

2. The default in prior mortgage clause in a junior mortgage is for the protection of the mortgagor.

3. A mortgage is personal property.

4. Fire losses up to the amount of the mortgage are payable directly to the mortgagee.

5. In the sale of property by foreclosure, the mortgagee is paid first.

6. The bond is usually recorded.

7. The mortgage is usually recorded.

8. By "equity of redemption" is meant a period of grace after default in which the mortgagor may redeem his property, provided it has not been foreclosed.

9. If a new owner buys a parcel of real property "subject to" an existing mortgage, he is personally liable thereon in case of his default.
10. If a new owner buys a parcel of real property "subject to and assuming" an existing mortgage, he is personally liable thereon in the event of his default.

Answers

1. T. 2. F. 3. T. 4. T. 5. F. 6. F. 7. T. 8. T. 9. F. 10. T.

LIENS, EASEMENTS AND OTHER ENCUMBRANCES

Short questions

1. What is a "lien"?
2. Name and describe two broad classes of liens.
3. Outline examples of specific liens and general liens.
4. Define an easement.
5. How may easements be created?
6. What is meant by an "easement by prescription"?
7. How may easements be terminated?
8. What is the effect of a restrictive covenant in a deed to real property?
9. How may restrictive covenants be used and what purpose do they serve?
10. How may a mechanic's lien be enforced?

Answers

1. A lien is a right given by law to a creditor to have his debt satisfied out of the property belonging to the debtor.
2. Specific liens which affect only certain property of the debtor, and general liens which affect any property belonging to the debtor.
3. Specific liens include mortgages, taxes, mechanic's liens, vendor's and vendee's liens, assessments, water charges, and attachments. General liens include judgments, liens for corporate franchise tax, liens for inheritance tax, and liens for decedent's debts.
4. An easement is a right to use the real property of another.
5. By express grant, by implication or necessity, and by prescription.
6. If there is an actual open, notorious, exclusive, and continuous use of land for a statutory period of time during which the owner of the land does not object, an easement by prescription is acquired.
7. By express or implied contract, by merger of the dominant and servient tenement, by non-use beyond a statutory period, by destruction of the servient tenement, by expiration of the purpose or necessity of the easement.
8. The effect is to limit the ownership or use of the property.

9. Restrictive covenants may be used to specify the character, location, and use of buildings erected or to be erected and maintained. They are thus used to protect and preserve the neighborhood and the property.
10. By foreclosure and sale.

True or False

1. When a seller defaults, the type of lien that may be enforced is known as a vendee's lien.
2. A vendor's lien is an example of a specific lien.
3. As a rule a mechanic's lien expires unless it is renewed within 6 months.
4. An easement appurtenant is the right acquired by the owner of land to use the adjacent land of another for a special purpose.
5. The maintenance of a utility pole by the telephone company on the land of another is an example of an easement in gross.
6. An easement appurtenant runs with the land, as does an easement in gross.
7. The priority of liens depends upon the time of their creation.
8. A judgment is a determination of the rights of parties as the result of an action at law.
9. The effect of a mortgage is to create a lien.
10. A lien is always an encumbrance.

Answers

1. T. 2. T. 3. F. 4. T 5. T. 6. T. 7. F. 8. T. 9. T. 10. T.

TAXES AND ASSESSMENTS: VALUATIONS AND APPRAISALS

Short questions

1. Define the term "assessment."
2. What is meant by an "ad valorem tax"?
3. In its broadest sense, what is the nature of a tax?
4. What is the effect of non-payment of real property taxes?
5. Indicate at least four items for which special assessments may be levied against real property.
6. State the formula for determining the tax rate.
7. What is a tax roll?
8. What is meant by value?
9. Distinguish between value, price, and cost.
10. List the three methods whereby cost of real property may be estimated.
11. Indicate the four approaches to valuation.

12. What is the formula for value under the cost approach?
13. What are the factors that cause depreciation of real property?
14. In addition to cost, what are some of the other important factors that affect value?
15. Indicate by example the use of a different approach to value depending upon the need for such valuation.

Answers

1. When specific properties are benefitted by public improvements, the charge or tax levied to pay for such improvements is called an assessment.
2. An ad valorem tax is one that is levied in accordance with the value of the property.
3. A tax is a charge assessed against persons or property for public purposes.
4. Unpaid taxes or real property become a lien thereon.
5. Sewers, curbs, street paving, sidewalks.
6. $\dfrac{\text{Budget}}{\text{Assessed Valuation}} = \text{Tax Rate}$
7. A tax roll is a record of the tax levies in a taxing area.
8. Value is the power that goods command because of utility, scarcity, demand, and transferability.
9. Value describes a barter relationship, whereas price is the measurement of the commodity in terms of dollars. Cost is a measure of past expenditures for a commodity.
10. (a) Quantity survey method. (b) Unit in place. (c) Comparative method.
11. (a) The cost approach. (b) The market approach. (c) The income approach. (d) The rule of thumb approach.
12. Value = Replacement Cost less Depreciation.
13. Physical wear and tear, loss due to natural elements, such as rain, snow, wind, hail, etc., functional and economic obsolescence.
14. The social economic and political forces in the particular area where the property is located.
15. If the valuation is for insurance purposes, the cost approach is of prime importance; if for the resale of property, the market approach would carry more weight; if the valuation is sought for investment purposes, the income approach is paramount.

True or False

1. An appraisal is an expression of opinion of the value of property as of a given date.
2. In analyzing a parcel of land to estimate its value, the first thing to determine is its highest and best use.

3. The tax on a parcel of real estate is arrived at by multiplying the tax rate by the selling price.
4. Physical deterioration of real property results from tax liens.
5. An appraiser in his work determines value.
6. "Highest and best use" may be defined as that use which will yield the highest return on the investment.
7. The income approach to valuation would be most widely used in the determination of value of one-family residential properties.
8. Economic obsolescence is not a factor in land values as land does not depreciate.
9. An office building with a poor floor plan would suffer a loss of value due to functional obsolescence as soon as it is built.
10. Restrictions against real property are of no concern to an appraiser since they are rarely enforced.
11. In most districts, taxes are assessed against properties by the names of the owners.
12. Assessed valuations are an excellent guide to property values.
13. Assessments for local improvements are apportioned according to the front footage of the land benefitted.
14. Assessments against property become a lien when they are confirmed and entered as provided by law.
15. As provided by ordinance or state law, notice of assessment is given by advertisement.

Answers

1. T.   2. T.   3. F.   4. F.   5. F.   6. T.   7. F.   8. F.   9. T.   10. F.
11. F.   12. F.   13. T.   14. T.   15. T.

LEASES, LANDLORD AND TENANT

Short questions

1. Andrews leases premises to Brown for five years. At the expiration of the period, Brown remains in possession. Brown claims the lease is automatically renewed for another five years. Andrews claims Brown has a lease only for one additional year. Who wins?
2. Jones leases premises to Brown for one year. The lease provides that if Brown remains over he shall be a tenant from month to month. After 14 months' occupancy, Jones gives Brown 30 days' notice to vacate. Brown claims he has a lease for an additional 10 months. Is Brown correct?
3. Can a tenant for life make a valid lease?
4. What are the interests of the landlord and tenant in a lease called?
5. Ash leases certain premsies to Blake for a three-year term at $200 monthly. At the expiration of three months, a flood damages the

premises to such an extent that the premises are uninhabitable for five months. What, if any, is Blake's liability?

6. In what ways may a lease be terminated?

Answers

1. Andrews. The lease is not renewed for 5 years, but from year to year.

2. No. The lease contract determines Brown's rights. It specifically provides that upon Brown's holding over, the tenancy shall be upon a monthly basis and this provision will be enforced.

3. Yes, if he does not extend it beyond the term of his own life. Since the tenancy of the life tenant is uncertain, the joinder of the reversioner or remainderman should be had.

4. Landlord's Interest = Reversion
   Tenant's Interest = Estate for years

5. He is liable for rent for the 5 month period. If the lease has no act of God clause, Blake would also be liable for the cost of repairing the premises unless exempted by statute.

6. (a) By performance; automatically terminates at end of term. (b) By surrender; by mutual cancellation of lease before end of term. (c) By breach; lessor may evict. Lessee may declare forfeiture.

Short questions

1. List the essential elements of a valid lease.
2. What is a leasehold? What type of right does it convey?
3. What is a tenancy by sufferance?
4. What is a percentage lease?
5. What is rent?

Answers

1. (a) Parties (lessor & lessee) with capacity to contract. (b) Agreement to let and take. (c) Adequate description of premises. (d) Term of the lease. (e) The rent. (f) Form (if required) in accordance with law. (g) Delivery by lessor and acceptance by lessee.

2. A leasehold is a contractual relationship whereby the tenant obtains the right to use, occupy, and possess the leased premises. This right is a personal property right.

3. A tenancy by sufferance arises where legal possession under a lease has ended and the tenant holds over and continues in possession wrongfully. Said person is not truly a tenant and has only naked possession.

4. A percentage lease is one whereby the rent is based upon a percentage of the tenants gross receipts—generally set over a fixed minimum.

5. Rent is a definite periodic return for the use and occupation of real property. It is the consideration for the lease and may be payable in money or products of the land.

Multiple choice

1. A Lease must be in writing if its term is for:
   a. Six months
   b. A year
   c. An indefinite period
   d. A year and a day
2. Where a tenancy is terminable at the volition of either party, the tenancy is known as:
   a. A tenancy at will
   b. A tenancy at sufferance
   c. A monthly tenancy
   d. An indefinite tenancy
3. When premises reach a physical condition whereby the tenant is unable to occupy them for the purposes intended, the situation is legally recognized as:
   a. A dispossess eviction
   b. An actual eviction
   c. A constructive eviction
   d. A passive eviction
4. Fixtures and machinery installed by the tenant are usually considered:
   a. Personal property
   b. Real property
   c. Mixed property
   d. Real fixtures
5. In every lease the landlord must specifically covenant:
   a. Possession
   b. Quiet enjoyment
   c. Fitness for use
   d. Habitability

Answers

1. d. 2. a. 3. c. 4. a 5. b.

True or False

1. A broker and a salesman may actively engage in the real estate business as a partnership.
2. The license law is a police measure.
3. If one solicits listings by ringing door bells, he is subject to suspension of license.

4. The Code of Ethics is part of the Real Estate License Law.
5. Reciprocity is not compulsory upon any state in the granting of a license to a non-resident licensed applicant.
6. A single separate bank account only is adequate for the deposit of monies held by a broker for others.
7. A broker must immediately notify the Secretary of State when he changes his business address.
8. The Real Estate License Law prohibits a real estate salesman from working more than 40 hours a week.
9. A developer who employs salesmen must be licensed as a real estate broker.
10. A broker must notify the Secretary of State when he changes his residence address.
11. The license law requires that every real estate broker maintain a definite place of business.
12. A broker's license cannot be converted into a salesman's license and vice versa.
13. A real estate broker may be disciplined for the misconduct of his salesman.
14. A licensed real estate salesman may go to work for another broker without requesting the Secretary of State to transfer his license.
15. A real estate broker is required to report cessation of employment of his salesman to the Secretary of State.
16. A real estate broker may employ another real estate broker in the capacity of a salesman.
17. A broker's license and a salesman's license are identical and mean the same thing.
18. The obtaining of a broker's license by fraud is a misdemeanor.
19. The broker must obey all the lawful instructions given to him by his principal.
20. A broker may not act for anyone whose interests in the transaction are adverse to his principal.
21. A broker need not disclose that he is actually the owner when dealing with a prospective purchaser.
22. A person who works as a real estate broker only part time need not be licensed.
23. Two brokers registered individually may occupy the same office space and need not have individual signs.
24. A broker is not permitted under the license law to use unlicensed persons merely to show properties.
25. A salesman may not renew his license until the license of his employing broker is renewed.
26. A broker's right to collect commission is not affected on a deal made after the expiration of his license and before the renewal of same.

27. A broker's license remains in force if he moves his place of business.
28. If two brokers share office space but conduct their business separately, they may, under the license law, use the same letterheads.
29. The void license of an officer of a corporation or a member of partnership does not affect the license of the corporation or the partnership.
30. The Secretary of State may refuse to renew the license of a broker who has refused to stop selling by a method which is dishonest or untruthful.
31. A person who has been convicted of certain felonies may be refused a license even though he presents recommendations from several friends and brokers.
32. A broker's license may be suspended but not revoked for representing both buyer and seller and receiving commissions from both without their knowledge and consent.
33. Any licensee is entitled to a hearing before having his license revoked.
34. A broker who collects rents for clients and co-mingles the money with his own so that he cannot make a proper accounting may have his license revoked.
35. A real estate broker's license should be kept in a safe deposit box for safekeeping.
36. It is a violation of law for a broker to pay commissions directly to a salesman employed by another broker.
37. A clerk in a real estate office who prepares real estate listings and simple sales agreement need not be licensed as a salesman.
38. All real estate licenses must be renewed in May.
39. A real estate salesman may be put in jail for engaging in the real estate business without a license.
40. Brokers employing salesmen are relieved of all responsibility for the acts of the salesmen if the salesmen are all bonded.
41. Realtors are members of the National Association of Real Estate Boards.
42. A real estate salesman who desires to transfer to another broker merely picks up his license from the first broker and places it upon display in the office of the second broker.
43. A salesman may advertise listings in his own name without mentioning his broker.
44. A broker should consent to the transfer of a salesman's license even though the salesman owes him money which the broker loaned to him.
45. A salesman may receive a commission from a broker other than his employer for assisting in a transaction.
46. A real estate salesman's license may be issued to the vice-president of the ABC Realty Corporation.

47. A real estate broker's license can be issued only to a person who maintains a place of business in the state.
48. The Secretary of State may hold a hearing on its own volition even if it does not have a verified written complaint from a complainant.
49. A salesman must carry his license with him at all times for identification. (Must carry pocket identification card at all times.)
50. A person who sells property under a court order is not required to have a license.
51. The placing of a For Sale sign on a vacant property without the consent of the owner may jeopardize the broker's license.
52. All sales of real estate must be handled through a licensed real estate broker or licensed salesman. (Handled through brokers only.)
53. The real estate licensing law is not an act designed to raise revenue.
54. A licensee paying a commission to an unlicensed person may lose his license on that account.
55. The license law is the greatest single factor in elevating the real estate business to a profession.
56. A decision of the Secretary of State upon a complaint in favor of the licensee is final.
57. An unlicensed person making a real estate transaction cannot collect a commission.
58. A real estate salesman must turn over to his broker all money received in a real estate transaction.
59. A person who is not licensed may sell real estate for a friend, if he does not charge any fee.
60. A salesman may split a commission with any other licensed salesman or broker.
61. The purpose of the license law is to protect the public from irresponsible and untrustworthy brokers.
62. A real estate broker, not licensed when employed to negotiate a transaction, but who procures a license before he renders service, may recover commissions.
63. An unlicensed person who acts as a real estate broker is not entitled to compensation for his services and is guilty of a misdemeanor.
64. An applicant for a license may not legally act as a real estate broker until his license is actually issued to him.
65. A trust company which acts as a real estate broker must be licensed as such.
66. A building and loan company which undertakes to procure loans upon real property it is developing, to assist purchasers in financing homes thereon, must be licensed.
67. An advertising agency, which mails circulars describing and illustrat-

ing real estate for sale to selected lists of possible purchasers for which service a varying fee is charged, must be licensed.

68. An unlicensed broker is not entitled to commissions for procuring an advertiser for wall space of an owner's building for a specified period.

69. The Secretary of State may grant a license to a person who is operating under an assumed name, if he is convinced that the change of name was in good faith and for an honest purpose and that the licensee intends to be known by that name by all persons and in all his affairs.

70. The Real Estate License Law does not apply to brokers who negotiate the sale of business establishments, even where the sale includes the transfer of the lease of the place of business.

71. One who negotiates the sale of cemetery lots must either be a real estate broker or an employee of the owner of the cemetery.

72. Where the relationship of master and servant exists, such a servant as a janitor, in addition to his regular duties, may lawfully show space to and collect rents from his master's tenants without being licensed as a real estate broker.

73. A person, corporation, or co-partnership employed to secure the reduction of rent or other modification of a lease must be duly licensed.

74. The failure of a broker to plead and prove that he is a duly licensed broker is a sufficient defense against a broker's action for commissions on a real estate transaction.

75. A licensed broker cooperating with an unlicensed broker is not entitled to compensation rendered in the negotiation in which the unlicensed broker participated.

76. The exemption of the license law in favor of attorneys at law does not apply to those attorneys duly admitted in another state but not admitted to the Bar of the State of New York.

Answers

1. F. 2. T. 3. F. 4. F. 5. T. 6. T. 7. T. 8. F. 9. T. 10. F.
11. T. 12. T. 13. T. 14. F. 15. T. 16. T. 17. F. 18. T. 19. T.
20. T. 21. F. 22. F. 23. F. 24. T. 25. T. 26. F. 27. F. 28. F.
29. F. 30. T. 31. T. 32. F. 33. T. 34. T. 35. F. 36. T. 37. T.
38. F. 39. T. 40. F. 41. T. 42. F. 43. F. 44. T. 45. F. 46. F.
47. T. 48. T. 49. F. 50. T. 51. T. 52. F. 53. T. 54. T. 55. T.
56. T. 57. T. 58. T. 59. T. 60. F. 61. T. 62. T. 63. T. 64. T.
65. T. 66. T. 67. T. 68. T. 69. T. 70. T. 71. T. 72. T. 73. T.
74. T. 75. T. 76. T.

BIBLIOGRAPHY

Brown, Robert K. *Real Estate Economics*, Houghton Mifflin, 1965.

Bryant, Willis R. *Mortgage Lending*, 2nd ed., McGraw-Hill, 1962.

Case, Frederick E. *Real Estate*, rev. ed., Allyn & Bacon, 1962.

Hoagland, Henry E. *Real Estate Principles*, 3rd ed., McGraw-Hill, 1955.

Husband, William E., and Frank R. Anderson. *Real Estate*, 3rd ed., Irwin, 1960.

Kahn, Sanders A., Frederick E. Case, and Alfred Schimmel. *Real Estate Appraisal and Investment*, Ronald, 1963.

Lusk, Harold F. *Law of the Real Estate Business*, rev. ed., Irwin, 1965.

Maisel, Sherman J. *Financing Real Estate*, McGraw-Hill, 1965.

Martin, Preston. *Real Estate Principles and Practices*, Macmillan, 1959.

Ratcliff, Richard U. *Real Estate Analysis*, McGraw-Hill, 1961.

Ring, Alfred A. *The Valuation of Real Estate*, Prentice-Hall, 1963.

Ring, Alfred A., and Nelson L. North. *Real Estate Principles and Practices*, 6th ed., Prentice-Hall, 1967.

Semenow, Robert W. *Questions and Answers on Real Estate*, 5th ed., Prentice-Hall, 1966.

Unger, Maurice A. *Real Estate*, 3rd ed., South-Western, 1964.

Weimer, Arthur M., and Homer Hoyt. *Principles of Real Estate*, 5th ed., Ronald, 1966.

Wendt, Paul F. *Real Estate Appraisal*, Henry Holt, 1956.

INDEX

A

Abstract of Title, 92
Acceptance, 47, 49, 98
Accretion, 17
Acknowledgment, 86
Action of Foreclosure, 109, 110
Additional Extended Coverage, 185
Administrator's Deed, 91
Ad Valorem Taxes, 137, 139
Adverse Possession, 14, 16, 91
Advertising, 41, 44
  policy, 45
  types of, 45
Affidavit of Heirship, 120
Affidavit of Title, 120–122
Agency, 19
  actual, 19
  by appointment, 21
  by estoppel, 19, 22
  by necessity, 22
  by ratification, 22
  duties and obligation in, 22, 23, 24
  express, 19
  general, 19, 20
  implied, 19
  liability, 24, 25
  ostensible, 19
  special, 19, 20
  termination of, 26
  third parties, 24
Agreement, 58
AIDA Formula in Advertising, 45
Alienation of Real Property, 13
Aliens, 52
Alteration of an Instrument, 57
American Bankers Association, 2
American Institute of Real Estate Appraisers, 2, 143

American Society of Real Estate Counsellors, 2
Amortized Mortgage, 108
Apportionment clause, 79
Appraisal, 1, 2, 36, 139
Appraisal Journal, 144
Appraisal Practice, 139
Appraisal Process, 146
Approaches to Valuation, 141–143
  cost approach, 141
  income approach, 143
  market approach, 142
  rule of thumb, 143
Appurtenances, 1
Arbitration, 60
Assessed Valuation, 137
Assessment Clause, 78
Assessment Roll, 137
Assessments, 81, 93, 114, 136
Assessor, 137
Assignee, 57
Assignee for the Benefit of Creditors, 90, 94
  deed by, 90
Assignment of Contract 57, 82
Assignment of Lease, 157
Assignment of Mortgage, 122, 123
Attachments, 114

B

Bankruptcy, 14, 58, 94, 161, 162
Bargain and Sale Deed, 89
Bargain and Sale Deed with Covenants, 89
Base Line, 71
Beam Right Agreement, 124
Bilateral Contract, 54
Bill of Sale, 124
Binders, 61
Blanket Mortgage, 109

Bonds, 100
Boundary Line Agreement, 124
Breach of Contract, 60
Breach of Lease, 160
Broker, 27, 34, 81
Brokerage, 1, 9, 26
Budget, 137
Budget Mortgage, 108

C

Capacity to Contract, 47, 50
Certificate of Reduction of Mort-
    gage, 124
Chain of Title, 93
Chancery Court, 102
Chattel Real, 152
Check, 71
Checks, 59
City Planning, 181
Closing, 80, 94
Closing Fees, 96
Closing Objections, 95
Closing Statement, 97
Cloud on Title, 92
Collateral Bond, 125
Commission Merchant, 20
Commissions, 29
    conflicting claims for, 30
    default, 31
    deferment of, 31
    rate of, 30, 81
    when earned, 30
Committees Deed, 89
Common Law Mortgage, 103
Community Property, 7, 8
Condemnation Proceedings, 17
Conditional Bill of Sale, 93, 116,
    117
Condominium, 172–176
Condominium Mortgage, 175
Confiscation, 18
Consideration, 47, 52, 85
    adequacy of, 53
    good, 53
    past, 53
    valuable, 53
Consolidation Agreement, 125
Construction, 1
Contingent Remainder, 10

Contract of Sale, 13, 46, 64
Contracts, 46
Contract Under Seal, 55, 56
Conventional Mortgage, 108
Conversion, 63
Convicts, 52
Cooperatives, 171
    appraisal of, 171
Corporate Real Estate, 11
Corporation, 35, 36, 51
Corporation Franchise Tax, 116
Corporeal Rights, 12
Correction Deed, 90
Cost, 140
Court of Equity, 102
Covenant, 56, 77, 90
Covenant of Quiet Enjoyment, 90
Covenant Running with the Land,
    90
Creation of Easement, 118
Crimes, 62
Current Trends in Real Estate, 167
Curtesy, 8

D

Damages, 61
    general, 61
    liquidated, 61
    nominal, 61
    special, 61
Decedent's Debts, 116
Deceit, 63
Declaratory Judgment, 16
Dedication, 14
Deed, 46, 84
    Bargain and Sale, 89
    Bargain and Sale with Cove-
        nant, 89
    delivery of, 80, 98
    Full Covenant and Warranty, 86
    history of, 84
    of confirmation, 90
    of gift, 89
    of release, 90
    of surrender, 90
    parties to a, 85
    Quitclaim, 89
    requirements, 85
Defeasance Clause, 101

Deposit Monies, 32
Descent, 14
Description of Real Property, 65, 85
  government survey, 65
  lot and block number, 68
  metes and bounds, 69
  monuments, 74
Development, 164
  rururban, 165
  suburban, 164, 165
  urban, 164
Development Costs, 165
Development Financing, 165, 166
Direct Taxes, 136
Discharge of Contracts, 59
Dispossess Proceedings, 162
Dower, 8, 94
Drivement Easement Agreement, 125
Drunken Persons, 51
Dual Employment, 29
Duress, 50

E

Easement, 12, 112, 117
  appurtenant, 117
  by implication, 118
  by necessity, 118
  by prescription, 17, 118
  creation of, 118
  extinction of, 118
  in gross, 118
Elements of a Contract, 47
Eminent Domain, 17, 161
Encumbrances, 112, 117
Enemy Aliens, 18
Enforceable Contract, 55
Equitable Rights, 12
Equity Mortgage, 103
Equity of Redemption, 110
Erosion, 17
Escalator Lease, 152
Escheat, 117
Escrow, 95
Escrow Holder, 21
Estate for Years, 9
Estate in Expectancy, 9
Estate in Reality, 5

Estate Less than Freehold, 5, 8, 9
Estate pur autre vie, 7
Estate Tax, 116
Estoppel Certificate, 125, 126
Eviction, 161
  actual, 161
  constructive, 161
Exceptions to Title, 94
Exchange of Real Property, 36
Executed Contract, 54
Execution of Contract of Sale, 82
Execution of Deed, 86
Executor's Deed, 91
Executory Contract, 54
Expiration of Lease, 160
Express Agency, 19
Express Contract, 53
Extended Coverage, 185
Extension Agreement, 126
  purpose of, 126
  contents of, 126, 127

F

Factors, 20
Federal and State Governments, 51
Federal Estate Tax, 116
Federal Housing Act, 3, 105
Federal National Mortgage Association (Fannie Mae), 180
Fee, 7
Fee Simple, 5, 7
Fee Simple Absolute, 7
Fee Tail Estate, 7
FHA Mortgage, 3, 105
Finance, 1, 136
Financial Adjustments, 95
Financing Sale of Real Estate, 75, 110
Fire Clause, 156
Fire Insurance, 185
First Right of Refusal, 157
Fixed Lease, 152
Foreclosure, 14, 109
Foreign States and Sovereigns, 51
Forgery, 62
Franchise, 13
Franchise Tax, 116
Fraud, 50, 63

Fraudulent Practices, 62
Freehold Estates, 5
   not of inheritance, 5
   of inheritance, 5
Fuel, 95
Full Covenant and Warranty
   Deed, 86

G

General Damages, 61
General Liens, 115
Geodetic Survey, 69
Gift of Real Property, 13
G.I. Mortgage, 105
Government Survey, 69
Ground Lease, 154
Guarantors on Lease, 159
Guardian's Deed, 89

H

Habendum Clause, 85
Homeowners Insurance, 187
Homestead, 8
Horizontal Property Act, 173
Housing, 3

I

Identity of Parties, 95
Implied Agency, 19
Implied Contract, 54
Implied Warranty, 77
Impossibility of Performance, 57
Improvements, 1, 155
Incorporeal Rights, 12
Indemnification against Damages,
   159
Indenture, 84
Independent Contractor, 20
Indirect Loss Coverage, 186
Individual Proprietorship, 35
Infants, 51
Inheritance Tax, 116
Insane Persons, 51
Institute of Farm Brokers, 2
Institute of Real Estate Manage-
   ment, 2
Insurance Premiums, 95
Interest on Mortgage, 95
Interests in Realty, 5

Internal Revenue Stamps, 91
International Real Estate Federa-
   tion, 2
Intestacy, 91
Involuntary Alienation of Real
   Property, 13, 14

J

Joint and Several Contract, 54,
   55
Joint Contract, 54
Joint Tenants, 11
Judgments, 14, 55, 56, 93, 115
Junior Mortgage, 109

L

Laches, 102
Land Contracts, 46
Landlord and Tenant, 151
Land Trust, 11
Lease, 13, 36, 46, 77, 94, 151
   requirements of, 151
   termination of, 160
   term of, 151, 152
Leasehold, 152
Legal Aspects of Real Estate
   Transactions, 46
Legality of Contract, 47, 53
Legal Rights, 12
Legal Tender, 60
Liability Insurance, 186, 187
License, 13
License Law, 38
   bonds and surety, 39
   constitutionality, 39
   examination, 39
   expiration of license, 39
   fees, 39
   non-residence license, 40
   qualifications for license, 39
   regulating bodies, 39
   suspension or revocation of license, 39
Liens, 14, 112, 155
   mechanic's liens, 112, 155
Lien Theory of Mortgages, 104
Life Estate, 7
Life Insurance Association of
   America, 2

Lis Pendens, 93, 109, 119
Listing Contracts, 27, 46
   exclusive agency, 27, 28
   exclusive right to sell, 27, 28
   multiple listing, 27
   net listing, 27
   open listing, 27
Liquidated Damages, 61
Livery of Seizin, 84
Long Term Lease, 154
Lot and Block Number Description, 68

M

Management, 36
Marketing, 1
Market Value, 140
Married Woman, 52
Measure of Damages, 61
Mechanic's Lien, 93, 112
   discharge of, 113
   enforcement of, 113
Member of the Appraising Institute (MAI), 144
Merger, 57, 82
Meridian, 71
Metes and Bounds, 69
Misrepresentation, 50
Mistake, 49
Monthly Tenant, 152
Month to Month Tenant, 152
Monuments, 74
Mortgage, 13, 46, 76, 100, 101, 112
   lien theory, 103
   requirements of, 104, 105
   title theory, 103
   types of, 105
Mortgage Bankers Association, 2
Mortgage Foreclosure, 109
Mortgage Index, 93
Mortgage Market, 3
Mortgage of Lease, 105, 157
Mortgage on Crops, 109
Mortgage Participation Agreement, 130
Mortmain Statutes, 10
Multiple Line Coverages, 187
Mutuality of Assent, 47

N

National Association of Home Builders, 2
National Association of Real Estate Boards, 2, 34, 143
National Housing Act of 1934, 105
National Institute of Real Estate Brokers, 2
Net Lease, 152
Nominal Damages, 61
Non-Conveyance, liability for, 82
Novation, 58, 157

O

Offer, 47
Office, Real Estate, 34
Open End Mortgage, 109
Open Mortgage, 109
Operation of Real Estate Office, 34
Option, 48
Owner in Severalty, 10

P

Package Mortgage, 109
Paper Subdivision, 163
Paramount Lien, 162
Parol Evidence Rule, 56
   exceptions to, 56, 57
Partnership, 35
Party Wall Agreement, 130, 131
Payment, 59
Percentage Lease, 152
Performance, 58
   satisfactory, 59
   substantial, 59
   tender of, 60
Personal Property Clause, 78
Plat, 163
Possession, 83
Power of Attorney, 19, 131
Price, 140
Principal, 21
   undisclosed, 25, 26
Principal Meridian, 71
Priority of Liens, 117
Property Insurance, 184–187
Property Interests, 5
Property Management, 1, 147
   development of, 147

Property Manager, 148
  fees, 149
  functions, 148
  selection of, 149
  types, 148
Property Rights, 5, 12
Prospects, 42
Public Sale, 14
Purchase Money Mortgage, 109
Purchaser, 64

Q

Quantum meruit, 60
Quasi Contract, 54
Quid Pro Quo, 53
Quitclaim Deed, 89

R

Range, 71
Rate of Commission, 30
Real Estate Broker, 26, 34
Real Estate Business, 1
Real Estate Investment Trust, 176
  advantages, 176
Real Estate Market, 1, 2
Real Estate Salesman, 27, 34
Reality of Consent, 49
Real Property, 1
Real Property Taxes, 136
Realtor, 34
Reappraisal Lease, 152
Recission, 58
Recognizances, 55, 56
Recording, 98
Rectangular Survey, 69
Redemption, 158
Reduction Certificate, 78
Reentry, 158
Referee's Deed in Foreclosure, 89
Referee's Deed in Partition, 89
Rejection of Offer, 48
Release of Mortgage, 131
Remainder, 9, 10
Remainderman, 10
Rent, 95, 102
Repairs, 155
Restriction, 77

Restriction Agreement, 132
Restrictive Covenant, 91, 118
Reversion, 9
Revocation of Offer, 48
Right of Survivorship, 11

S

Sale and Leaseback, 167
Sale Clause in Lease, 157
Sale of Real Property, 13, 36
Salesman, 27, 34
Salesmanship, 41
Satisfaction of Mortgage, 133
School District Taxes, 137
  rates, 138
Seal, 56
Section, 72
Security, 156
Seller, 64
Separate Property, 7
Serviceman's Readjustment Act of 1944, 106–108
Several Contract, 54, 55
Sewer Rents, 81, 95
Society of Industrial Realtors, 2
Society of Residential Appraisers, 2, 144
Special and Allied Fire Lines, 185, 186
Special Damages, 61
Specialties, 55
Specific Liens, 112
Specific Performance, 60
Spendthrifts, 52
Spreading Agreement, 133, 134
Squatters' Rights, 17
Stamps on Deed, 91
Statute of Frauds, 21, 47, 53, 55, 56, 61, 64
Statutory Tenant, 9, 153
Straight Lease, 152
Street Rights, 75
Sub Agent, 20
Subdivision and Development, 36, 163
"Subject to" Clause, 76
Subletting, 157
Subordination, 159, 160
Subordination Agreement, 134

Substituted Contract, 58
Surety Bail Bond Lien, 114
Surety on Lease, 159
Surrogate's Court, 94
Survival Clause, 82
Syndicate Investment and Return, 169
Syndicate Investor, 169
Syndications, 167
  advantages, 170
  alienation of interest, 170
  regulation of, 170
  tax benefits, 169
Syndicator, 168

T

Table of Land Measures, 74
Tax Collections, 138
Tax Deficiencies, 138
Taxes, 81, 93, 95, 112, 136
Tax Liens, 93, 94, 112, 138, 139
Tax Rate, 137
Tax Rolls, 138
Tax Sale, 14
Tenancy at Will, 9, 153
Tenancy by Sufferance, 9, 153
Tenancy by the Entirety, 11
Tenancy from Month to Month, 9, 152
Tenancy from Year to Year, 9, 152
Tenancy in Common, 11
Tenancy in Partnership, 11
Tenants, 77, 94
Tender of Performance, 60
Termination of Lease, 160
  actual eviction, 161
  agreement, 160
  bankruptcy, 161, 162
  breach, 160
  constructive eviction, 161
  destruction, 161
  eminent domain, 161
  expiration, 160
  paramount lien, 162
Testamentary Trust, 11
Time of Performance, 58
Time of Essence, 58, 80
Title, 77

Title Insurance, 92, 94
Title I, Housing Act of 1949, 179
Title Search, 92, 109
Title Theory of Mortgages, 103
Torrens System, 98
Torts, 62
Township, 72
Transfer Tax, 116
Trespass, 62, 63
Trustee, 20
Trusts, 11

U

Undisclosed Principal, 25
Undue Influence, 50
Unenforceable Contract, 55
Unilateral Contract, 54
United States Savings and Loan League, 2, 144
Unjust Enrichment, 54
Unopened Street, 77
Urban Renewal, 179
Urban Renewal Legislation, 180

V

Valid Contract, 55
Valuation, 141
  comparative method of, 141
  cost approach to, 141
  methods of, 141
  quantity-survey method, 141
  unit in place method, 141
Value, 140
  factors affecting, 141
VA Mortgage, 3, 105
Variances, 184
Vendees Lien, 80, 114
Vendors Lien, 114
Vested Remainder, 10
Violations, 79, 118, 119
Voidable Contract, 51, 55
Void Contract, 51, 55
Voluntary Alienation of Real Property, 13

W

Water Charges, 81, 93, 95, 114
Will, 14, 91
Words of Conveyance, 85

Writing, 53

Y

Yearly Tenant, 152

Z

Zoning, 183
  control, 183
  ordinances, 183